CONNECTIONS:
The Life and Times of B.A. Packard in 1880s Tombstone and on the Arizona-Sonora Borderlands

by
Cynthia F. Hayostek

CONNECTIONS:
The Life and Times of B.A. Packard
in 1880s Tombstone and on
the Arizona-Sonora Borderlands
by
Cynthia F. Hayostek

Foreword by
J.C. Mutchler

Goose Flats Publishing ~ Tombstone, Arizona

Connections:
The Life and Times of B.A. Packard in 1880s Tombstone and on the Arizona-Sonora Borderlands

by Cynthia F. Hayostek

Foreword by J.C. Mutchler

Copyright © 2015 by Cynthia F. Hayostek
ISBN# 978-1-939345-02-8
Library of Congress Control Number: 2014954877

Published and printed in the **U.S.A**.

First edition - February 2015

Published by
Goose Flats Publishing
P.O. Box 813
Tombstone, Arizona 85638
(520) 457-3884
www.gooseflats.com

Book layout & cover design:
Keith Davis
Goose Flats Graphics
Tombstone, Arizona

All rights reserved. This book or any portion thereof may not be reproduced or used in any manner whatsoever without the express written permission of the author or publisher except for the use of brief quotations in a book review.

*Dedicated in loving memory of my father,
John H. Davis Jr., best friend of
Ashley B. Packard Jr.*

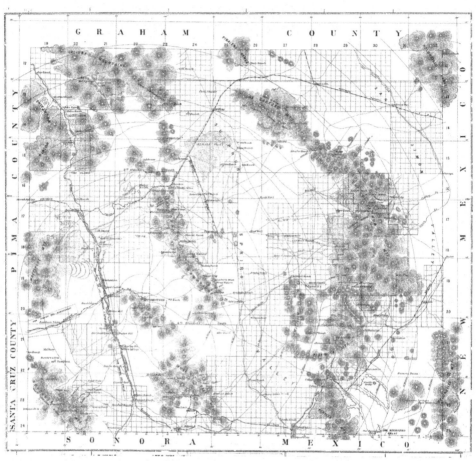

Cochise County, Arizona in 1904.

Cochise County Treasurer's Office

Table of Contents

Foreword - ix

Introduction - 1

Early Years - 3

Miner - 13

Transition - 42

Agriculturist - 64

1893 - 93

Politics and Greene - 110

Banker - 145

Revolution - 173

Final Years - 202

Epilogue - 230

Connections - 235

Bibliography - 273

Index - 280

Connections: The Life and Times of B. A. Packard

Cynthia F. Hayostek

Foreword

B.A. Packard was certainly one of the crucial players in the formation of Southern Arizona, especially in and around Cochise County, the town of Douglas, Arizona, and in northern Sonora, Mexico.

An interesting character in and of himself, the story of Packard's life and his many adventures – as a rancher, banker, mining investor, engaged citizen and politician – might be enough for an engaging narrative that would hold the interest of many regional historians. But Ms. Hayostek does much more with Packard, using the narrative arc of his life to help us understand the complexity of bi-national interactions that helped form southern Arizona and northern Sonora into today's singular region.

Through much of the late 19th and early 20th centuries, the Arizona-Sonora border was a zone of fluidity rather than a rigid international boundary, a place of interaction rather than exclusion. True border citizens like Packard and William Greene conducted business and lived their lives in a single region that encapsulated the border rather than was divided by it.

Packard's many and varied business and political interests on both sides of the U.S.-Mexico border made him a true border citizen, equally influential and at home in either nation. Again and again, as Ms. Hayostek writes, "Packard's varied and large body of international experience undoubtedly made him 'the go-to guy' for borderland ranchers, miners and political figures."

Biographies are among the trickiest narrative forms within the historian's craft, fraught through with methodological challenge. Imposing a chronological logic on the quotidian events and actions that make up the day-to-day life of individuals and collective societies is at the crux of what historians do in trying to make sense of the past.

Picking and choosing from the overwhelming number of facts and details that make up the past to impose a meaningful narrative that aids in our comprehension and understanding of who we are as a society today, or within any particular historical period, is daunting.

Using a particular individual who was a central historical actor within a period is one particular approach to this task and one wrought with both possibility and peril. The best of biographies not only help us understand the particularity of the individual experience and how their historical period impacted them, but also give us new comprehension of a particular time period and give us greater understanding of a particular society itself.

Ms. Hayostek does a remarkable job of pulling together an impressive variety of primary sources, the inescapable "dross of facts" that grounds the historian's tale in reality, to render an engaging story of one man's incredible life as a border citizen and to enrich our understanding of the Arizona-Sonora borderlands in the past and the present.

J.C. Mutchler
Associate Research Historian
Southwest Center
Associate Research Professor
Department of History
University of Arizona

Cynthia F. Hayostek

Introduction

Late in 1922, my paternal grandfather accepted a new job and moved his family to Douglas, Ariz., and into a house in the 1100 block of 10th Street. After my father's bicycle was unpacked, he began riding it, thus attracting the attention of neighborhood boys. One of them, Ashley Packard, lived across the street from my dad's new home.

The friendship Ashley and my dad, Jack Davis, developed more than 90 years ago was just the first of several multigenerational relationships between the Packard and Davis families. In one sense, this book, a biography of Ashley's remarkable grandfather, Burdette Aden Packard, is merely a continuation of Jack and Ashley's friendship.

B.A. Packard was a man of medium height who'd grown portly by the time my dad knew him. Although B.A.'s hair was silver then, in his younger days it had been blond. He had a square face with a strong jaw. This determined-looking appearance was accentuated by large eyes of a penetrating blue that observed the world confidently and with twinkling good humor.

My dad used to tell me stories about B.A. Packard. He owned the First National Bank in Douglas. Ashley and my dad would walk five blocks downtown to the bank. B.A. would usher them into a room where there'd be burlap sacks on a table. The sacks contained large silver Mexican coins called 'dobe dollars, and the two friends spent hours counting the coins. Packard paid them with an American dollar that they used to buy sodas at the Owl Drug ice cream fountain.

B.A. had a ranch about 15 miles west of Douglas. He'd drive the boys to the ranch in his car, which you knew was coming, said my dad, because of the way B.A. drove. In town, he'd keep the vehicle in first gear no matter what, and you could hear the engine loudly revving and straining long before the car appeared.

At the ranch, the boys helped work cattle. Ashley's mount was a retired racehorse named Barney, whose age – 16 years – was the same as his height in hands. Ashley's saddle was an old-fashioned heavy one. This was a difficult combination for a young boy and it took both friends to heave the saddle onto Barney's high back.

B.A. used his car to work cattle. My dad vividly described B.A. rescuing one of his purebred Hereford calves caught in barbed wire. He untangled the calf and put the exhausted critter in the car's backseat, where it bled on the upholstery, but B.A. didn't seem to care about that. He slowly drove to ranch headquarters so the calf's mother could walk along the car near her baby.

Those two facets of B.A. were what I usually came across as I read local and regional history books: "B.A. Packard, the banker and cattleman... ." But I suspected there was more to B.A. than just those two things, and so I started researching his life.

Who's Who-type entries provided enticing glimpses of B.A.'s accomplishments, as did a survey of Cochise County records. But I soon discovered the truth of something my dad said, "B.A. played his cards close to his chest." My dad always accompanied these words with a gesture of a poker player holding a slightly splayed handful of cards and pulling them toward his body so only he could see them.

It was true; books and official records didn't completely convey the essence of B.A.'s life and times. So I started reading newspapers. I began with 1880 Tombstone papers, for that was the year B.A. arrived in Arizona. I switched to Bisbee papers in 1898, and to Douglas papers in 1907.

I looked for flaws but never found any. I gradually discovered an extraordinary man, the notable people with whom he associated, and the momentous times they shared. Here is his story and their stories.

Cynthia F. Hayostek

Early Years

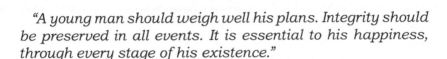

"A young man should weigh well his plans. Integrity should be preserved in all events. It is essential to his happiness, through every stage of his existence."
— John Adams, 1735-1826, second U.S. President

Late on March 26, 1880, people gathered to see who would alight from a stagecoach arriving in Tombstone, Arizona Territory. Among those disembarking were two men with dust in their fashionably generous sideburns and on their stylish jackets.

The pair undoubtedly resembled Eastern tenderfoots, but no one made fun of them. They were in Tombstone to buy silver mines, and most everyone in the boomtown knew it because B.A. Packard and A.A. Hopkins were, as the Tombstone *Weekly Nugget* put it, "from the oil regions of Pennsylvania."[1]

Packard and Hopkins were just two of a couple dozen Keystone State oil producers who invested in 1880s Tombstone and Cochise County. Most of the oil men soon returned home, but Packard settled permanently in Arizona. He started farming and ranching, held political offices, acquired banks, and became an individual who influenced state, national and international events. Today, few know of Packard or his connections, which is the way he would have wanted it. He was an unpretentious individual, and that was the result of his upbringing and education.

Burdette Aden Packard was born Nov. 1, 1847 in Portville, a town in western New York close to the Pennsylvania border. He was the only child of Ashley Giles and Virtue V. (Crandall) Packard. The Packard family line extended back into 1600s Massachusetts and Rhode Island to the man who was progenitor of all Packards in the United States. Virtue Crandall's ancestors were also multi-generational New Englanders who claimed relationship to Daniel Webster.[2]

Ashley moved to Portville in 1844, just a few years after it became a separate township from Olean, a Cattaraugus County settlement on the Allegheny River famed for its stands of white pine. Ashley worked first as a sawyer and then as a raftsman, which meant each spring he gathered cut timber on the river, roped the logs together and floated the rafts down the Allegheny to sell in Pittsburgh – a dangerous job he did for 36 years, 30 of them as a raft pilot.

Ashley farmed when he wasn't on the river. After retiring from the lumber business, he worked the land full-time. He also served as Portville Justice of the Peace and as an assessor. He built a home in a part of Portville known as Main Settlement. His multi-story Stick Style house was the only slate-roofed dwelling in the area, and was on land Virtue acquired from her family.[3]

Young Burdette went to school in his native town amid the increasing tensions preceding the Civil War. When war broke out, he was 12-years-old and four paternal uncles and his father enlisted in the Union Army. Burdette, however, had little to do with the war.

One reason was that his mother's family included Quaker members. During the winters of 1864 and 1865, Burdette attended a school run by Maria King, a Quaker, in Ceres, N.Y., southeast of Main Settlement. The lessons Burdette learned included living an honest, unassuming life that was of service to others.

Another reason Burdette didn't participate in the Civil War was that he'd entered the business world. Around his 10th birthday, he acquired his first horse and soon began horse trading and training. His dealings gave him a discerning eye when it came to equines, and a deep appreciation for race horses. That term, for B.A., always meant Standardbreds, a breed developed in rural New York in the mid-1800s that trots or paces in harness rather than gallops under saddle as Thoroughbreds do.

When he was not in school, Burdette worked on his father's farm. In 1864, at age 16, Burdette helped with that year's log raft. Apparently, the work didn't suit Burdette because the next year, just before lumber season started, he became a clerk in a store owned by John R. Archibald of Mill Grove, a hamlet near Main Settlement.[4]

Archibald, the same as Ashley, got into the lumber business as a sawyer and log raft pilot. Archibald bought a grocery and general provisions store, shortly before Burdette began working for him. The obvious links between Archibald and Ashley must have helped Burdette get the job – the first known instance of connections in Packard's long life.[5]

Burdette A. Packard as a young man in the 1870s.

Packard family photo

By age 19, Burdette was manager of Archibald's store. In 1873, B.A. went into business for himself by joining an ancient and honorable trade. He bought two wagons and became a wholesale hawker in the Western Reserve (the five western New York counties) and Pennsylvania.

Hawkers peddled goods from a cart or wagon instead of from their backs. In the 1800s, both hawkers and peddlers sold horses, household goods, and tin pots and pans to people living in isolated places.

While he was a hawker, connections again played a role in Packard's life. In 1875, 27-year-old B.A. boarded with E.W. Middaugh, a farmer in Steuben County, N.Y. William C. Middaugh, a 20-year-old student, lived with Ashley and Virtue in Portville at the same time.[6]

Connections: The Life and Times of B. A. Packard

Unfortunately, B.A. started his business at the wrong time. In 1872, a company named Montgomery Ward began publishing mail order catalogues that reached into every community, no matter how small or isolated. That, combined with mass production and railroad transportation, eliminated many peddler and hawker routes.

Then in September 1873, a financial panic swept the United States. America had enjoyed a booming economy during the Reconstruction following the Civil War, but the growth had dubious underpinnings. The breakdown started when the prominent banking firm of Jay Cooke and Co. collapsed. Soon almost half the nation's iron furnaces shut down and over half the nation's railroads went into receivership.

The depression lasted until 1878 and had long-lasting effects. One consequence was the "labor question" came to dominate societal thought, and this changed the nation's political agenda and balance of power between political parties. The labor question resulted from some cities' 25 percent unemployment rate, which forced many workers and their families into vagrancy. Wage cuts prompted violent strikes, which so alarmed metropolitan businessmen they demanded enactment of law and order regulations as protection against vagabonds and strikers.

Small-town businessmen and local officials, who deeply resented the disruptive influence of "big business" in their communities, often allied with labor. So did farmers who faced plummeting land and commodity prices. These groups wanted government regulations to control inflation and rising railroad rates.

The way the Democrat and Republican parties responded to these demands (or in the case of the GOP, didn't respond) resulted in the Republicans losing their massive Congressional majority in 1874. Reconstruction was over. Stalemate politics became the order of the day. Without federal guidance, Americans came to rely upon local efforts when dealing with economic and other difficulties during the next decade.[7]

Cynthia F. Hayostek

The 1873 panic and subsequent recession marked Packard in several ways. Chief amongst these was his life-long affiliation to the Democratic Party. Because he grew up in rural New York, it's easy to understand why he registered that way.

Although the Democratic Party in New York City had a cozy relationship with the corrupt Tammany machine, an equally iniquitous Republican cabal dominated the state's rural areas. Republicans were so unresponsive to the demands of farmers and small businessmen that they flocked to the Democratic Party.

Once in Arizona, Packard encountered much the same situation. Silver prices that were tied so closely to currency inflation concerned miners, and railroad charges to ship cattle to distant markets caused ranchers much angst. When political means proved inadequate to solve such difficulties, B.A.'s innate self-reliance caused him to forge onward and do what he thought was right, even if it was at odds with government policy.

The 1870s depression crippled Packard's fledgling hawker business, and he sold it. In later years, he said merely it developed too much "red fringe." Packard meant there was too much red ink (debt) in his ledger book, and he resolved to never be caught out again. He kept enough reserve so he survived difficult financial times in the early 1890s, expanded during the 1907 panic, and eased through an early 1920s recession. Packard always made sure, especially when he was running his own bank, that he had enough assets to ride out bad times – even the Great Depression of the 1930s.$_8$

In the mid-1870s, however, Packard's financial difficulties led him to manage a hardware store in Coleville, Penn., and then a store owned by Rixford, Penn., businessman Marcus B. Bennie. Eventually, Packard acquired his own oil well supplies and hardware store in Rixford.$_9$

Coleville and Rixford were in McKean County, immediately south of Portville. So was Titusville, where Edwin Drake had drilled the world's first oil well in 1859. Technological inadequacies then limited development of subsequent oil fields. By the mid-1870s, however, everything was in place for an oildorado. Whale oil used in lanterns was becoming scarce, well drillers had developed the tools and resolve required to tap into oil bodies, and new refinery techniques shifted production from odorous coal oil to clean-burning kerosene processed from petroleum.

In 1875, an oil well near Bradford, Penn., began producing 25 barrels a day. Although the price was just cents per barrel, the well was a moneymaker. In just months, Bradford and McKean County transformed from a pastoral farming region into a landscape devoid of vegetation and dominated by more than 5,000 oil derricks, noisy steam engines, raucous boom

The frenzied development of Pennsylvania oil produced a chaotic landscape that to modern eyes looks environmentally devastated.

Library of Congress

towns, and roads so muddy horses could sink up to their bellies.[10]

Into this maelstrom came Packard. He partnered with Bennie and Frank E. Tyler to buy an Otto Township farm. The partners then sold rights to portions of the farm, which by 1877 was the site of tanks and pumps sending oil by pipeline to Buffalo, N.Y. Packard received royalties on oil moved.[11]

He formed another partnership with Alphonius A. Hopkins and William J. McCullagh. They drilled an oil well in Kendall Creek and another near Rixford. The wells produced about 50 barrels a day, with a barrel selling for 58 cents to $4 ($13-91 in 2013). Hopkins put in a number of wells by himself, and lived in a Bradford farm house with Packard to gain oil rights.[12]

Through Hopkins, Packard developed connections with other oil entrepreneurs. Among them were John M. Armstrong, Charles H. Filkins, Fordyce A. Roper and Casper Taylor. They were among the men responsible for the remarkable growth of Bradford's oil production. In 1878, it was 6.5 million barrels; in 1879, 14.2 million barrels. Pennsylvania black gold accounted for half the world's total oil production before 1901.[13]

The affluence these statistics suggest had personal meaning for B.A. Once established in the oil business, he decided to marry. On Nov. 27, 1879, he wed Ella Lewis.

Ella, a dark-haired, petite woman, was the daughter of Israel T. and Elmina (Worden) Lewis. The same as the Packards, the Lewises originally were Rhode Islanders who moved to New York in the early 1800s. Ella was born Jan. 7, 1851 in Alfred, N.Y., 35 miles northeast of Portville. Alfred's founders were Seventh Day Baptists, many of whom were War of 1812 veterans.[14]

Alfred's pride and joy was its academy, founded in 1836. A history of now-Alfred University points out it took an "act of faith to start an institution of higher learning in the days when an eighth-grade education was considered lofty; it was an act of daring to decide to admit women students on an equal basis with men. However, even before the Civil War began, more than 40 percent of Alfred's students were women."[15]

One of those women was Ella, whose family moved in the late 1870s to Genesee, N.Y., east of Portville. After their marriage, Ella and B.A. split their time between New York and Pennsylvania, while B.A. sold most of his oil holdings.[16]

B.A. later said he made $72,000 ($1.7 million in 2013) in Pennsylvania. This, plus his network of oil business friends, undoubtedly made him receptive to something new. In March 1880, Filkins traveled to Tombstone. Within days of his arrival, he bonded several silver mines.[17] Bonding was a form of financial assurance that a mine would produce marketable ore.

Also in March, Packard and Hopkins traveled to San Francisco and then Tucson. The Southern Pacific Railroad tracks reached Tucson March 17, 1880, only 10 days before Packard and Hopkins' visit. So when they arrived, Tucson's passenger depot was under construction, and so was much of Tucson.

But what B.A. remembered about 1880 Tucson was a poker game. That Packard remembered a card game as the highlight of his first visit to Tucson says much about his passion for poker.

He came across three men playing poker under a tree, and they invited him to join them. Two of the men were professional gamblers, and the third was Robert N. Leatherwood, then Tucson's mayor. He was the first Democrat to hold that office, which made an immediate connection between him and B.A.

"'I never saw them before in my life,' Packard recalled, 'but I accepted the invitation and we played throughout the afternoon. I don't remember the outcome, it doesn't matter, but we had one of the most enjoyable afternoons I have ever spent.'"[18]

Cynthia F. Hayostek

Packard and Hopkins' trip from Tucson to Tombstone included a lengthy stagecoach ride. This part of their trip wasn't comfortable due in part to the many people crowded in and on the vehicle. The stagecoach road paralleled the San Pedro River part of the way, but the road was bumpy and dusty. With primitive springs and glassless windows, a stagecoach required its riders to endure nonstop jostling and constant grime.

Nor was the trip safe. In 1880, Apaches controlled rural southern Arizona. Miners, ranchers and farmers, even those who lived only a short distance from Tombstone, could become Apache victims – something B.A. would soon learn.

Another danger was armed robbery. On March 15, 1881, bandits attempted to rob the Tombstone stage, killing a passenger and driver. The incident was one that led up to a gun battle near Tombstone's OK Corral seven months later.

Packard would play a minor role in that now-famous gunfight. But Packard didn't know that on March 26, 1880 when he and Hopkins got out of the stagecoach and brushed the dust out of their sideburns and off their jackets. Nor did B.A. know he was stepping into a life-changing experience.

NOTES

1. In biographical material he supplied during his time in the Arizona legislature, Packard said he arrived in Arizona on May 10, 1880. He gave the same date in newspaper interviews late in his life, but for James H. McClintock's compendium, *Arizona*, Packard specified March 26. Packard gave May 10 for reasons revealed in Chapter 2.

2. Both the Packard and Crandall families contain many names associated with Seventh Day Baptists. Packard genealogical information supplied by Ashley B. Packard, Lions Bay, British Columbia, Canada.

3. Adams, William, ed., *Historical Gazetteer and Biographical Memorial of Cattaraugus County, N.Y.* Syracuse, N.Y.: Lyman, Horton & Co., 1893, pp. 72-73, 1002, 1005. *A History of the Town of Portville, 1805-1920*, Portville Historic and Preservation Society, 1986, pp. 116-118, 127.

4. The account of B.A.'s boyhood is a compilation from: *Arizona, The Youngest State*, Vol. III. Chicago: S.J. Clark Publishing Co., 1916, p. 30; "Col. B.A. Packard, An Old Cowman of Cochise," *Bisbee Daily Review*, Aug. 5, 1934;

Connections: The Life and Times of B. A. Packard

"Col. B.A. Packard, Pioneer, Banker and Cattleman, ...," *Dispatch*, March 13, 1935; *Press Reference Library, Notables of the West, Vol. II.* No publication data, 1915, p. 235.

5. Adams, p. 1007.

6. 1875 New York state census, pp. 162 and 207.

7. Foner, Eric, *A Short History of the Reconstruction.* New York: Harper & Row, 1990, pp. 217-221.

8. Red fringe: Nichols, Charles A., *Dear Old Cochise.* Unpublished manuscript written in 1950s; copy in possession of author.

9. Partnerships: *Press Reference Library.* Evidence of Packard's own hardware business is letterhead stationery in possession of Dorothea Watkins, Douglas, Ariz.

10. Hatch, Vernelle A., *Illustrated History of Bradford, McKean County, Penn.* Bradford: Burk Bros., 1901, pp. 58-65 and 86-93. Miller, Ernest C., *Pennsylvania's Oil Industry.* Gettysburg, Penn.: Pennsylvania Historical Association, 1974, pp. 25-41.

11. Deeds involving Otto property are: McKean County, Penn., Grantee Book Misc. E, pp. 155-57; Book Y, pp. 71-72; Book 4, pp. 76-78; Book 3, pp. 247-248; Book 6, pp. 56-58; Book 4, pp. 329-331; and Book 6, pp. 177-179.

12. Other deeds naming Packard are: McKean County Grantee Book Misc. E, pp. 16-162; Book 2, pp. 520-521; Book 23, pp. 542-544; and Book 3, pp. 681-682.

Production figure and price quote: "Colonel Packard Recalls ...," *Dispatch*, Dec. 2, 1928. Article mentions "Indian Creek," but I used information in recorded deeds, not reminiscences 50 years after the fact.

13. Hatch, pp. 66-83.

14. Lewis genealogical information supplied by Ashley B. Packard.

15. "A Tradition of Distinction: Alfred University, 1836-Present," accessed July 2008 at: http://herrick.alfred.edu/special/archives/histories/history_of_au.shtlm.

16. Miller, pp. 42-52.

17. *Tombstone Weekly Nugget,* March 18, 1880.

18. "Col. B.A. Packard, An Old Cowman," *Review*, Aug. 5, 1934.

Cynthia F. Hayostek

Miner

"[T]here are a number of Olean and Bradford men in town. These oil men take very naturally to a new mining camp; they are real speculators with plenty of nerve to back it."
– John A. Rockfellow, 1858-1947, Cochise County pioneer

To Packard and his oil country colleagues, Tombstone must have reminded them of Bradford, Oil City, Titusville, and other raw Pennsylvania boomtowns where they'd lived. So undoubtedly, the Pennsylvanians easily fit into early-day Tombstone. Perhaps because of this, their involvement in 1880s Tombstone has been overlooked by historians.

More than two dozen Pennsylvania oil men contributed to Tombstone's boom. In just a few years, they invested more than $1 million ($2.5 billion in 2013) in Tombstone and southern Arizona. About half of them lived in, or at least visited, the region during the 1880s. They formed a web of business connections with each other and with other investors, and they all used the legal system to protect their property.

The names of Packard and Hopkins, and their friends Filkins, Roper and Taylor, appear on about 100 southern Arizona mining records. That's because Filkins and Roper acted as brokers, and Packard and Hopkins speculated; they were the most active buyers and sellers of their oil country contemporaries.

Although prices are listed on only some deeds (a common subterfuge to avoid taxes was "$1 and other valuable considerations"), some amounts mentioned are large. For example, the 1881 sale of three mines by Packard, Hopkins and William W. White to Boston residents Edward H. Dunn and J. Henry Sleeper was for $100,000 ($2.5 million in 2013). Potential amounts are even bigger. White, along with fellow

Pennsylvanians Jonathan Smithman, James Amm and William A. Pullman, bought, went to court over, and then sold Bisbee's Atlanta claim, which became a major copper producer for Phelps Dodge Corp.[1]

Other Pennsylvanians invested their considerable talents toward the progress of Tombstone and Arizona Territory. A prime example is Artemis E. Fay. He edited the Titusville *Daily Courier* before moving to Arizona, where he established Tombstone's first newspaper, the *Weekly Nugget*, on Oct. 2, 1879. Democratic in its political viewpoint, the *Nugget* served Tombstone for seven months before a Republican-leaning newspaper with a more clever name, the *Epitaph*, printed its premier issue.[2]

Fay, the same as all editors of the time, routinely exchanged issues with newspapers at which he'd previously worked. Thus news of Tombstone appeared in Pennsylvania oil country. This subtle bit of public relations undoubtedly encouraged oil men to think silver when they wanted to invest their profits.

Such a connection was important because, although the oil men were strongly entrepreneurial, they did need information before deciding to invest money in a capital-intensive venture in the Arizona desert. Their willingness to plunk down thousands of dollars in a chancy proposition thousands of miles away from home called for a certain adventuresomeness.

Adventuresomeness was certainly a characteristic of Ed Schieffelin, the prospector generally credited with discovering Tombstone's treasure trove. Although warned all he would find was his tombstone at the hands of Apaches if he prospected some unprepossessing hills a few miles east of the San Pedro River, Schieffelin ignored the naysayers.

In August 1877, Schieffelin found silver ore rich enough to convince his brother, Albert, and Richard Gird, a civil engineer and assayer, to brave the Apache threat and return with him to southeastern Arizona early in 1878. Their exploratory work produced claims they named the Lucky Cuss, Toughnut and Owl's Nest.

Prospectors who trailed behind the Schieffelins and Gird included Henry Williams and Oliver Boyer. They located the Grand Central claim which, because of a dispute with the Schieffelins and Gird, became known as the Contention.

Despite this, Williams and Boyer participated with the Schieffelins, Gird and Gird's cousin, Thomas E. Walker, in establishing the Tombstone Mining District. The district's formal foundation plus its ore body attracted capital with which to develop mines and build mills. By 1879, Tombstone was the site of numerous mines employing hundreds of men.

Water flowing down the San Pedro generated the power to run a mill of Gird's design that processed ore at Charleston, seven miles southwest of Tombstone. Another Charleston mill, this one steam powered, was part of a company whose directors included former Arizona Gov. Anson P.K. Safford and Connecticut industrialists Frank and Elbert Corbin.

Early in 1880, not long after their mill started up, the Corbin brothers, Marcus and Willis Hulings of Oil City, a few Philadelphians, and two individuals from Boston formed a syndicate. This syndicate bought stock in the Schieffelins' company, and the two entities merged on May 20, 1880 into the Tombstone Mill and Mining Co.[3]

Most likely, Fay and the Hulings were the connections that brought Filkins from Oil City to Tombstone early in 1880, just as Filkins was a connection who encouraged his friends Packard and Hopkins to join him in Tombstone in late April that year.

The April 8, 1880 issue of the *Nugget* announced commencement of work on the Vizina (pronounced Vie-zee-nah) Mine in a bond arrangement. On April 28, 1880, Filkins purchased the Vizina outright for $41,500 on behalf of "Pennsylvania parties," who incorporated the Vizina Mining Co. in New York.[4]

Thanks to Hopkins, Packard owned shares in this company – although he didn't know it until he got to Tombstone. He'd been against investing in the Vizina while in Bradford. Once in Tombstone, however, he saw the possibilities and told Hopkins so.

"Thereupon Hopkins took an instrument in writing from his pocket and said: 'Well, Pack, I bought stock in it before we started and made up my mind if it was good, you were in, but if it was no good then I'd forget it and say nothing about it. We're partners, and you're in half on this interest.'

"After recounting the incident, ... Packard said, 'that was the sort of partner I had. He was a fine fellow. None better.' "₅

Packard was correct on both counts. Hopkins was a good man and the Vizina did indeed have potential. But the same as with all mines, investment was extremely risky. It was all too easy then (as it still is today) not only to lose the initial investment, but for bankruptcy to overtake a nascent mining company.

Three factors (other than ore amount) controlled the destiny of mining companies late in the 19th century: access to capital and professional management, inexpensive (rail) transportation, and market conditions. Tombstone mining companies in the 1880s had precious little influence over the last two factors. Therefore, it was imperative to do everything right when it came to the first factor.

B. A. Packard wearing his sideburns in the 1880s.
Packard family photo

Capital had to be invested wisely. Upper-level management needed to be on site, or at least make regular visits, particularly if the corporation headquartered some place other than Arizona. Hiring a professional superintendent was wise, especially if dealing with metallurgically-complicated ore bodies, as in Tombstone.

Professional services, however, often ranked low on company directors' priority lists, and many commonly made the mistake of spending more money on mill and concentrator construction than on mine development.[6] An example of this flawed emphasis was the firm put together by the Eastern investors who took over from the Schieffelins and Gird; it was the Tombstone Mill (first) and Mining (second) Co.

The Pennsylvanians, on the other hand, generally hired professional superintendents and kept management local. That was one reason why Packard remained in Tombstone; he was a local administrator for several companies in which he held an interest. Another reason was that some companies became entangled in legal difficulties, which required close supervision.

One Pennsylvania corporation that emphasized mill over mine was the Sunset Silver Mining Co. Its directors hurried to build a mill, then apparently figured out they'd made a mistake and tried to rectify it by selling the mill. But it was too-little-too-late and, combined with declining ore, the Sunset Co. became a has-been in less than two years.

Packard was not involved in the Sunset Mine, which occupied 12.27 acres of ground on the western slope of Lucky Cuss Hill, southwest of the mine of the same name. But several of Packard's connections, most notably Asa W. Say, were deeply involved in the Sunset.

The Schieffelins and Gird located the Sunset on May 13, 1878. The trio gave the property to Gird's cousin Walker, who sold it to Pennsylvanians during the spring of 1880.[7]

"Speculators of the oil regions who have paid attention to the silver stocks," said the April 8, 1880 *Nugget* quoting the Bradford, Penn. *Era*, "are aware of the present value attached to shares in the Sunset Mine... . It is said a share recently changed hands at $10,000... ."

Stirring up some of this excitement was Say. The April 29, 1880 *Arizona Star* describes Say showing off in Tucson a large specimen that was a mass of bright yellow chloride ore held together by native silver. Say claimed the specimen came from a Sunset vein 23 inches wide and 100 feet long.

Smithman and B. Frank Hall (also a Pennsylvanian) paid $10,000 to buy into the Sunset, whose official incorporation took place Sept. 7, 1880 in Oil City. Shares were $50 each. Marcus Huling purchased 4,200 shares and so, not surprisingly, became the corporation's president. Other investors included Huling's son Willis, Say, W.P. Book, White and Taylor.[8]

The Sunset owners were so confident of their mine they decided to enlarge its ground. "[A] number of capitalists have purchased three claims that nearly surround the Sunset," reported the April 8, 1880 *Nugget*. "They are the Longfellow, Luck Sure and Sunnyside, and promise to prove as valuable as the Sunset. They have been consolidated and stocked to $65,000."

The Luck Sure, Sunnyside and Longfellow, the *Nugget* informed its readers, had been purchased by James S. Book, a Pennsylvanian. He'd been offered more money for the Luck Sure than what he paid for all three mines, apparently because assay values from the Luck Sure ran between $300 and $1,000 per ton.[9]

On April 29, 1880, James K.P. Hall, Say and B. Frank Hall applied for a patent from the U.S. Land office for the Sunset. The *Nugget* issue that day, in addition to the patent application notice, published a paragraph that was, in essence, a request for bids for erection of a hoist at the Sunset mine and for a mill on the San Pedro.

In its May 13 issue, the *Nugget* reported, "The lower shaft of the Sunset Mine is now down 145 feet, all in ore, which is a sight to look upon." A week later, the *Nugget* said, "Since our last issue, the Sunset Mine has been showing to better advantage than before. In the upper shaft, the ledge has widened, and the body of ore strengthens in proportion. ... The Company are arranging for the erection of a mill on the San Pedro. Mr. [J.W.] Pender has secured the contract for erection of hoisting works, and he and Asa W. Say are now in San Francisco purchasing the machinery."[10]

The "powerful set of hoisting works," according to the *Nugget*, consisted of "a double set of engines with double reels, gearing, etc." purchased from Rankin, Brayton & Co. of San Francisco. That firm installed custom mill machinery for the Boston & Arizona Smelting & Reduction Co., about three miles north of Charleston.[11]

The 10-stamp Sunset Mill, erected immediately after the Boston & Arizona Mill, was about eight miles down the San Pedro from the Boston Mill, and 10 miles north of Charleston. According to the April 1881 *Arizona Quarterly Illustrated*, the Sunset Mill included an amalgamation set-up and two retorts. These items meant Sunset ore underwent several concentration steps and the final product was bullion (a mixture of silver and gold), which, beginning in June 1880, was hauled to Benson's railroad depot.

A small settlement called Bullionville sprang up around the Sunset Mill, but it soon was considered part of Contention City, since that place was situated between the Sunset Mill and Contention Mill. Contention City's population peaked at around 200 – not even close to Charleston, the mill town upriver which had about 400 residents.

The Sunset Mill probably did pay for itself. The July 27, 1880 *Tombstone Epitaph* said that when the Oil City men bought the Sunset Mine for $60,000, everyone laughed because its shaft was only 12 feet deep. Four months later, 150 feet of levels radiated off a 100-foot shaft. The ore found was enough to pay the purchase price five times over, the *Epitaph* assured its readers.

During September 1880, the Sunset's optimistic directors spent $60,000 buying into two claims near the Lucky Cuss, and Say bought two claims adjacent to the Longfellow. In

November 1880, the pragmatic Halls sold their rights in the Sunset Mine to the company.[12]

On Jan. 5, 1881, the Sunset sold its mill for $25,000 to the Head Center Mining Co., which was owned then by four Tucson men. The deal involved two promissory notes, which the Head Center Co. paid off by Dec. 12, 1881.[13]

So what happened? In September 1880, the Sunset Co. was on top of the world. Three months later, it sold its mill – a major asset. Why the company did this could be that the ore lode pinched out in October. The ore's disappearance could be what caused the experienced Halls to sell in November.

Undoubtedly, miners tried to find a new lode, but when exploration turned up nothing, the Sunset directors leased the mine to the Des Moines and Tombstone Mining & Milling Co., composed of individuals who picked out ore fragments remaining in the mine. These scavengers, known then as chloriders, also worked dumps and tailings.

In 1883, one of those chloriders, D.W. Cunningham, received a notice from the Des Moines Co. that, since he'd not worked in the Sunset the previous year, the company demanded he pay $200 as his share to the total or forfeit his interest in the mine. It was an ignoble end to what had been a bonanza, especially since in mid-1883, the federal government granted the patent the Sunset Co. applied for in 1880.[14]

While the Sunset presented operational obstacles, two mines in which Packard was directly involved, the Vizina and Stonewall, presented legal challenges. That Packard remained in Arizona to deal with these difficulties changed his life.

In 1880, after Filkins bonded the Vizina for his fellow Pennsylvanians and they incorporated, the Vizina's directors did everything right. They hired a professional superintendent who focused on mine development instead of building a mill.

"The work of developing the Vizina Mine," reported the April 8, 1880 *Nugget*, "commenced on Monday last, under the direction of Dr. [James W.] Steinburn, a mining engineer of many years' experience on the Pacific coast."

Steinburn set men to digging a shaft and cut about 40 feet away that angled toward the shaft. Both excavations reached ore that contained "three thousand dollars to the ton, picked rock, while an average assay clings to the hundreds," said the *Nugget*. Undoubtedly, this strong show of ore was what convinced Packard that Hopkins had involved him in a profitable mine when they first arrived in Tombstone.

By early May 1880, the Vizina consisted of two shafts. The northern one contained a five-foot-wide ore vein that dipped toward Tombstone. As May wore on, blasting inside the Vizina alarmed Tombstone pedestrians.$_{15}$

This happened because "the mine takes in a large portion of the lower [southern] end of the business part of our city,"

This 1881 photograph of Tombstone looks north, down from the hillside property of the Tombstone Mill & Mining Co. On the left is the Vizina Consolidated Mining Co. plant. Note the seven-team wagon on the road to the right of the Vizina. Newly-constructed Schieffelin Hall is the two-story building with peaked roof on the northern edge of town.

Author's collection

explained the *Nugget* on April 8, 1880. The newspaper added, "rent from business houses and private residences [on the surface] will remunerate the price paid for the mine in a year or so."

In September 1880, Alfred H. Emanuel, who'd been Steinburn's assistant, took over from him as Vizina superintendent. Also that month, a 20-horsepower steam engine and other machinery arrived. The engine, which powered the mine's hoist, went into a building on the southwest corner of Toughnut and Fourth streets that was tall enough to cover a 52-foot headframe.[16]

Before October arrived, the Vizina had sent 200 tons of ore to the Boston & Arizona mill for processing, said the Oct. 1, 1880 *Epitaph*. The ore, noted the Aug. 26, 1880 *Epitaph*, was richer than any other district mine – "15 tons gave $410 per ton from the battery samples." The $410 figure was impressive because Tombstone's average value ranged between $45 and $70 per ton.[17]

Such bounty allowed the Vizina Co. to pay for its new office building that faced Toughnut Street and included several apartments with attached bathrooms. Across the street was a building that contained Packard's office.[18]

He lived in as well as worked out of a three-room apartment. He'd become the local manager for the Vizina Co., as well as several other mining firms in which he was involved. Because Ella stayed back East, and B.A. traveled between Tombstone and New York often (he did so three times in the last six months of 1880), an apartment for him made sense.

As 1881 began, the Vizina consisted of three shafts more than 100 feet in depth; two shafts were in ore. A drift connected the shafts, which had produced 800 tons of ore and $60,000 for the company. The Vizina was the Tombstone district's third largest mine.[19]

This, plus its location on part of the town site, made the Vizina the target of opportunists. One such was James B.

McGowan who, on Aug. 1, 1880, moved onto two Vizina-owned lots at Allen and First streets, and repelled all comers. The company took him to court.

The U.S. First District Court declared McGowan presented no usable facts in his defense since he was not "a man of ordinary understanding." John H. Lucas, McGowan's attorney, said his client would leave if no damages were demanded, and the court dismissed the case for costs.[20]

The Vizina used the Sept. 30, 1880 *Epitaph* to warn squatters such as McGowan off company property. After Cochise County split off from Pima County on Feb. 1, 1881, the Vizina Co. complained about other squatters to the newly formed Cochise County Board of Supervisors, which repeatedly asked County Attorney Lyttleton Price for an opinion about the validity of the company's title.

Price told the supervisors that Vizina land fronting Toughnut clearly belonged to the company because "the Vizina Mining Claim was located under the Act of Congress of 10th May 1872 prior to the location of the Townsite of the Village of Tombstone ... and ... the locators of said mining claim and their successors in interest have complied with all the requirements of the law under which the said claims was located."

The Vizina Co. owned the surface land, said Price, despite "a deed ... executed by the Mayor of said village to certain persons (the so-called Townsite Company) conveying the premises in question, and those persons claim, by reason of said conveyance, title to the premises in question, as against the owners of the Vizina Mine."[21]

Price's opinion makes it clear that the Vizina Co., the same as many Tombstone property owners of the time, was embroiled in the Townsite Controversy. This dispute began in 1879, when Safford and some other men created a company that sold lots on what developed as today's Tombstone. But this company did not obtain legal title to the land it sold. People who bought land from this company discovered their deeds were faulty after a second company, the Tombstone Townsite Co., began selling the same real estate in May 1880.

The Tombstone Townsite Co. was set up so that the mayor (in 1880 a man named Alder Randall) held all company deeds in trust. In October, Randall sold his deeds to the Townsite Co., which attempted to transfer most of them to non-resident company partners. To protect their real estate, many Tombstone landowners took up armed residence on their property to prevent lot-jumping.

John Clum, *Epitaph* editor, led a vigorous protest against the scheme, which affected not only private parties but also mining companies holding property within Tombstone – the Vizina, Mountain Maid, Way Up, Good Enough and Gilded Age.

Edward Field, Gilded Age owner, cited the 1872 Mining Law in his suit against the Townsite Co. and one of its owners. Citation of the 1872 Mining Law in the Vizina case was easier to back than Field's, as the Vizina had a proven lode within its claim and the Gilded Age did not.[22]

The Vizina produced steadily from its lode throughout 1882 – the year of peak production in Tombstone. Packard's friend Taylor took over as Vizina superintendent in January of that year. Taylor's wife, Jennie, joined him after Packard purchased a house for them.[23]

The Nov. 4, 1882 *Epitaph* said a 350-foot stope (room) dominated the Vizina, which daily produced a wagonload of ore sent to the Boston & Arizona mill. The Nov. 25, 1882 *Epitaph* declared the Vizina had paid $100,000 in dividends, and shipped $154,200 in bullion.

An omen these halcyon days wouldn't last long appeared in the Nov. 28, 1882 *Epitaph*, which reported a fire in the Vizina plant. Because a fire station was only a block away, a quick response insured all miners were hoisted out of the mine safely, and structural damage was slight.

This fire was in the middle of a half-dozen conflagrations occurring at the Vizina plant. Given that the blacksmith shop had a constant fire and all the steam that ran the machinery was fire-produced, it's surprising firefighters didn't call more often than they did.

At the time of the 1882 blaze, a difficulty already confronted the Vizina that was completely opposite from fire, and would eventually end Tombstone's boom days. The Dec. 16, 1882 *Epitaph* reported a pump installed in the Vizina removed 10,000 gallons of water every 12 hours.

The first Tombstone mine to encounter excessive water was the Sulphret, south of the Vizina, during March 1881. As other Tombstone mines reached 500 feet in depth, they too confronted prodigious amounts of water.

Initially, mining companies welcomed the flow since it could to be used in mills built near Tombstone, thus eliminating the cost of shoveling ore into canvas sacks and loading the sacks into wagons for a trip to mills along the San Pedro. By mid-1886, Charleston's mills were closed and the town abandoned.

The first of Tombstone's new mills was the Girard, which began utilizing water from the Grand Central and Contention mines in early 1882. Installing additional pumps in 1883 temporarily suspended operations in the two mines, but by 1884 the new pumps again lowered the water level.[24]

Mines such as the Vizina benefited from the Grand Central/Contention pumping, but the oil country men didn't wait to find that out. On Nov. 27, 1883, the Vizina directors sold the property for $11,600 to a New Yorker, Henry A. Tweed, who kept Taylor as superintendent.[25]

Taylor hired chloriders, 25 of them, according to the Sept. 15, 1885 Tombstone *Record-Epitaph*. He also overcame a variety of difficulties. One began around 4 a.m. on Dec. 15 with "pistol shots, followed by the alarm bells of the fire department, and the shrill screeching of the whistles of various hoisting works [which] advised residents ... that a serious conflagration was in progress.... . [T]he Vizina hoisting works ... [was] enveloped in flames."

The hoist building was a total loss, although adjoining structures were saved. Taylor estimated it would cost $20,000 to replace the hoist house, but the company carried only $3,000 insurance.[26]

Tweed produced the money for a new Armstrong hoist, but shortly before it became operational, he sold the Vizina to Taylor. Beginning in February 1886, Taylor leased the Vizina to 18 chloriders, and shipped their output to a Socorro, N.M. smelter. He left Tombstone for good in 1890 upon receiving appointment as postmaster of Santa Paula, Calif.[27]

Although the chloriders occasionally found a pocket of rich ore, clearly the Vizina's producing days were numbered. Early in 1888, Tombstone merchant Lewis W. Blinn bought the mine for $4,000.[28]

The Vizina, which had been the district's third largest mine, thus suffered an ignominious end – the same as the Sunset. It was a far cry from the exhilaration people felt during Tombstone's first few years as a boomtown.

Toward the end of his life, Packard recalled how people in 1880 Tombstone were wild with excitement. B.A. became infected too since just days after learning of his Vizina stock "purchase" as Hopkins' partner, his next move was to purchase other mining properties.[29]

Early in May 1880, "B.A. Packard and A.A. Hopkins ... [i]n a quiet manner have secured some very valuable property in different localities in this district, among them the Baker, Haley and Thunderbolt claims, belonging to Baker, Haley and Slattery, and the Stonewall by bond. Actual purchases, one-fourth of the Orneo, and one claim in the Turquoise [district, 15 miles east of Tombstone], and they have a bond on nine claims in the Dragoon Mountains. Thorough, energetic businessmen," opined the *Nugget*, "they will prove a valuable acquisition to our camp."[30]

Only the Stonewall developed into a top-rank producer. Of the Baker, Haley and Thunderbolt claims, just the Thunderbolt incorporated, with James Vizina and three others as principals.[31]

The nine claims (plus three not mentioned by the *Nugget*) were in the Dragoon Mountains and made in the names of Packard, W.S. Mollison and Richard R. Richardson, the latter of Franklin, Penn. The nine claims were in the Turquoise district, which was also the site of the Silver Cloud Mine. Packard and Hopkins, with fellow oil men Hiram W. Hoag and John S. Hunter and Tombstone residents John R. Duling and Silas M. Leavenworth, invested in the Silver Cloud, but the ore quickly petered out.[32]

In the Orneo, Packard, Hopkins and Richardson confronted another mining world difficulty – apparent fraud. When the trio bought into the Orneo on Say's recommendation, Richardson and Say purchased half the mine, and Packard, Hopkins and Say bought a quarter.

Richardson recalled Say telling him the Orneo had a good title with no claims against it. Say "pointed out to [Richardson] a ledge or vein of valuable ore," stating it was part of the Orneo. On the strength of this, Richardson bought his share and received a deed.[33]

The ore he saw, Richardson said in a suit he later filed against Say, was really on the Prompter claim, just south of the Sunset. Richardson insisted the Orneo was never a valid claim, and that when Say said it was, he committed fraud. Richardson asked the court for $2,000 and expenses.

As the Orneo was properly located, the First U.S. District Court dismissed Richardson's suit in June 1882. He had to pay court costs.[34]

Packard and Hopkins didn't join Richardson in this suit; they filed their own against Say as part of a legal whirlwind that enveloped the Stonewall Mine. That extensive litigation shows that while some shot it out on the streets of Tombstone, Packard fought in court.

The Stonewall was a small property southwest of the Sunset. South of the Stonewall was a claim located May 6, 1878 by R.C. Jacobs. It was 1,500 feet of "mineral bearing ledge" and Jacobs claimed "300 feet on each side of the center of the ledge... ." He marked his claim with four stone monuments, and named it the Knoxville. When he recorded his claim, Jacobs mentioned the monuments, but not the Stonewall since it was located a week *after* the Knoxville.$_{35}$

On May 10, 1880, Hopkins, Say and Packard bought the Knoxville for $16,000 from T. McPherson, H. Lines, Thomas J. Jones and A. Ames. The Pennsylvanians, however, may not have known it as the Knoxville, for the property was never called that in a deed recording the transaction. Instead, it's described as 1,500 by 500 feet and delineated by stone monuments. Then the deed says, "also the Stonewall No. 2 Mine located May 6, 1880 by the parties of the first part," meaning McPherson and his partners.$_{36}$

Why there was a Stonewall No. 2 and why it was located in 1880, not in 1878, the same as many other Tombstone claims, was central to Packard and Hopkins' stance in the litigation that followed their purchase. Another part of the problem, as Packard ruefully noted, was 1880s Tombstone investors, including him, were in so big a hurry to make a fortune that they didn't bother with mundane matters such as checking for clear title.

With what they thought was a good deed in hand, the Pennsylvanians wasted no time putting the Stonewall into production. The May 20, 1880 *Nugget* reported, "Say, Hopkins & Packard ... have put a force of men to fully develop [the Stonewall]. Only a few days work disclosed large bodies of good ore, the extent of which is not yet fully determined as the excavations are all in ore."

Cheered by this good fortune, Packard and Hopkins left Tombstone in mid-June and headed for Pennsylvania to find investors. Within days of their departure, trouble visited their property. Two items in the June 24 *Nugget* tell what happened; both items mention shotguns in their headlines.

"During a few days last week, there was considerable excitement over on the Unexpected-Owl's Nest-Minerva Mine, (it is claimed by different people under all three names.) The same ground is claimed to have been originally located by Andy Baldridge on April 11, 1879. Messrs. Corbin and Richard Gird claim the mine under the name of Owl's Nest, and Dr. Stainborn [sic] claims it under the name of Minerva. The latter has been in possession of the mine for months, and during that time has done a great deal of work.

"Last week the Corbin-Gird men went on the property, removed the Stainborn windlasses from the shafts, and took possession. Stainborn, being informed of the proceedings, went up to the mine, and of course was told to leave the ground, the argument being backed more forcibly by a shotgun. After some parlaying with Horner, the shotgun expert, Stainborn returned to town, had Horner arrested and lodged in the lock-up, and during the same night Stainborn put a force of men on the property, and the two parties held together, four on a side, all well armed.

"During the following day, a consultation took place between Doc Stainborn and Messrs. Corbin and Gird downtown while their forces were at the mine, and the result was, as a suit for title is proceeding in the courts, that Stainborn's men were withdrawn from the property, and the other side ... is now in possession... ."

Another *Nugget* article began, "And now the Stonewall mine, located on the hill opposite town, comes in for its share of notoriety in the shotgun policy.

"The property was recently sold to A.B. [sic] Packard and H.H. [sic] Hopkins and others, of Pennsylvania, on a working bond, and the developments during the past two or three weeks has made the property very valuable. Messrs. Corbin and Gird claim a prior right to the property, and one or two men, accompanied by their attorney, Harry B. Jones, went upon the ground and demanded possession.

"Harry Jones looked down the muzzle of a shotgun for a brief period, but it didn't frighten him much, as he had been there before. However, after a time Jones and party retired, leaving the property in the same possession as before. Here the matter ends for the present, and in all probability the courts will decide the title question."

U.S. District Courts did become involved, although it took five cases and four years before all disputes pertaining to the Stonewalls and Knoxville were cleared. The first of the five cases stemmed from the attempt to seize the Stonewall.

Although the *Nugget* article didn't say Jones represented the Orion Silver Mining Co., the newspaper implied this when it mentioned "Messrs. Corbin and Gird." The Orion was a corporation whose principals were the Corbin brothers – Frank, Elbert and Philip. Frank and Elbert also controlled the Tombstone Mill & Mining Co., a syndicate formed May 20, 1880 by merging with the Schieffelins and Gird's interests.

On June 28, 1880, Philip Corbin and Orion Co. sued Hopkins, Say and Packard. Orion stated it was an Arizona corporation with a valid claim to the Knoxville. The defendants had no right to eject Orion and so the company sought $5,000 in damages and possession of the Knoxville.[37]

These preliminaries show Orion thought it was dealing with the Knoxville. The *Nugget* newspaper article shows Packard, Hopkins and Say thought they were dealing with the Stonewall.

The U.S. First District Court issued summons. Pima County Sheriff Charles A. Shibell told the court he'd personally served Say, but Hopkins and Packard were out of county. Presumably, they were served when they returned to Tombstone in late July.[38]

In September, the trio hired attorneys who responded to Orion, saying there were no grounds for the complaint and insufficient facts in it. On Feb. 18, 1881, Orion filed an amended complaint that included a telling detail – after ejecting Orion in June 1880, the three men had been in possession of the Knoxville "ever since." Packard and Hopkins must have mined the Knoxville for all it was worth, all the while stalling in the court system.

On May 5, 1881, Packard and Hopkins filed a supplemental location notice for the Knoxville, "made for greater certainty being desirous of obtaining a patent for said mine... ." They hired Cochise County Surveyor H.G. Howe to survey the property, which eliminated all references to stone monuments that could be moved.

Signing with Packard and Hopkins as Knoxville owners were White, C.W. Pratt and Thomas Liggett, whose investment occurred during Packard and Hopkins' June 1880 trip east. Missing was Say, as his partnership with Packard and Hopkins was dissolving.[39]

Packard and Hopkins' response to Orion's amended complaint went to the heart of the dispute. After denying Orion was an Arizona corporation, the duo said the trouble was not over the Knoxville but instead was over the Stonewall. Orion's ownership claim, said Packard and Hopkins, was based on a location which Orion's owners "pretend was made by their grantors."

Even if the location was made by whom Orion alleged, Packard and Hopkins said, Orion forfeited that location because its grantors had not worked the claim once during the previous 365 days – a requirement of the 1872 Mining Law. The ground therefore became open to claim by anyone who was savvy enough to realize the situation, and Packard and Hopkins' grantors (McPherson and the others) had done just that.

On Aug. 11, 1881, Orion, from its Philadelphia office, quitclaimed the Knoxville to Packard and Hopkins for $1 and "diverse considerations." On Oct. 29, White, Hopkins and Packard sold the Knoxville, Stonewall and Stonewall No. 2 for $100,000 to Dunn and Sleeper. On April 9, 1882, the

U.S. First District Court granted Orion's withdrawal from its Knoxville suit, and Packard and Hopkins consented.[40]

A related case made its way through the court system beginning in late 1881. This case began with a complaint filed by John Haynes and Lucas, Packard and Hopkins' attorneys in the Orion case. Haynes and Lucas wanted $1,000 for their services, but said they'd received only $10.

After receiving a summons, Hopkins and Packard responded to Haynes and Lucas' complaint, saying it was "ambiguous, unintelligible and uncertain." Packard and Hopkins said they weren't certain the complaint was meant for them since it listed only initials and not first names, or that the complaint was from Lucas since only his initials were given and not a first name.

After Haynes and Lucas filed an amendment taking care of that deficiency, Packard and Hopkins were unavailable to receive a subsequent summons. It was December 1881 and they'd left Arizona to spend the holidays with their families back East. Next, Packard and Hopkins protested that Haynes and Lucas were not partners when they took the case, so they shouldn't be paid that way.[41]

Perhaps Packard and Hopkins considered $1,000 an excessive charge. Perhaps Haynes and Lucas thought $1,000 was reasonable since B.A. and Hopkins kept the Knoxville through their efforts and then sold it. Packard and Hopkins must have paid Haynes and Lucas for no other record has yet been found about the case.

The Haynes-Lucas suit seems laughable when compared to three intertwined Stonewall cases. When Packard and Hopkins sold the Stonewall and Stonewall No. 2, their partners were White, Liggett and Hunter.

The buyers were Dunn and Sleeper as trustees of the Boston & Arizona Co. The firm's founder was W.A. Simmons, a former U.S. Customs collector in Boston.

~ 32 ~

"[A]s President of the Empire [Mining Co.]," the May 6, 1880 *Nugget* said, "he is pushing the work vigorously; as President of the Sycamore Water Company, he has organized and equipped that company; he is also the head of the Contentment mine, ... owner and director of the Sulphret, Tranquility and Townsite companies... ."

Simmons and his associates were "some of the heaviest business men of Boston," said the *Nugget*, and they acted it. For example, after the Tranquility Co. (a California corporation dominated by Wells Fargo interests) won a court judgment in 1882 against the Head Center Co. (purchaser of the Sunset mill), Tranquility within months arranged what apparently was a hostile take-over of Head Center by obtaining 100,000 shares of its stock.[42]

Boston & Arizona, eventual owner of the Knoxville, was Tombstone's custom reducer.[43] That is, if a mining company didn't have its own mill, it sent its ore to be concentrated and turned into bullion at Boston & Arizona. Ore from the Knoxville/Stonewall/s went to Boston & Arizona.

After Packard returned from his Eastern fund-raising trip during the summer of 1880, Stonewall development began in earnest. Packard hired Augustus Barron, a well-regarded mining man, as Stonewall foreman. West of the original shaft, workers began digging a double compartment shaft with drifts and crosscuts planned off its 300-foot depth.

Although only one wagonload of Stonewall ore went to Boston & Arizona daily during the summer of 1880, 3,000 tons waited for processing on a dump.[44] While Packard, Hopkins and White owned the Stonewall, said the Nov. 3, 1880 *Nugget*, the mine "yield[ed] them about $20,000 in cash, the ore milled having averaged a little over $80 per ton... ."

The Dec. 12, 1880 *Nugget* reported progress on Stonewall No. 2. Miners had found a rich ore vein when the shaft was only 20 feet deep.

These successes attracted attention and, early in 1881, Boston & Arizona offered to purchase the Stonewall/s/Knoxville from Packard and Hopkins. The $100,000 transaction, however, did not take place until Oct. 29. Why this was so relates to the Orion court case.[45]

Boston & Arizona must have been satisfied with its purchase. The June 1 and June 15, 1882 *Epitaph*s reported the Stonewall's new shaft reaching 290 feet with levels at 100 and 160 feet. Two winzes (steeply inclining passageways) were added at the 160-foot level, and 22 miners produced 25 tons of ore each day.

At the Knoxville, production reached 14 tons per day, reported the Oct. 28, 1882 *Epitaph*. Miners dug a shaft to the 90-foot level so a hoist could be installed that would connect to a 200-foot level.

Then legal difficulties came to the forefront.[46]

When Packard and Hopkins sold the Stonewall, the contract stipulated they would hold Boston & Arizona harmless in a suit then pending in U.S. District Court, which had been filed against them by Lavina C. Holly.

She was proprietress of Rural House, a boarding establishment on Allen Street near Fifth. Board there was $9 a week, with single meals in her dining room costing 50 cents each.

An indication that Holly could be a tough-minded businessperson was a claim she filed against Jessie E. Brown, manager of the Grand Hotel. In an 1881 decision, the court decreed Holly was to get a sofa bed from Brown or $50 plus costs.[47]

Packard and Hopkins met Holly when they first arrived in Tombstone, since they bought the Stonewall from her on May 10, 1880 – just two weeks after their arrival. The deal was for $8,000, with $4,000 up front and another $4,000 due when the mine began to produce or was sold again. Holly took an initial payment, gave Packard a receipt, and on June 22,

1880, hosted a lavish supper and then a dance for all her Tombstone friends in the new Vizina & Cook building.[48]

Packard and Hopkins refused to pay Holly the second $4,000 because, within days of their purchase, they realized the Stonewall had a clouded title and they'd receive no legal deed from Holly. Almost a year later, on April 22, 1881, Holly sued Say, Packard and Hopkins, demanding $8,000.[49]

So, just as they had at the Knoxville, Packard and Hopkins mined the Stonewall at a furious pace while stalling their appearances in court. This was not easy since opposing attorneys initially were Haynes and Lucas, and papers served on Packard and Hopkins bore their first names.

In autumn of 1881, Packard and Hopkins appeared in court, as summoned, but Say never showed. On Oct. 11, Holly withdrew her demurrer, and two weeks later Packard and Hopkins sold the Stonewall to Boston & Arizona.

Although Holly withdrew her suit, her assignee, John M. Miller, did not. He'd become Holly's partner on April 12, 1881 – shortly before she sued Packard and Hopkins.

On March 3, 1883, the U.S. Second District Court awarded Holly-Miller $9,466.66, which was the $8,000 asked for, plus taxes and costs, but minus Packard's initial payment. On April 13, Holly-Miller received $5,531.80, which was Packard and Hopkins' share, but not Say's.

His non-participation indicated that the trio's partnership had fallen apart. Say left Tombstone July 12, 1881. Packard and Hopkins formally called an end to the partnership on Nov. 1. No accounting was done, although Packard and Hopkins claimed Say owed them money and was in debt to many others.

Holly also had debts – $607 to M. Levi and Co., $1,371 to Shromp and McCann, and $430 to J.D. Culph and Co. – all San Francisco businesses. After getting Packard and Hopkins' money, Holly paid her creditors and attorneys, then gave $1,705 to Benjamin F. Maynard and the remainder to Say.

Maynard was an assignee Holly gained during August 1881 in place of Miller. That Holly gave Say money was proof Holly and Say were in collusion, said Packard and Hopkins. It also explained, they said in their suit against Say and Miller, why Say never appeared in court.

This suit came about after two other court cases over the Stonewall. In one of them, Boston & Arizona sought an injunction against Cochise County Sheriff J.L. Ward, who was selling the Stonewall at auction.

That happened because Holly filed a writ of attachment on April 25, 1881.[50] It went into effect after Miller won the case. Although Packard and Hopkins paid their share of the settlement, Say did not and so the attachment process began. After Ward published a notice in a Tombstone newspaper of his intent to auction the Stonewall, Boston & Arizona sought an injunction to prevent that.

In its motion, Boston & Arizona said it believed Holly's dismissal of her suit made all further action unnecessary. With apparent guilessness, Boston & Arizona asserted that if Ward sold the Stonewall at auction, this would cloud its title, thus decreasing the mine's value.

The court was not sympathetic, and denied the injunction on March 27, 1883.[51] At the auction, held Oct. 11, Boston & Arizona bought its own mine for $6,527.52. Boston & Arizona then sued Hopkins and Packard for this amount, but got nowhere.

The opposite was true in Packard and Hopkins' suit against Say and Miller. In a decision filed Dec. 26, 1884 that included Maynard, the U.S. Second District Court held that Holly's assignment to Maynard was not a "bona fide transaction but was made merely to cover up and conceal" her ongoing interest in the case.

The court pointed out that Packard and Hopkins had paid Holly and Miller what the court had ordered. Since Say was living in Tombstone when the suit began, Holly and Miller could have approached Say for money then. That they didn't indicated they were in cahoots, the court said. It placed an injunction on Holly, Miller and Maynard, prohibiting them from seeking anything more from Packard and Hopkins.

The court did order Packard and Hopkins to pay costs of $20.65. It must have been something they were happy to do since the decision cleared their good names. That undoubtedly was all they were after when they sued Say and Miller.

After all the turmoil surrounding the Knoxville/Stonewall/s, it was probably refreshing for Packard to deal with the Old Guard Mine. Although never a major producer like the Vizina or Stonewall, the Old Guard held its own amongst smaller corporations.

The same as the Sunset, the Old Guard was one of the first mines located in Tombstone, and the oil country men purchased it in 1880 via Roper's brokerage efforts. Roper was also an incorporator of the Old Guard Mining Co.[52]

That firm pushed work in its mine, north of the Lucky Cuss. By August 1880, the Old Guard included a shaft, a drift developing from the 80-foot level, and a winze connecting the 150 and 220-foot levels. Among those who purchased a portion of the mine was Packard.[53]

Mining continued steadily throughout 1882. The Oct. 28 *Epitaph* of that year reported the Old Guard's shaft was 235-feet deep. At the southeast drift off the 90-foot level, the company was installing a whim to begin hoisting again. The Dec. 16, 1882 *Epitaph* told of a new raise in the Old Guard.

The next year, as in all other Tombstone mines, excessive water became an increasingly insurmountable problem. The Old Guard Co. leased its property to chloriders, who picked over the mine's bones for several years.

By the end of the 1880s, scavenging of the Old Guard, Vizina, Tranquility and Bunker Hill mines provided almost all the district's production. Tombstone's population, generally estimated at more than 10,000 in 1882, fell to less than 650 by the end of the 1890s.[54] There were a couple of mining revivals in the early 20th century, but mining in Tombstone never flourished again as it had in 1882.

This demeaning end to what had been a prosperous town makes it easy to overlook the fact that mining jump-started Cochise County's, and thus Arizona's, development. Everything came from mining: soldiers were at Fort Huachuca to protect mines, farms and ranches; farmers and ranchers thrived by supplying food to miners and soldiers, and fodder to their animals. For the next 100 years, copper mining in Bisbee was the engine that powered Cochise County's economy.

Packard and his oil country compatriots were part of this. Their money and values helped shape Cochise County and southern Arizona. They were law-abiding businessmen who relied on the court system instead of street gun play to achieve their aims. They worked to install civilization as they understood it, and eventually they were successful.

Packard entered Tombstone late in March of 1880, probably expecting to stay a few weeks. In his later years, B.A. said he arrived in Tombstone on May 10, 1880. That was the date he bought the Knoxville/Stonewall/s and, after that, his life was never the same. Sometime during the ensuing litigation, Cochise County worked its magic on Packard, and he decided to never again live in any other place.

NOTES

1. Knoxville: Cochise County Mine Deeds, Book 3, p. 595-8. Atlanta: Cochise County Mine Deeds, Book 3, pp. 133-145.

Atlanta court case: Arizona Historical Society Archives, Tucson, MS 180, file 507, William W. White, Jno. A. Smithman, James Amm, Wm. A. Pullman vs. George A. Atkins, Pat J. Delaney and Samuel Shaw. Plaintiffs said they received clouded title from defendants; the court agreed and gave the Pennsylvanians the mine.

2. *Arizona Quarterly Illustrated*, July 1880, Arizona Historical Society Library.

3. Shillingberg, Wm. B., *Tombstone, A.T. A History of Early Mining, Milling and Mayhem*. Spokane, Wash., Arthur H. Clark Co., 1999, pp. 54-56.

4. Original deed in Arizona State Archives, Phoenix. The deed says the Vizina was located Aug. 6, 1878 by James Vizina and Benjamin Cook as an extension

of Good Enough Mine.

Cochise County Incorporations Book 1 pp. 195-201 lists Vizina incorporators as Thaddeus E. Sumner, Judson E. Haskell and Amm – all Pennsylvania oil men – and Fred E. Borden and Saul H. Bradley.

5. "Colonel Packard Paints Rosy Picture...," *Dispatch*, Nov. 2, 1928. This is the first appearance of this story; it shows up at least three other times in the *Dispatch* and once in the *Tombstone Epitaph*. All the articles were written by Nichols.

6. Farrell, Mary M. and others, *Tearing Up the Ground With Splendid Results: Historic Mining on the Coronado National Forest.* Heritage Resources Management Report No. 15, USDA Forest Service Southwestern Region, 1995.

7. Sunset acreage: Cochise County Mine Deeds, Book 7, p. 110. Location: Pima County Mine Records, Book D p. 28.

8. $10,000 share: Cochise County Mine Deeds, Book 1, p. 452. Sunset incorporation: Cochise County Articles of Incorporation Book 1, pp. 76-85. Hulings: A paragraph in the Dec. 3, 1880 *Nugget* mentions the arrival of Marcus Huling and son, W.J., in Tombstone to look after their mining interests. The Sunset incorporation document lists Willis J. Huling.

9. "Luck Sure, Sunnyside And Longfellow Mines," *Nugget*, May 6, 1880.

10. "The Sunset," *Weekly Nugget*, May 20, 1880.

11. "Machinery for the Boston and Arizona Mill...," *Weekly Nugget*, June 3, 1880.

12. Say purchases: Cochise County Mining Deeds Book 2, pp. 607-09, 611-13, 697-699, 699-701. These were: portion of claim adjacent to Longfellow sold by C.W. Pratt and H.H. Hollock to Say for $5,000; claim adjacent to Longfellow sold by William W. White to Say for $5,000; claim near Lucky Cuss sold by Say to Sunset Co. for $40,000; and portion of claim near Lucky Cuss sold by Smithman to Sunset Co. for $10,000. Hall sale: Cochise County Mining Deeds Book 2, pp. 733-35.

13. Mill sale: Cochise County Misc. Book 1, p. 9- 13; promissory note satisfaction, pp. 189-90.

14. Forfeiture: Cochise County Misc. Book 2, pp. 230-31. Patent: Cochise County Deeds of Mines, Book 7, pp. 107-13.

15. Two shafts: "Mining Review Of The Week," *Nugget*, May 6, 1880. Alarmed: "Weekly Review Of Mines," *Nugget*, May 20, 1880.

16. Emanuel: Cochise County Misc. Book 1A, p. 206. Machinery: *Arizona Quarterly Illustrated*, January 1881, p. 21.

According to Oct. 1, 1880 *Epitaph*, Steinburn resigned from Vizina to prospect in Winchester District in Dragoon Mountains. He filed a claim there in 1882 (Misc. Book 1A, p.325).

17. Blake, William P., *Tombstone & Its Mines*. New York: Cheltenham Press, 1902, p. 71.

Connections: The Life and Times of B. A. Packard

18. Vizina office: "Mining Review Of The Week," *Nugget*, Oct. 13, 1880. Packard's office: "Douglas Pioneer Tells Story ...," *Epitaph*, Oct. 15, 1929.

19. *Arizona Quarterly Illustrated*, January 1881, p. 21.

20. Manuscript 180, file 504, AHS.

21. AHS Manuscript 180, Series No. 1.

22. Shillingberg, pp. 76, 92-93.

23. Taylor: Cochise County Power of Attorney Book 1, p. 325. Purchase house: Cochise County Deeds Book 4, p. 8. The clue the property was for Taylor is that he recorded the deed.

24. Faulk, Odie B., *Tombstone Myth and Reality*. New York: Oxford University Press, 1972, pp. 165-166.

25. "Vizina," *Epitaph*, Oct. 15, 1887.

26. "The Fire Fiend," *Daily Tombstone*, Dec. 15, 1885.

27. Tweed to Taylor: "Vizina," *Epitaph*, Oct. 15, 1887. Activity details: *Daily Tombstone*, Jan. 26, Feb. 24, March 2 and 7, 1886. To California: *Prospector*, April 19, 1890.

28. Ore pocket: "Rich Ore Out of Vizina Mine," *Epitaph*, Sept. 24, 1886. Blinn: "Vizina Sold," *Epitaph*, Jan. 14, 1888.

29. "Col. B.A. Packard: An Old Cowman of Cochise," *Bisbee Review*, Aug. 5, 1934.

30. "Mining Purchases," *Nugget*, May 13, 1880.

31. Cochise County Incorporations, Book 1, pp. 224-26.

32. Nine claims: Cochise County Mine locations Book 5, p. 504-13 and 518-19. Silver Cloud: Cochise County Mine Deeds Book 1, p. 471-475; Book 2, p. 148-9; Book 3, p. 484-86; Book 6, p. 776-79. The Silver Cloud is mentioned *Epitaph*, July 22 and Aug. 6, 1880, and *Nugget*, June 10, July 29 and Oct. 22, 1880. That mine didn't produce much is clear from Cochise County Mine Deeds Book 2, p. 148-9, which records Packard purchasing the Silver Cloud from Leavenworth in 1885 for $100.

33. AHS Manuscript 180, file 445.

34. Orneo: Pima County Mine Records Book D, p. 535. Dismissal: "District Court," *Nugget*, June 1, 1882.

35. Stonewall: Pima County Mine Records Book C, p. 338. Knoxville: Pima County Mine Records Book D, p. 62. Although the two locations were made only a week apart (the Knoxville on May 6 and the Stonewall on May 14), for some reason they appear in two different books. This probably contributed to subsequent confusion.

36. Cochise County Mine Deeds Transcribed from Pima County, Book 2, pp. 494-5.

37. Pima County Recorder's Office, Book 1, Civil Case No. 365.

38. "Local Intelligence," *Nugget*, July 29, 1880.

39. Cochise County Mining Locations Book 1, pp. 584-5.

40. Knoxville: Cochise County Mine Deeds Book 3, pp. 595-8. Orion: Pima County Superior Court, Civil Case No. 365.

41. AHS Manuscript 180, file 520.

42. Court: AHS Manuscript, 180, file 562. Merger: Cochise County Deeds of Mines Book 7, p. 22-31. Wells Fargo: Cochise County Articles of Incorporation filed March 15, 1883.

43. Deposition of R.N. Leatherwood in Boston & Arizona Smelting & Refining Co. vs. Robert A. Lewis et al. in Cochise County Civil Case No. 504. Leatherwood described his ownership and assessment work on the Knoxville in 1878. He declared there was no Merry Christmas claim then – a crucial point since Lewis and other Merry Christmas owners insisted most of their claim was on Knoxville ground.

44. Barron: "Notes," *Epitaph*, Aug. 26, 1880. Operations: "Stonewall," *Epitaph*, Aug. 26, 1880.

45. Packard said Boston & Arizona approached him in "Col. B.A. Packard, An Old Cowman of Cochise."

46. Documents relating to the Stonewall legal tangle are in AHS Manuscript 180, files 708, 778 and 787. One portion of the 778 file is Cochise County Superior Court Civil No. 44 with the balance as Cochise County Superior Court Civil Case No. 911.

47. Boarding house: Front-page ad *Nugget*, May 6, 1880. Holly vs. Brown: U.S. District Court Minute Book 1, p. 18; Cochise County Superior Court Civil No. 40.

48. "Local Intelligence," *Nugget*, June 24, 1880.

49. Within days: "Col. B.A. Packard, An Old Cowman of Cochise." No deed: A day after Packard and Hopkins bought the Stonewall from Holly, she sold them seven claims in the Dragoons. There are recorded deeds for the claims (see No. 32), but not for the Stonewall.

50. Cochise County Lis Pendens Book 1, p. 18-20.

51. AHS Manuscript 180, No. 708.

52. Location: Pima County Mine Records Book D, p. 123 and 32. Incorporation: Cochise County Articles of Incorporation Book 1, pp. 147-49.

53. "Old Guard," *Epitaph*, Aug. 26, 1880. Packard share: Cochise County Mine Deeds Book 4, pp. 475-8.

54. Shillingberg, p. 340.

Transition

"All things must change to something new, to something strange."
— *Henry Wadsworth Longfellow, 1807-1882, American poet*

Since they were veterans of Pennsylvania's oil boomtowns, it seems unlikely that life in an Arizona silver boomtown caused Packard and Hopkins much anxiety. Even so, the world they entered when they got off the stagecoach in March 1880 Tombstone contained elements both familiar and strange.

For instance, a little more than a week after their arrival, two trotting mares raced for a $1,000 ($23,500 in 2013) purse in Tombstone Driving Park. This familiarity for Packard contrasted strongly with a man he perhaps saw who cadged drinks by putting a tarantula in his mouth.[1]

Tombstone was certainly full of such incongruities. But to Packard, Hopkins and many others, the place was also full of opportunity. Finding and developing mineral wealth gave everyone the possibility of becoming rich or, at least, making good wages.

Tombstone, the same as other western mining boomtowns, followed a pattern of development. The discoverers of the area's silver ore, the Schieffelins and Gird, made fortunes. So too could those who arrived early enough to get in on the ground floor; that is, when surface mineralization made it easy to obtain a viable claim. Jim Vizina was a good example of this.

Once it became necessary to extract ore from underground, the secondary phase of development began. Sinking shafts, building hoists and tunneling with blasting equipment required capital, technology and crews of paid laborers. Individual prospectors/miners had none of those things, and they sold their claims to corporations, wealthy individuals or partners who did.[2]

Packard and Hopkins were definitely in the last category. But they were mine owners with humble beginnings who'd come up through the ranks, unlike "robber baron" owners, such as the Corbins.

Packard entered the Pennsylvania oil fields with a shrewd business sense gained during almost two dozen years as a horse trader, hawker and rural merchant. He made his first fortune in Pennsylvania oil through hard work and auspicious timing.

He made his second fortune in Tombstone silver the same way, while displaying unusual regard for the men who worked for him. For instance, men employed by the Stonewall Mine in 1880 worked eight-hour shifts instead of the 10 that was the norm with other companies.[3]

By and large, hardrock mining was repetitive, physically wearing and dangerous. An underground shift usually began in a stope with miners shoveling ore into wheelbarrows or carts for a trip to the hoist. Once this mucking was done, drilling began.

Miners pounded the sharpened ends of iron bars into rock walls. In tight areas, miners singlejacked, using short drill bars and lightweight sledgehammers to gradually bore holes into which blasting powder was placed and ignited, thus creating the loose ore which the next shift removed before drilling.

In large stopes, doublejacking – with one miner holding a long drill bar and exchanging it with another as the bit dulled in between blows of a second miner's heavy sledgehammer – was possible. Whether single or doublejacking, all work was done with candles providing the only illumination in pitch-black stopes.

On the surface, laborers picked over excavated ore, discarding that which appeared to be without value. Rocks bearing signs of ore (what miners called "color') were thrust into sacks, loaded into wagons and hauled to the mill. Production could reach 12-14 tons a day.

Tombstone wages for such work were generous, which attracted many people. In its July 1880 issue, the *Arizona Quarterly Illustrated* reported Tombstone miners (those underground) earned $4 a day ($94 in 2013), and ordinary laborers (on the surface) received $3 a day. Skilled workers, such as blacksmiths (sharpening drill bits) and engineers (running steam engines or machinery such as hoists), made $6 a day.

Thus in 1880 Tombstone, a miner earned $24 each week. If he lived in a boarding house, which provided him a bed and meals, he paid $8-9 a week. If he could find a house to rent, he gathered friends to live with him because rent was $25-40 a month.

The May 8, 1880 issue of the *Epitaph* listed Tombstone food prices. Flour was $4 per 100 pounds, with sugar at 18 cents a pound. Dry fruit was 15-20 cents per pound, cheese 30 cents a pound and macaroni 20 cents per pound. Beef was the most expensive meat and antelope the cheapest. (In 1880, few major cattle operations were close by, but there were large antelope herds.) Whiskey cost $2 ($47 in 2013) a barrel.

The latter item was doled out in 75 saloons that 1880 Tombstone newcomer Henry B. Maxson estimated were part of the 105 businesses he counted.[4] It's easy to understand why miners drank after they came off shift; liquor eased their aching muscles and dulled their minds to the danger in which they worked in daily.

Another pastime was gambling. Faro was popular as was Packard's favorite, poker. That too is easy to understand given that almost everyone living in Tombstone was gambling. Mine owners bet their money the ore would hold out long enough for them to make a large profit. Saloon owners and other merchants gambled on the same thing – that the ore would last long enough so their investment in a remote location would pay off.

Miners who followed the Schieffelins and Gird to Tombstone bet they'd be as lucky as those three and make fortunes. The odds, of course, were against them. Most of the men who flocked to Tombstone hoping to become rich ended up as "wage slaves."

Those with the best chance of lucking into a pay-off at the gaming table that was Tombstone were the ones somehow involved in table management. Professional gambler was a recognized profession in early-day Tombstone; so was prostitute. Such occupations were not acceptable in polite society but, the same as store owners, they retained more control over their destiny than did mere wage earners.

Whether soiled dove, merchant or miner, early-day Tombstone residents lived in tents or hastily built wooden shacks lining streets littered with rocks and horse apples. The streets were constantly dusty and only occasionally muddy after Tombstone's infrequent rain storms.

During 1880, conditions improved rapidly. Merchants installed plank sidewalks in front of their establishments. Others erected more substantial buildings. One example is the Vizina building, which Jim put up after he sold his namesake mine to the oil country men.

The building bearing Vizina's name and that of his partner, Ben Cook, was at Fifth and Allen streets. It included, said the July 17, 1880 *Epitaph*, a handsome porch on a plastered and painted structure. The businesses occupying the Vizina Building included a saloon, men's clothing store and the Safford, Hudson & Co. bank. The latter was Tombstone's second bank with, as the name implies, former-Gov. Safford as an owner.

Another large edifice, said the Aug. 12, 1880 *Weekly Nugget*, was "J.V. Vickers' new two-story building next to the Nugget office [which] will be an ornament to Fremont Street when completed." Along with Vickers' real estate agency, building occupants included noted physician Dr. George E. Goodfellow and the Sycamore Water Co.

The Oct. 9, 1880 *Nugget* notified its readers that Sycamore was selling tickets for water purchases. Twenty-seven tickets, good for one gallon each, cost $1.

Sycamore was the middle of three arrangements made to provide Tombstone with water. The first had been freelance entrepreneurs such as David S. Chamberlain. He hired a man to dig one of Tombstone's first wells and then sold water for $2 per 50-gallon barrel. Soon, however, competition from others equipped with 500-gallon tank wagons sent the price down.[5]

J.V. Vickers, 1880s Tombstone businessman
Cochise County Treasurer's Office

As Tombstone's population grew, so did the demand for water. Boston & Arizona president Simmons and others organized the Sycamore Springs Water Co. In early 1880, the firm constructed a 500,000-gallon reservoir at its springs in the Dragoon Mountains and an eight-mile iron pipeline to 120,000-gallon storage tanks on Tombstone's north side.[6]

This array, however, was inadequate to fight a fire that on June 22, 1881 consumed more than 70 buildings. Tombstone had a volunteer fire department, but feeble water flow limited members' efforts.

Packard's office/apartment escaped the flames, as did Vickers' building. But the Vizina & Cook Building was among those reduced to ashes. Losses were $15,000 worth of goods at Chas. Glover & Co., and $10,000 at both the Oriental Saloon and Meyers & Co. The Safford, Hudson & Co. Bank lost only $1,000, thanks to cashier Milton B. Clapp, who crammed money into a safe and then helped other employees carry records out the back door.

Clapp's friend, George W. Parsons, suffered serious injury during the fire. After learning in perilous fashion that Clapp did not need rescuing, Parsons turned his fire-fighting attentions to the balcony of Abbott House (a boarding hotel owned by another friend). Falling debris knocked Parsons unconscious, but bystanders pulled him clear of the flames.[7]

Parsons recovered and, undoubtedly, became among Tombstone citizens demanding a better water system. Another volunteer fire company formed after the 1881 fire, but it took an even worse fire in 1882 before the town got a new water system.

This fire, which occurred May 25, 1882, burned out the business district's heart. More than 100 establishments, including Vickers' building, were incinerated. Damages totaled about $500,000.[8]

Following this fire, efforts by the Huachuca Water Co. to complete a pipeline took on new urgency. Formed in 1881, the company used $500,000 to lay wrought-iron pipe 25-30 miles from the Huachuca Mountains to Tombstone. The seven-inch-diameter pipe could deliver 45,000 gallons an hour at 160 pounds pressure. The system was so effective it was in use 100 years later.[9]

This three-part story of Tombstone's water system is reminiscent of the pattern that developed its mines. That is, individuals such as Chamberlain were squeezed out because deep-pocketed corporations, such as Huachuca Co., could pay for the technology necessary to deliver product more efficiently.

Such evolutions – entrepreneurial individuals coming up against wealthy, powerful and (sometimes) corrupt entities – are part of what some historians call the Western Civil War of Incorporation. This conflict included mine employees versus corporate owners, range wars between small and large-scale ranchers, and urban property owners trying to force order upon chaotic boomtowns.[10]

In Tombstone, the force-order-upon-them incorporators tended to be Republicans and Northerners who were urban and modern in their outlook. Their opponents generally were Democrats, Southerners, rural and believers in "the doctrine of no duty to retreat; the imperative of personal self-redress; the homestead ethic; the ethic of individual enterprise, the Code of the West, and the ideology of vigilantism."[11]

Packard fit into both groups. He was a Northerner but a Democrat. He was modern in outlook but rural in background. This combination placed him uniquely in Tombstone's Civil War of Incorporation, of which an 1881 gunfight near the OK Corral is the most famous feature.

The events leading up to the now-famous gun battle are colored by the bias of whoever is relating them. John P. Gray, a non-incorporator, bad mouthed the Earp brothers in a memoir he wrote in the 1930s. Incorporator Clum's description of Wyatt, Virgil and Morgan Earp, both at the time and later, gave them a heroic cast since they were the incorporators' "enforcers."

Clum, in the Oct. 9, 1880 *Epitaph*, claimed Tombstone was not a violent town. He wrote that in the first 1½ years of the town's life, there'd been only four fatal shootings, and three of the perpetrators were imprisoned. This contrasts strongly with "the man for breakfast every morning" view held by many then and today.

No matter who's telling the story, it's clear a long string of incidents created animosity between the Earp brothers and their friend John Holliday, and the Clantons, a non-incorporator ranch family. On Oct. 25, 1881, "Ike" Clanton harped on those incidents to his younger brother Bill, friends Tom and Frank McLaury, and anyone else in Tombstone who'd listen to his alcohol-fueled tales.

Ike was still at it the next day, and people who heard him began warning the Earps and Holliday about Ike's repeated threats. In violation of city ordinance, Ike retrieved his pistol and rifle from where he'd checked them and began carrying them about town. That afternoon, he met with the McLaurys, his brother Bill and self-styled badman Billy Claiborn in an open lot west of photographer C.S. Fly's boarding house on Fremont Street.

Around 2:30 p.m., Virgil Earp, as city marshal, walked west on Fremont with his brothers and Holliday. Once they spotted the Clantons and McLaurys, Virgil demanded their weapons. Claiborn didn't participate in the ensuing gun battle. Neither did Ike, who ran to the east side of Fly's building after the first volley and disappeared.[12]

In about 30 seconds, six men were shot. The McLaurys and Bill Clanton died within minutes; Virgil and Morgan Earp and Holliday recovered from their wounds. Only Wyatt Earp was unscathed.

Just a handful of Tombstone residents witnessed the action. Some heard the noise, but the majority knew nothing of the gun battle. Among those was Packard. He was in Tucson that day on business and when he returned to Tombstone late in the afternoon, he got a surprise. Ike was hiding in the rear room of Packard's office/apartment and was, in Packard's words, "scared almost to death.

"My office was directly across the street from the office of the Vizina Mining company office," Packard recalled, "and the fighting took place in about the same part of the block on the next street, and Clanton ran through the block and hid in my office. He was not in a mood to talk and he made no statement to me about the trouble. I allowed him to remain there that night and the next morning he was gone. All I knew about the fight was the street report as Clanton never talked of it to me."[13]

Packard thus downplayed what became known as the gunfight at the OK Corral. But many in the 1880s carried on about it because it was a shocking event. Even today, three men killed and three wounded in a single incident would make the news.

Two days after a well-attended funeral, Ike signed a complaint leading to the arrest of the Earps and Holliday. Their acquittal followed a preliminary hearing that lasted through November. Then they tried to resume their lives.

At the end of December, Virgil survived an assassination attempt that would leave him with a permanently crippled arm, and he departed Tombstone. In mid-March 1882, unknown assailants killed Morgan, and Wyatt and Holliday left Tombstone. Then the men suspected of Morgan's murder began meeting violent ends.

All the carnage prompted a fact-finding trip by Gen. William Tecumseh Sherman, who arrived in Tombstone on April 7, 1882 while on his way to Fort Huachuca. Tombstone leaders wined and dined Sherman and his party, leading the general to say "he was much astonished and greatly pleased to find a number of fine looking, intelligent citizens in this place so badly thought of outside."[14]

Clearly, one outsider who thought badly of Tombstone was President Chester A. Arthur. On Dec. 6, 1881, the Republican President asked Congress to deploy Army troops to southern Arizona. The Democratic Congress didn't grant Arthur's request, so on May 3, 1882 (likely after receiving Sherman's report) Arthur issued a proclamation ordering Arizonans to cease "aiding, countenancing, abetting or taking part in ... unlawful proceedings." He threatened to use "military forces for the purpose of enforcing ... the laws" of the United States.[15]

Tombstone's Democrats, and particularly Packard, undoubtedly considered Arthur's proclamation as yet another attempt by the Republican government to disrupt their lives. Packard certainly saw Arthur in an unfavorable light because, before he became President, Arthur had been the right-hand man of Roscoe Conkling, the boss of the Republican cabal that ran upstate New York.[16]

There'd been so little federal presence before the OK gunfight that Tombstone citizens had come to rely upon their own efforts to deal with lawbreakers, which included volunteer posses as well as vigilante action. Following the OK gun battle, Tombstone inhabitants continued to conduct their lives in ordinary fashion.

For instance, Packard concluded sale of the Knoxville/Stonewall/s just three days after the shoot-out. He then fully participated in Tombstone's most prosperous year – 1882 – when the top three mining companies alone produced almost $11 million ($3 billion in 2013).[17]

This made Tombstone a hustling, bustling place, and Packard got in on the prosperity in ways both familiar and strange. The familiar was he returned to the hardware business. The strange was he bought a newspaper.

Packard became a merchant again by joining Bothin, Tweed & Co. Probably Packard wished he had not done so because the business became involved in court actions whose messiness resembled the Knoxville/Stonewall/s.

Early in 1885, Tombstone merchant Julian C. Bothin had the opportunity to buy out his partners, George Gillson and J.T. Preddy, both of Carson City, Nev. Their large store filled the southwest corner of Allen and Fourth streets. Bothin, however, didn't have enough money to consummate the deal, so he persuaded Tweed to join him.

Tweed had arrived in Tombstone in 1881. He became friends with Packard even before Tweed bought the Vizina Mine in late 1883.[18]

Bothin, Tweed & Co. advertisements began appearing in *The Tombstone* newspaper on June 18, 1885, touting general merchandise, clothing, Studebaker wagons and hardware. The latter was Packard's portion of the store, which he had inventoried during August 1885 by Parsons, who was fully recovered from his fire injuries.[19]

An inventory was necessary because Tweed took Bothin (owner of much Tombstone real estate) to court, claiming he'd been totally misled. Tweed said he'd paid over $35,000 to get into the business after receiving assurances from Bothin that "there was a handsome profit in the transaction" since the store contained "clothing, hardware and groceries worth at least $52,000" which "had been purchased at exceedingly low figures" yet were of high quality. Bothin had also promised Tweed that the store's debts were manageable and money owed the store was easily collectible.[20]

None of it was true, Tweed told the Cochise County Superior Court in an attempt to retrieve his money. For example, Bothin, Gillson and Preddy owed William Steinhart of San Francisco $19,759.28 with nine percent per year interest. In addition, Bothin's declaration of easily collectible debts was belied by court charges he'd filed during attempts to collect money owed the store in the months preceding Tweed's purchase.[21]

Tweed acknowledged he'd been duped by Bothin because they "had been for a long time on terms of business and social intimacy and mutual confidence... ." So Tweed took Bothin's proposal at face value and didn't review the ledgers until after he'd paid into the partnership. Then he learned the store was struggling.

The court placed an injunction on Bothin so he couldn't collect any business money, and appointed a receiver to supervise the store's appraisal. It was a large chore, said the Aug. 29, 1885 *Epitaph*, because of the "immense stock carried by the firm." A thorough inventory revealed assets worth $98,198.11, so at least one of Bothin's claims was valid.

In late October, Tweed decided to make the best of a bad deal and rescinded his action. Tweed's wife, Harriet, managed the store until May 1888, but she encountered the same things Packard had faced in the 1870s – too much red fringe and a declining economy. The Tweeds compounded their difficulties by buying another store shortly before it became apparent Tombstone's boom days were over.[22]

Tombstone mining companies began to struggle in 1882 or 1883 when they had to cope with flooding tunnels. If the firms survived an 1884 strike, they then confronted dwindling ore bodies in 1885. Companies laid off workers, which affected mercantiles such as Bothin & Tweed.

As often happens during recessions, Tombstone residents searched for a scapegoat for their economic distress and settled upon foreign immigrants. During a February 1886 meeting, those in attendance declared a boycott against Chinese-owned businesses. This quickly expanded to include those who opposed the boycott, such as Tweed.

In a large ad in the April 15, 1886 *Epitaph*, Tweed declared his store's motto was "Live and Let Live." Two days later, Tweed told *The Tombstone* that his stance actually increased his store's business.

Tweed tried other things to bolster business. The Aug. 25, 1885 *Tombstone* reported Tweed, "Pack" and "Steb" (Asa H. Stebbins) were entertaining

Tweed's store ad in the *Tombstone Epitaph*

Fort Huachuca visitors. Since the Army men included the quartermaster's clerk and post trader, Tweed was currying their favor in hopes of winning a government contract – a common ploy.[23]

On Dec. 10, 1887, the *Epitaph* said Tweed was among the incorporators of the Cochise Fair Association, which intended to buy Doling's horse race track and build a grandstand there. This gambit to boost the local economy, however, apparently came to naught.

Bothin retained his share in the store but apparently was minimally involved in its management. Harriet Tweed kept the mercantile going until mid-1888 when five creditors took her to court within two months. This forced the Tweeds to declare the store bankrupt, and Paul B. Warnekros bought all its stock in July. The Tweeds moved to Phoenix in 1889.[24]

Financial difficulties of another sort pulled Packard into the newspaper world. This came about through his friendship with John and Thomas Dunbar. Thomas farmed at Tres Alamos, a San Pedro River settlement north of Benson. John held a variety of occupations, including stagecoach station manager, newspaper editor and restaurant manager.[25]

The Oct. 17, 1880 *Nugget* announced John's arrival in Tombstone with horses he'd purchased from Henry C. Hooker, whose Sierra Bonita Ranch, northwest of Willcox, was famous for quality stock. Dunbar established the Dexter Stable with partner John H. Behan.[26] Both had political ambitions that would bring them difficulties.

In 1881, upon creation of Cochise County, the Democratic Behan became its sheriff. That, plus his maneuverings to get the job, put Behan into conflict with the Republican Earps, and particularly Wyatt, since he and Behan were interested in the same job and the same woman.

Dunbar's troubles were different. He became Cochise County's first treasurer in 1881. When he left office in 1883, Parsons audited the books and "Found money errors and some striking ones. Several warrants, if not forged, were paid with knowledge of parties. [County] Treasurer [John O. Dunbar] was very anxious today. Also one of the supervisors [M.E. Joyce]. Showed Supervisor Blinn glaring things. D.[unbar] was anxious to make good deficiencies."[27]

Parsons' insinuation that Dunbar misappropriated county funds perhaps stemmed from Parsons' remembrance of the sumptuous way Dunbar furnished the treasurer's office in 1881.[28] Parsons may also have assumed Dunbar had financial worries after a wild hay cutting loss.

At the time, cutting the stirrup-high grass that covered southern Arizona valleys was a cheap way for large fodder consumers, such as livery stables, to fill equine stomachs.[29] The April 30, 1882 *Nugget* reported Apaches burned 300 tons of hay, worth $6,000, that Dexter employees had gathered in the Sulphur Springs Valley, 10 miles east of Tombstone. Three days later, another *Nugget* item announced dissolution of Dunbar and Behan's partnership.

Unlike Behan, Packard stood by Dunbar when he got into trouble. So did his brother Tom, who'd served in the Territorial House during the same term John had been treasurer. Both supported John following his arrest and trial on forgery charges.

In court, it came out that Board of Supervisors chairman Milt Joyce habitually signed blank warrants. Dunbar paid two such warrants, and was arrested before the warrants were repaid. A jury found Dunbar not guilty of forgery and subsequently he placed into the county coffers the amount involved.[30]

Packard loaned Dunbar $10,000 with which he made restitution. Packard warned Dunbar the loan "would not be cheap money."[31] He meant it.

In 1881, Packard had loaned $3,000 to Mark P. Shaffer and Frank H. Lord so they could buy a Chiricahua Mountains saw mill from Tombstone's leading citizen E.B. Gage. Packard charged only three percent interest, but Shaffer and Lord couldn't make the payments. The sawmill was sold at public auction, letting Packard and Gage recoup at least part of their money.[32]

That situation didn't happen with Dunbar. Cochise County records show how he paid Packard back completely.

On Jan. 13, 1883, John sold half of his *Tombstone Republican* newspaper to Tom for $3,500, and the other half to Packard for $3,000. Tom came out okay in the deal because on Jan. 25, 1883, he sold a Tombstone lot to Packard for $3,500. The same day, John sold the Dexter Stable for $8,000 to Packard and $10,500 to Tom. Packard, Tom and Casper Taylor sold the Dexter five months later to T.W. Ayers.[33]

John published the *Republican* until late 1885, when he leased the *Record-Epitaph* and began editing it.[34] The *Republican* venture, plus purchase of Tombstone real estate, drew Packard deeper into the community.

He'd first bought property in June 1882 with a lot and house on Tombstone's east side belonging to Frank Wallace and his wife, Ellen.[35] The connection was Wallace held shares in the Silver Cloud Mine. Packard probably purchased the property for Taylor, who'd become Vizina superintendent in January, and thus needed a place where he and his wife, Jennie, could live and run a boarding house.

As Vizina supervisor, Taylor dealt with a miners' strike in 1884. By then the Vizina had installed water pumps, the same as many other companies. This considerable cost (the April 29, 1884 *Epitaph* said $300,000 for the big three companies) was one reason why the Vizina and other firms cut miners' wages from $4 to $3 a day. The miners walked out in May.

The miners' union threatened violence; the companies hired scabs. On Aug. 9, a gun battle erupted between strikers and those in the Grand Central compound. Two days later, troops arrived from Fort Huachuca. Work resumed, but the strike marked the beginning of the end for the big three mining companies in Tombstone.[36]

On June 1, 1885, B.A. bought lots and a house on Second Street in which he installed Ella and his family, who'd arrived during autumn 1884. Why Packard waited 3½ years to bring them to Tombstone probably had little to do with the violence-prone men involved in the OK Corral gunfight, and more to do with other factors.

Packard once told a friend he knew the Clantons, MacLaurys, "Curly Bill" Brocius, Zwing Hunt and other outlaws, as well as the Earps, Holliday, Behan and his deputy Billy Breckenridge. But, emphasized Packard, he didn't associate with them.

Ella Lewis Packard
Packard family photo

In this, Packard took the same stance as many other Tombstone residents. Some of the people and things that happened in Tombstone "were not attractive to me and I tried to avoid them," Packard said in his later years.

"First and last, there was a well-defined line between the tough element and the people who recognized the merit of the law," said Packard. "I have said I knew the characters named. But that does not imply anything like an intimate acquaintance or familiarity on my part with their activities. I merely knew their reputation in the community and, for some of them, such as Doc Holliday and Zwing Hunt and Billy Grounds, any honest man would have had to say under oath that 'it was bad.' "[37]

Clara Spaulding Brown, a Tombstone resident who wrote for the San Diego *Daily Union*, echoed Packard's stance. In a Jan. 29, 1882 report, Spaulding said, "In reality, an ordinary, sober citizen, who minds his own business and keeps good company – there is just as good company here as anywhere – is as safe as in San Diego or Boston."[38]

The fact that early-day Tombstone was a male-dominated culture in which Packard hesitated to place the well-educated Ella, must have been a factor in his thought process. In 1880 Tombstone, there was little "society" other than carousing.

Two ads in the March 18, 1880 *Nugget* clearly convey this. An ad for Vizina & Cook, "Dealers in Choice Liquors and Cigars," promised "Happiness for the jovial and a shady bower for rest and recuperation." An ad for Jack Doling's Saloon suggested, "Call Frequently, Drink Moderately, Pay on Delivery, Take Your Departure Quietly."

Other pastimes, such as billiards or cards played by whiskey-imbibing men, usually took place in smoke-filled saloons such as Doling's. Drinking and cigar smoking could even dominate Tombstone's theaters, as this paragraph from the Dec. 2, 1881 *Nugget* illustrates:

"We question very much if any one of the many persons who persisted in smoking in the theater last evening would not indignantly resent the imputation that they were not gentlemen. Yet blowing clouds of tobacco smoke into the hall, partially filled with ladies, and possessing no ventilation, smacks of ill breeding to say the least. We trust it will not occur again."

Doling's held bets on Tombstone's horse races. Animals from as far away as San Diego arrived in Tombstone to trot on its Driving Park track, which was near Charleston. Packard and his contemporaries all raced trotters on the course.[39]

An Aug. 18, 1886 *Tombstone* article promoted a half-mile race with a $350 purse. Entered were a Tweed colt, a black mare owned by firewood contractor and teamster Victor H. Igo, and trotters owned by William Humphries and Maynard. Tweed's colt won with a 59.5-seconds time, but lost a rematch on Aug. 24.

Dunbar and Behan used their trotters to publicize the Dexter. The July 4, 1882 *Epitaph* reported a Dunbar horse winning a race held during the holiday festivities. The Dec. 5, 1880 *Nugget* mentions Behen's "fast mare" running away with a sulky Behan was driving.

Gradually, Tombstone assumed more genteel trappings that made it attractive to reputable females. A circulating library opened in 1880 and a roller skating rink in 1882.[40] There were occasional dances, theater performances and other events suitable for respectable women, but their main social outlet remained church. By 1883, there were four of them – Episcopalian, Presbyterian, Methodist and Roman Catholic. That year, Tombstone's two schools had five teachers and 275 pupils, making it larger than Tucson's school district.

By then, the pumps in Tombstone's mines were producing streams of water which were diverted to residential gardens and yards. Following the lead of Michael Gray, Tombstone pioneer who established cottonwoods in his yard in 1881, home owners also planted trees. Tombstone gradually began to lose the dusty barrenness that visitors often mentioned upon their arrival.[41]

These changes probably helped persuade Ella to move west. Two other factors played a major role in B.A.'s decision to stay in the West. One is easy to define, but the other is not.

Packard's first child, Gertrude Louise, was born March 23, 1883 in Portville, where Ella was living with B.A.'s parents. Although business demands caused Packard to return to Tombstone after Gertrude's birth, he must have missed his family.

Every October, Packard attended the birthday celebration of his grandmother, Rebecca (Rose) Packard. In 1884, following Rebecca's 89th birthday party, B.A. returned to Arizona, bringing Ella and Gertrude. Ella was pregnant then with her second child, a boy born Dec. 22, 1884 in Tombstone whom the couple named Ashley Burdette, for his grandfather and father.[42] It must have been a joyful Christmas for B.A. because on Dec. 26 came his vindication in the last of the Stonewall court cases.

Being able to enjoy family life undoubtedly was one factor that caused B.A. to settle in Tombstone, but there was another reason. In his later years when he mentioned it, he spoke succinctly.

"I wasn't satisfied back there," Packard said of the East. "I longed for Arizona."[43]

What in 1880 was new to Packard soon became strangely familiar, even comfortable. This transition was caused in part by the expansiveness of Cochise County's landscape.

New York's Cattaraugus County and neighboring Pennsylvania counties consist of mile-wide river valleys squeezed between hills. The composition of southeast Arizona is also valleys and mountains, but the valleys' length ranges between 100 and 130 miles, and the width from 30 to 40 miles. The narrow valleys of Cattaraugus County must have felt confining to Packard after his time in Cochise County.

Living in wide-open country tends to produce a wide open mind set. New York and Pennsylvania offered a limited lifestyle to Packard, but Cochise County promised almost limitless possibilities. Packard began seizing them soon after he settled his family permanently in Arizona.

NOTES

1. "The Races, Commencing Tomorrow," *Weekly Nugget*, May 6, 1880; "Foolhardy," Epitaph, July 20, 1880.

2. Limerick, Patricia Nelson, *The Legacy of Conquest*. New York: W.W. Norton & Co., 1987, pp. 105-06.

3. "Stonewall," *Epitaph*, Aug. 26, 1880, "Three shifts will be put to work... ."

4. "Tombstone," *Arizona Daily Star*, Dec. 3, 1880. Maxson, a U.S. minerals surveyor, said Tombstone had 75 saloons, 30 stores, 8,000 people, two newspapers, 10 lawyers, 20 doctors and dentists, and three stagecoach services.

5. "First Wells in Old Tombstone...," *Dispatch*, Oct. 19, 1930.

6. "Personal," *Star,* April 28, 1880, included a request-for-bids to dig an eight-

mile trench from Dragoon Springs to Tombstone in which to install a water pipeline. The *1883-84 Tombstone General and Business Directory*, p. 108, provided other details.

7. Parsons, George W., *A Tenderfoot in Tombstone*. Tucson, Ariz.: Westernlore Press, 1996, pp. 155-57 and 240-44.

8. Clements, Eric L., *After the Boom in Tombstone and Jerome, Arizona*. Reno, Nev.: University of Nevada Press, 2003, p. 37. According to *Epitaph*, June 27, 1882, Vickers was rebuilding by then.

9. Blake, p. 23.

10. Brown, Richard Maxwell, "Violence," in *The Oxford History of the American West*, edited by Milner, Clyde A.; O'Connor, Carol A; and Sandweiss, Martha A. New York: Oxford University Press, 1994, p. 404.

11. Brown, p. 393.

12. Shillingberg, p. 243-53.

13. "Colonel Packard Recalls ...," *Dispatch*, Dec. 2, 1928. Packard repeated story in *Dispatch*, Aug. 24, 1932.

14. "General Sherman," *Epitaph*, April 8, 1880. The general's speech was enlivened by a stagecoach arrival. The spectators' cheering frightened the horses and they ran away. Fortunately, all the passengers had disembarked.

15. Faulk, pp. 156-7.

16. Zimmerman, Warren, *First Great Triumph, How Five Americans Made Their Country A World Power*. New York: Farrar, Straus & Giroux, 2002, pp. 134-5.

17. Clements, pp. 23-4. The big three were Tombstone Mill & Mining Co., which was Schieffelins-Gird combined with Safford-Corbins; the Contention Consolidated Mining Co., which had been Western Mining Co. until it absorbed the Contention in 1881; and Grand Central Mining Co., headquartered in Youngstown, Ohio.

18. 1880 Census Kings County (Brooklyn), New York City-Greater; 1882 Cochise County voting registration.

19. Chafin, Carl, editor, *The Private Journal of George Whitwell Parsons, Vol. II*. Tombstone: Cochise Classics, 1997, p. 291-2. Parsons declared Tweed was buying Packard out, but a court case (see No. 20) indicates otherwise.

20. Owner: Abstract of Title to Real Estate in Tombstone book, Arizona State Archives, Phoenix. Much of Bothin's property was lots within the Vizina claim, including Russ House and Dexter Stables. Tweed: Cochise County Superior Court Civil Case No. 25. This case is incorrectly indexed as No. 1095; portions are in AHS Manuscript 180.

21. Owe: Cochise County Misc. Book 2, p. 422-28. Debt: In 1884-85, Bothin instituted debt collection in Cochise County Superior Court against Prompter Gold & Silver Mining Co. and New Jersey & Sonora Reduction Co., and fraud

charges against Summerfield Bros. These cases are files in Manuscript 180.

22. Rescind: "Our Pot-Pourri," *Daily Tombstone*, Oct. 31, 1885. Second store: *The Tombstone*, Dec. 14, 1885. It was The Mechanics Store at Fourth and Allen. The *Epitaph*, March 17, 1886, said Tweed restocked the store and opened it as a general merchandise market.

23. Fritz, Scott, "Impact of Economic Change on the Anglo, Jewish and Hispano Mercantile Communities in New Mexico and Arizona, 1865-1929," 2003 Arizona Historical Society convention.

24. Five creditors: Cochise County Superior Court Civil Nos. 940, 941, 942, 943 and 947; all Manuscript 180. Warnekros: "Buys Stock," *Epitaph*, July 28, 1888. Tweeds to Phoenix: *Prospector*, April 13 and 23, 1889.

25. Dunbar's stage stop jobs: *Epitaph*, July 10, 1880, and *Star*, June 24, 1880. Restaurant: *Epitaph*, Sept. 14, 1880.

26. Dec. 17, 1881 *Nugget* places the Dexter Stables, with "J.O. Dunbar and J.H. Behan" as managers, on Allen Street between Third and Fourth. An item later in month notes reduction in Dexter's food and water charge from 50 cents to 25 cents a day.

27. Chafin, p. 86.

28. "Local Splinters," *Epitaph*, April 1, 1881.

29. Bahre, Conrad J., "Wild Hay Harvesting in Southern Arizona," *Journal of Arizona History*, Spring 1987.

30. "Interesting History," *Tombstone Prospector*, Oct. 25, 1892. Dunbar was prosecuted by Cochise County Attorney Marcus A. Smith. Ten years later when Smith was Arizona's Congressional delegate, he related Dunbar's story to the *Arizona Republican*, which the *Prospector* reprinted.

31. "Colonel Packard Recalls ... ," *Dispatch*, Dec. 2, 1928.

32. Abstract of Judgment Book 1, pp.789-796, Cochise County Recorder's office.

33. The Dec. 9, 1882 *Epitaph* mentions Dunbar as proprietor/editor of the *Republican*. John sells: Cochise County Sales Book 1, pp. 99-101. Tom sells: Cochise County Deeds Book 4, pp. 389-391. John sells lot: Cochise County Deeds Book 4, pp. 391-395. Tom, B.A. and Taylor sell Dexter: Cochise County Deeds Book 5, pp. 73-5.

34. Lyon, William H., *Those Old Yellow Dog Days, Frontier Journalism in Arizona, 1859-1912*. Tucson, Arizona Historical Society, 1994, p. 75-6. This citation combined with article in *The Tombstone*, Nov. 28, 1885, provides: In 1883, Clum left Tombstone and Charles D. Reppy took over the *Epitaph*. In the first part of 1885, William J. Berry combined his *Tombstone Record* with the *Epitaph*. Dunbar leased the *Epitaph-Record*, with the first issue appearing under Dunbar's name Nov. 27, 1885. The *Republican* ceased publishing then. Dunbar ran the *Epitaph* until 1888 when W.J. Cheney bought it.

35. Cochise County Deeds Book 4, pp. 8-11.

36. Clements, pp.73-79.

37. "Colonel Packard Recalls Day ...," *Dispatch*, Dec. 2, 1928.

38. Brown, Clara Spaulding, *Tombstone from a Woman's Point of View*. Tucson, Ariz.: Westernlore Press, 1998, p. 49.

39. Bets: *Nugget*, May 6, 1880. San Diego: *Epitaph*, Aug. 3, 1880. Packard racer: *The Tombstone*, July 5, 1885. In its account of Fourth of July activities, *The Tombstone* said, "The next race was a match race between Packard's roan colt and A.T. Jones' sorrel Daisy for a purse of $40 a side, which was won by the colt."

40. Library: *Epitaph*, "Local Splinters," June 12, 1880. There are several skating rink mentions in *Epitaph*s of late 1882, including Dec. 9, 1882.

41. "A Wonderful Change," *Tombstone Prospector*, June 20, 1889; and *1883-84 Tombstone General & Business Directory*, p. 110.

42. Genealogical information supplied by Ashley B. Packard, Lions Bay, B.C., Canada.

43. "Colonel Packard Recalls Day...," *Dispatch*, Dec. 2, 1928.

Connections: The Life and Times of B. A. Packard

Agriculturist

"The great cities rest upon our broad and fertile prairies. Burn down your cities and leave our farms, and your cities will spring up again as if by magic; but destroy our farms and the grass will grow in the streets of every city in the country."
— *William Jennings Bryan, 1860-1925, American politician*

B.A. Packard and H.A. Tweed were already close friends when they dealt with the difficulties of Bothin, Tweed & Co. in 1885. Two years earlier, they'd developed a ranch in the Dragoon Mountains, and the resulting connections directed the rest of Packard's life.

Packard and Tweed had much in common. Born only four years apart, both had fathers who had been sawyers – Tweed's in Florida and Packard's in New York. Both fathers acted upon their ambitions – Charles A. Tweed became a judge, while Ashley G. Packard became a respected local politician.

Their sons displayed similar drive. Both sallied forth from rural roots to make fortunes in the industrial world – Packard in Pennsylvania oil and Tweed with a nickel-plating factory in New York City. Both migrated to Tombstone – Packard in 1880 and Tweed in 1881.[1]

When Tweed registered to vote in Cochise County that year, he gave his occupation as merchant. Two years later, he said "cattle raiser." That's because, during spring 1883, Tweed cobbled together a ranch on the Dragoon Mountains' west side, about 15 miles northeast of Tombstone.

His first step was to buy the rights to Bull Whacker Springs from A.B. and H.P. Shultz on March 1, 1883. From the latter, Tweed also bought a portion of what was known as Helms

Ranch, which included 245 head of cattle, two horses, harness and a mowing machine.

Then Tweed bought from Louis Duvall and Frank Samoniel the California and Slavin Gulch ranches, near Helms Ranch. Finally, Tweed purchased another portion of the "Helms Horse Ranch" from the estate of Charles E. Helms, who'd been killed by Apaches during a February 1882 raid.[2]

This conglomeration became the Tweed-Packard (T-P) Ranch, and both kept horses there. Packard's concern for them resulted in a March 1883 encounter with Apaches, which he later described to a friend.

"I was in town at the time and a hired man was at the ranch," said Packard. "The Indians came along and the [hired] man hurried to Tombstone to tell me. I had a fine saddle horse at the ranch of which I was very fond and proud, and the first thing I asked [him was] if he had brought that horse.

"When he told me he had not, I was somewhat out of humor and said so, and then I planned to go to get the horse the next morning. So I got my rifle and ammunition, my six-shooter and water can and field glass [telescope], and started early next morning for the ranch.

"I arrived there just at night and I did not dare sleep in the cabin, so I went out to a rocky spot and slept there. Next morning, I took my horse and rode to a low butte from which I could see all over the surrounding country with my field glass, planning to locate my horse from there.

"As I got toward the top of the knoll, I became suddenly aware that a group of three Indians was not more than 300 yards from me. I got off of my horse from the right side to make further observations, and it was apparent that the Indians had seen me.

"They did not wait for orders but they jumped upon their ponies and started then away on the run, taking each a separate course. As I saw them running, I suddenly became quite bold and I started firing at them, emptying my rifle and revolver but I think the Indians escaped injury.

"Without a doubt, those same three Indians continued their journey through the pass where they came upon a man named Dibbell, a prospector, and brutally killed him. I found my favorite horse a little later in good condition and took him back with me.

"But my horses had not escaped the ravages of the savage. I had a most promising two-year-old colt, a real beauty, that I found had been made a victim of Indian savagery as the Indians had caught the colt and had cut a great piece of steak out of one of its hips and then turned it loose again. The slice taken out was almost as large as one's hat.

"It seemed hardly probable the colt would live from the wound, but it did and later became a fairly good saddler. The place from which the meat had been cut off left a shrunken part of the leg."[3]

Packard's Apache encounter didn't frighten him because he and Tweed kept the T-P Ranch until May 1885, when they sold it for $34,500 to Ernest Storm, a Tombstone butcher. Included were 925 cattle, some equines and equipment, including a hay mower. With John Volz and Ernest Pascholy, Storm formed the Kansas Cattle Co., which evolved into the Tombstone Land & Cattle Co. that held the place almost 10 years.[4]

Tweed and Packard profited because of the cattle's fertility. It was a lesson not lost on Packard. In many ways, agriculture in the late 1800s was a calculated gamble with big payoff potential. Who better to play this game than Packard, the man who loved poker?

Mining and agriculture were economic gambles, but there were other parallels. Factors controlling farmers' destiny late in the 19th century – availability of capital and expert management, nature's good behavior, and transportation to market – were almost identical to what controlled mining companies' destinies.

Without capital, the only influence farmers had over variables was their own skill set. Packard's odds of success in Arizona agriculture increased because he had deep pockets as well as agricultural experience. He hired experienced managers – just as he had while mining.

Packard also realized the key to agriculture in Arizona's desert climate was (and still is) access to water. This made well-watered land scarce and thus expensive. The only people who could afford such land were those with money. This meant ordinary men became hired hands for wealthy owners who founded large corporations – another echo of the mining world.

Abundant capital could mitigate transportation and market difficulties. It could also blind the wealthy to small agriculturalists' often-desperate struggle. A prevalent attitude was that farmers ought to be imbued with the Jeffersonian ideal of self-reliance and spurn loans or similar assistance, despite coping with successive years of drought, grasshopper plagues or other trials.

The farmers who did borrow often received inflated, cheap dollars and then had to pay back in deflated, more expensive money. "Currency thus became the agent that delivered to farmers the message of their victimization," writes historian Patricia Nelson Limerick. Farmers' bitterness about this gave rise in the late 1880s and 1890s to Populism and its compelling spokesman William Jennings Bryan.[5]

Packard, having worked his father's upstate New York farm and survived the 1870s depression, empathized with the "little guy." But he also stressed self-reliance. This mix was something Joseph "Mack" Axford discovered in 1894 when he was 14-years-old, and Packard hired him as a ranch hand on his San Pedro River spread.

Packard took a chance on the orphaned teen, but then had him ride an untrustworthy horse 18 miles to the ranch with minimal direction. Axford earned a $10 gold coin each month (paid personally by Packard) and found – room and board – on the Half Moon Ranch.[6]

Connections: The Life and Times of B. A. Packard

The name described Packard's brand, which resembled inverted parenthesis marks.[7] How Packard acquired the brand and San Pedro land requires tracing his evolution from mine owner to agriculturist.

The process began while Packard and Tweed owned the T-P Ranch. Its main feature was an adobe building nicknamed the White House. It was a stop on the freight/stagecoach road between Tombstone and Dragoon, which was the Southern Pacific Railroad depot located in the range's northern end.[8]

Despite the road's traffic, those staying at the T-P ranch endured frequent Apache scares. This happened because the Dragoons, particularly the scenic northwest portion, dominated by pinkish tan cliffs and bulbous boulders, had been a citadel for the famous Chiricahua Apache leader Cochise. After his death and dismantlement of the Chiricahua Reservation, the Dragoons became a magnet for Apaches escaping southward from the San Carlos Reservation toward Mexico. Writers called the area Cochise Stronghold; Packard and Tweed's White House sat in the middle of the Stronghold's western entrance.[9]

Packard was familiar with the Dragoons. He located a mining claim there in his father's name, and on Jan. 1, 1883, he, Richardson and W.S. Mollison had recorded 12 mining claims.[10] Packard must have encouraged Tweed to obtain the Bull Whacker Springs rights, which occurred exactly two months after Packard and his partners recorded their dozen mine locations.

Three years later, a similar mining-to-farming progression pulled Packard into the upper San Pedro River country, south of Tombstone. It started when Packard helped Emanuel after he'd resigned as Vizina Mine superintendent.

During the next few years, Emanuel located some mining claims but by 1885 had become over-extended. His claim in Ash Canyon, in the southeastern Huachuca Mountains, included a 10-stamp mill but was on the 1885 delinquent tax list.

Packard purchased the property Feb. 27, 1886, after which workers moved the mill to Tombstone.[11] It thus shared the fate of all mills along the San Pedro, once water pumped out of Tombstone's mines started generating steam to power mills in town.

In June 1885, Packard, in his father's name (having obtained power of attorney), bought a Tombstone house and two lots for back taxes. The house, facing Second Street and near the Bruce Street intersection, was in the same block where, just months later, Tweed bought a house.[12]

After settling Ella and his children into the house, Packard rode regularly to Ash Canyon. He'd placed a few cattle on his new property and this, combined with the T-P Ranch, solidified Packard's appointment in July 1885 as cattle inspector for much of Cochise County.[13]

One reason for Packard's appointment was his connection with Asa Stebbins. He was a well-to-do Connecticut merchant who'd married a Western Reserve woman who was a niece of a Supreme Court Justice. This gave Stebbins some long-lasting political contacts.

Although a widower when he arrived in Tombstone in 1880, Stebbins' familiarity with Packard's portion of New York probably provided them with their first connection. Another connection was Stebbins' ownership and management of mines in the Dragoons and Tombstone. A third connection was the toll road Stebbins and two partners planned through Cochise Pass in the Dragoons.[14]

Stebbins obtained some of his mining property via tax or sheriff's sales. It was a technique Packard used to buy his Tombstone house and Huachuca ranch, and for the rest of his life. Stebbins also taught Packard how to establish and use political connections.

A portion of this procedure was building a persona, and the evidence includes the first mention of "Pack" in the Aug. 25, 1885 *Tombstone*, and "Old Boy Pack" in *The Tombstone*'s

Oct. 25, 1885 issue. Other chatty items about Packard began appearing in newspapers. An example is the April 30, 1886 mention in *The Tombstone* of Packard returning from a Sonoran trip minus his sideburns.

Stebbins encouraged Packard, as well as Tweed, to attend political gatherings. In October 1885, newly appointed Arizona Gov. C. Meyer Zulick (the first Democrat to hold the office) visited Tombstone. He'd just been rescued after being held hostage by copper mine employees in Pilares, Son., 75 miles south of where the international border crossed the Sulphur Springs Valley.[15]

According to the Oct. 19, 1885 *The Tombstone*, attendees at a banquet for Zulick included Packard and Tweed. Three days later, Packard attended another banquet for Zulick – this one in Tucson.

The end result of this was "The name of B.A. Packard is being mentioned for the position of Prison Commission," reported *The Tombstone*. "We know of no worthier gentleman in the territory than Mr. Packard for this position. Mr. Packard is a democrat, which is the only thing we have against him, but as it is a democratic administration, ... we heartily endorse Mr. Packard...."[16]

The prison job didn't come about, which was just as well for Packard was busy being a cattle inspector. Verifying cattle ownership through brand checks connected Packard to small ranchers as well as multi-partnered owners of large corporations. Among the latter were Walter L. and Edward L. Vail, Jonas H. and Enoch A. Shattuck, Theodore F. White, William H. and Charles H. Bayless, and Vickers.

Walter Vail had been a timekeeper in a Virginia City, Nev. mine. He saved his money, and in 1876 this enabled him and a partner to purchase a ranch 10 miles south of the Cienega stage stop.

With brother Edward, Walter developed the Empire Ranch so that by 1879 it became one of Tombstone's first beef suppliers. The Vails' efforts were greatly aided by discovery of silver on their property, and the Total Wreck Mine provided a monetary cushion that ensured the Empire's profitability and growth.[17]

Southeastern Arizona around the turn of the 20th Century was full of scenes such as this one. A sea of grass sweeping toward distant hills dominates the photograph and a small roundup of cattle isn't readily noticeable. Such a scene would have been quite familiar to Packard and his ranching friends.

Bisbee Mining and Historical Museum

The Shattuck brothers originally were Erie, Pennsylvanians who trailed cattle from Texas to Kansas in the late 1870s before moving to Cochise County. With partners, they established the Erie Cattle Co. in the southern half of the Sulphur Springs Valley.

The Erie was Cochise County's first range cattle corporation. Its success attracted Jonas and Enoch's half-brother, Lemuel C. Shattuck, from Pennsylvania. Eventually, his multi-faceted business deals made Lemuel a major economic force in

Bisbee.[18]

Theo White, another Pennsylvanian, arrived in Arizona in 1873 as a government surveyor. In 1878 with two brothers, he built El Dorado Ranch where West Turkey Creek flowed into the Sulphur Springs Valley. With Vickers' help, El Dorado became the foundation of the Chiricahua Cattle Co. (CCC), which dominated the Sulphur Springs Valley's northern half.[19]

Bayless family members arriving in 1879 Tombstone from Highland, Kan., were William H., his brother Alexander H., and William's son, Charles H. Father and son returned to Kansas but Alexander stayed, leasing the Mountain Maid Mine and then working for Vickers. William returned in 1883 to establish a cattle ranch on the Dragoons' east side.

William soon moved to the northern San Pedro Valley, closer to Tucson, to get away from the Apache threat. He acquired a partner then, and eventually involved son Charles in his enterprises, which came to include sheep.[20]

All four of these ranching enterprises had non-familial partners, which meant corporations were essential. That's where Vickers came in. He wrote the incorporation documents for the Erie and CCC, among others.

Born in the same Pennsylvania county as White, Vickers had considerable business experience before he arrived in 1880 Tombstone shortly after Packard. Vickers sold real estate and New York Life Insurance Co. policies in Bisbee and Tombstone while building his Fremont Street office.[21]

In addition to insurance, Vickers expanded into buying and selling mines (including the Old Guard), and making loans and investments. Business was so good that by 1882, John hired Milt Clapp to keep the books. When Clapp moved to California in 1884, Vickers replaced Clapp with Alex Bayless.[22]

This connection was just one indication of Vickers' growing fortune through association with cattlemen. He bought into the Whites' El Dorado Ranch late in 1883. Fifteen months later, John participated in formation of the CCC – Cochise County's second range cattle corporation – which eventually controlled almost 1.7 million acres.[23]

Vickers was closely involved with the Vail, Shattuck, White and Bayless ranches in many ways; one was livestock purchase loans. Vickers got his money back, with interest, when the animals sold.

Another Vickers' service was selling cattle. He was a popular broker because his contacts enabled him to negotiate the highest possible price in the era's rapidly developing Midwest stockyards and burgeoning California market.

Vickers could not, however, solve a problem that bedeviled southern Arizona cattle ranchers – high transportation costs. Paying $6 to a railroad to ship a steer to market where it brought $27.50 seemed excessive to southern Arizona ranchers.[24]

Walter Vail complained vociferously about railroad costs. In *The Tombstone* of July 31, 1885, he suggested dressing out animals in Arizona and then shipping the carcasses in refrigerated railroad cars to New York. In 1890, he and Edward bypassed the railroads and drove a herd across the western Arizona desert to California.[25]

Other ranchers grumbled about Southern Pacific Railroad rates but had no viable alternatives. The Shattucks and John H. Slaughter, a Texan who'd ranched along the San Pedro before procuring the San Bernardino land grant east of the Sulphur Springs Valley, trailed their cattle to Deming, N.M. This reduced the railroad charge somewhat.[26]

Packard undoubtedly knew all this because he inspected cattle bound for sale. Transportation difficulties were something he avoided as long as possible. He did not acquire a large ranch until the railroad's arrival in Bisbee.

That town had its start in 1877 when members of a U.S. Army patrol found evidence of silver ore in the Mule Mountains, southeast of Tombstone. Although Bisbee mines eventually produced more silver than Tombstone, copper was what made Bisbee.

Connections: The Life and Times of B. A. Packard

Almost from its beginning, Bisbee was dominated by several professionally managed corporations because much capital was necessary to mine copper profitably and wait out the ups and downs of a developing market. Bisbee's growth occurred as America switched from kerosene lamps to electrical power, and copper wire was an integral part of that.

Corporations such as Phelps Dodge, parent of Copper Queen Consolidated Mining Co. (CQ) in Bisbee, had the wherewithal to build its own railroad and thus reduce dependency upon the Southern Pacific and other railroads. CQ employees surveyed possible routes into Bisbee from Benson, and on May 24, 1888 the Arizona & South Eastern Railroad (A&SE) took shape. CQ superintendents (and brothers) Lewis (smelter) and Ben (mine) Williams were the A&SE's first president and agent.

Tombstone residents assumed the tracks would come their way with a line from Fairbank, west of Tombstone on the San Pedro. Some, including Stebbins, donated money toward a location survey. The amount collected, however, wasn't enough to start the work. The tracks laid went south, paralleling the San Pedro before curving around the Mules' southern end and reaching into the canyons hosting Bisbee's mines and homes.

The first train arrived in Bisbee on Feb. 1, 1889. A few years later, more than 10,000 tons of cattle, from both sides of the international border, shipped out yearly on the A&SE line. They left from the Osborn Station, where cattle pens were in flat country a few miles south of Bisbee. That made Bisbee a cattle town as much as a copper town.[27]

Initially, Packard participated in this growth mainly as a cattle inspector. The job let him observe the two ranching systems prevalent in southeastern Arizona in the late 1800s. The first, known as the Texas system, drew largely upon Mexican traditions.

Partially because the corriente breed, favored in northern Mexico, and its close relative, the longhorn, were "easy keepers," special care and supplemental feed were not part of the Texas system. Cattle generally were handled only twice a year during roundups, when equestrian skills such as roping and cutting were paramount. Cattle were sent elsewhere to fatten.

This system, with its "minimal amount of labor and capital required to raise cattle in the Texas manner, coupled with the rather considerable potential profits, made [it] attractive to neophytes," especially in the 1880s.[28] It was the system Packard encountered often during his brand inspection work in the field and during round-ups in Cochise County. But Packard also dealt with ranchers who followed the Midwest style of ranching.

That style, derived from British traditions, paid "greater attention to the welfare and quality of the livestock." Midwest-style ranchers provided supplemental feed and upgraded their stock with selective breeding and importation. They used stock pens to handle cattle, fattened animals before sale, and organized themselves in stockmen's associations.[29]

Packard came to use both styles, and why he did so had much to do with his connections in the San Pedro Valley and Tombstone. Chief among these was Vickers.

Vickers came from a wealthy Quaker family – a link for Quaker-educated Packard. Vickers had other ties with Packard, among them friendship with Parsons and ownership in what he called the "Old Guard racket."[30]

In addition to life insurance, Vickers sold fire and accident insurance. Purchaser of the latter was William C. Greene, a farmer/rancher along the San Pedro, south of Tombstone. Greene ran a thorn into his hand and ignored it, resulting in an infection so severe he was under a doctor's care. He subsequently provided a testimonial for Vickers and his insurance business in the *Tombstone Prospector*.[31]

Born in Wisconsin in 1853 into an old-line Quaker family, Greene grew up in New York. He was in Arizona by 1877, working in a mining camp near Prescott. He moved south late in 1880, winding up in Tombstone where he labored in the mines.

In 1883, he settled onto a farm along the San Pedro and, in 1884, married Ella Moson, sister of Ed J. Roberts. Ella has married William M. Moson in California and borne two children before divorcing him. She came to Arizona in 1882 with her brother Ed, who partnered with Greene who bought cattle in Mexico for Moson's ranch along the San Pedro.

Greene fathered two daughters, Ella and Eva, while adroitly managing his wife's interests and developing his own. That included a farm, house and share in Greene and Tanner's Ditch. That irrigation channel was slightly more than a mile north of today's Hereford Bridge.[32]

Packard must have visited the Greene homestead, which was approximately halfway between Tombstone and Ash Canyon. That 30-mile trip required an all-day ride, and a rest stop was welcome for horse and rider.

Packard also became friends with others along the upper San Pedro and on the Huachucas' east side. They included George A. Metcalf in Ramsey Canyon, and Thomas and William Farish, who lived in Ash Canyon.

The Farish brothers had mined all over the west before running Tombstone's Head Center Consolidated Mining Co., which bought the Sunset Mill. The Farishes later attempted to develop the Pilares copper deposits, north of Moctezuma, Son. Moctezuma played a role in Packard's life in the 1900s, but a more immediate connection was that Thomas Farish became Gov. Zulick's personal secretary in 1888.[33]

Metcalf's small farm was noted for strawberries. His fruit was the basis for a May 1886 fund-raiser for the Tombstone Methodist Church's Ladies Aid Society. Subsequently chosen principal of Tombstone's school, Metcalf married Bessie Tolman late in 1886. In June 1889, the Metcalfs moved to the Sonoran mining camp of Oso Negro.[34]

Ella was one of the women who sold cream and Metcalf's strawberries for the Ladies Aid Society. Although raised Seventh Day Baptist, she joined the Methodist women, and hosted Ladies Aid meetings in her home. Ella's circle of friends thus included Emma Dunbar, John's wife.[35]

During 1886, Packard, utilizing contacts made as brand inspector, followed Vickers' lead and began buying and selling cattle. Occasionally, Packard encountered problems. One such was a deal he made with Henry Whitbeck and John and William Robbins, owners of the Chicago-based Whitbeck Land & Cattle Co.

Late in 1886, Packard (in his father's name) sold 51 cattle to Whitbeck for $15.50 per head. Over a year's time, Packard delivered 48 head to Whitbeck but received no payment. Packard claimed Whitbeck even resold and butchered some of the cattle but still didn't pay, so Packard took Whitbeck to court.

The Second Judicial Court found for Whitbeck. Packard appealed, and the case dragged into 1891 before the higher court denied a motion for another trial. By then, Packard was well established in the cattle business and seldom had difficulties of this type.[36]

Packard began growing his cattle business in 1887, and he started in Sonora. He had contacts in the Mexican state through his job (since crossing Mexican cattle into the U.S. required an inspection),[37] and perhaps through old connections. One of those was, surprisingly, Bothin.

Before things fell completely apart between Bothin, Tweed and Packard, Bothin gained an interest Los Nogales de Elías. Originally a Spanish land grant, Los Nogales lay on both sides of the international border in Pima County. Owner was the Camou family, a prominent one in Sonora, as was the Elías family for whom the grant was named.[38]

Perhaps Bothin, through this connection, introduced Packard to the Pesqueiras, another important Sonoran family.

Or perhaps Packard came to know them during his cattle inspections along the border in the San Pedro Valley.

Whatever the method was, in late 1887, as tracks were laid for the A&SE Railroad, Packard took his first steps toward establishing a cattle domain. In December, he bought 2,000 cattle from Elena Pesqueria, widow of Gen. Ignacio Pesqueria, the famed Mexican independence leader and erstwhile developer of the Cananea copper mines.

Grass, water and towering cottonwood trees have always been part of the scenery along the San Pedro River, both in Packard's time and the present day.

(Bisbee Mining and Historical Museum)

About the same time, Packard and Vickers leased Ojo De Agua. That ranch, set in grassy, rolling hills a few miles east of Cananea, contains the "eye of water" that's the origin of the San Pedro River. Included in the deal were 1,750 Packard cattle and 27 horses already on the ranch as well as a wagon and harness, implements and improvements.[39]

Throughout 1888, Packard developed the dual ranching system he followed the rest of his life. His Mexican property became a quantity operation, with a large number of corrientes on large acreage managed Texas style. His American property was a quality operation, with mostly blooded animals on smaller acreage managed Midwestern style. Packard ran both ranches in the traditional manner. That is, he hired a foreman who gave orders to a wagon boss, who never took orders from anyone but the foreman. The wagon boss hired the cowboys or vaqueros, who didn't take orders from anyone but the wagon boss.[40]

Packard's first foreman was Henry J. Aston, one of three Texan brothers who incorporated the Reloj Cattle Co., headquartered on the Huachucas' east side.[41] Henry's older brother, John, drove the family cattle, bearing the turkey track brand, into the San Pedro Valley during spring 1887.

The brand didn't resemble a turkey footprint but a winged "T." John died late in 1887 after being accidentally shot near Ochoaville, at the border on the San Pedro. Ironically, another Aston brother, George, was shot and killed 14 years later in the same area, also during the holiday season.[42]

February 1889 brought incorporation of the Packard Cattle Co. It was capitalized for $100,000 by Vickers, Packard and Alex Bayless with the stated aim of raising, purchasing, and selling cattle and horses, and buying and selling land as well as "various products thereof."[43]

Two months later, Packard signed a series of deals enlarging his position in Cochise County's agricultural world. On April 16, 1889, Packard and Vickers gave Peter and Martha Moore a $1,000 down payment ($26,000 in 2013) and a $2,000 promissory note for their farm south of Crystal Springs, which is north of today's Hereford, Ariz.

The Moore farm, which had 75 acres planted in crops and 117 fruit trees, lay between the property of Greene and Charles Anshutz. Included was a one-third interest in a San Pedro dam and "the Tanner Ditch or Greene and Tanner's Ditch." The dam probably impounded 10-15 surface acres of water.[44]

In a separate contract, Peter Moore sold Packard one horse, one mule, one mare, two mowing machines, rake and harness, three hay racks, one harrow, two plows, one shovel plow, a lot of chickens and chicks, lumber and other building material, hand tools, and a patent seeder. Packard also secured a contract for 80 tons of alfalfa hay to be delivered to Fort Huachuca before July 1, 1889, and a right-of-way to his place through Greene's property.[45]

On April 17, 1889, Packard and Vickers transferred to Packard Cattle Co. all the Moore property they'd bought the previous day. Also on the 17th, Bayless deeded to Packard Cattle Co. 160 acres along the San Pedro south of Crystal Springs. He was obviously a "straw man" for this property that adjoined Greene's farm and that of James C. Burnett.[46]

Moore had a wood-cutting business that supplied the CQ smelter's insatiable furnaces. He thus knew the Mule Mountains intimately and so claimed a spring on the range's west side that still bears his name. The water from Peter Moore Spring flowed 10 or so miles into the San Pedro.

During July 1888, shortly before the A&SE tracks began snaking toward Bisbee, the railroad bought a right-of-way across Moore's property where the Moore Spring water ran toward the river. The deed specifically exempted from the sale a cistern on Moore's property, which by 1894 had a building or two erected nearby that became known as Packard Station.[47]

That scheduled stop on the A&SE was a great boon to those living in the borderlands of the southern San Pedro Valley. It was much closer, and thus easier, to board a train at Packard Station, or load or unload goods there, than go all the way to Osborn or Fairbank.[48]

That, however, was in the future. In April 1889, just days after Packard and Vickers bought the Moore farm, they sought a court injunction preventing Peter and Martha Moore from cashing any checks or notes. Packard and Vickers claimed the sale had been made under fraudulent circumstances.

Packard and Vickers said that while negotiating, they'd pointedly asked if there was any question about the farm's water rights. The Moores replied there'd never been any dispute, to which Packard and Vickers responded they wouldn't give $4.50 for the farm without water rights.[49]

After buying the property, Packard and Vickers said, they learned Moore was a defendant in John Hill et al. vs. H.C. Herrick et al.[50] Packard must have felt he'd fallen into the labyrinthine world of San Pedro water rights litigation, which undoubtedly reminded him of the Knoxville/Stonewall/s muddle.

In the 1880s, such a large amount of water flowed down the San Pedro that *The Tombstone* on Aug. 27, 1885 mentioned a 12-pound fish caught in the river.[51] The flow, however, wasn't limitless, as those associated with the Union Ditch, south of Contention, found out. Initially, water poured through the dam's head gate five feet wide and 1½-feet deep, even during the dry summer months.

Owners of the dam, constructed in 1877, and the ditch, dug in 1878, were John Hill, A.B. Wild, Samuel B. Curtis and Samuel Summers. The Contention Consolidated Mining Co. purchased a water right from the four men, and used its share to run its mill.[52]

In 1886, the four men and Contention went to court, complaining that Emile Lenormand and Anton Mariluis were siphoning water away from the Union Ditch. The two Frenchmen, both Tombstone saloon keepers, had a farm upstream from the Union Ditch. In 1884, they constructed a dam and irrigation ditch that utilized water previously reaching the Union.

In July 1886, the Cochise County Superior Court declared Hill et al. had the right to a two-inch flow over the Union head gate at all times. The court imposed a perpetual injunction, requiring Lenormand and Mariluis to reduce the water flowing into their ditch in order to maintain the two-inch level at the Union head gate. If they didn't, the court could impose fines and jail time.

Two years later, Hill, Wild, Curtis and Summers were in court again. This time, the quartet wanted H.C. Herrick, Peter and Carter Crane, Hop Kee and Boston & Arizona to stop taking water that would have flowed into the Union Ditch. The Contention Co. wasn't part of this action because it had closed its mill by then.

All five defendants had property south of Fairbank. But the case gained a sort of class action status since other users upstream apparently thought the 1886 injunction applied to them too because they were south of the Union Ditch. Involved in Hill vs. Herrick were:

– C.M. Bruce, J.C. Hayes, William C. Land, Robert Perrin, E. B. Perrin, G.F. Thornton, and Hugh Tevis. They comprised Tevis, Perrin, Land & Co., which then possessed the San Ignacio del Babocomari land grant along that stream which emptied into the San Pedro.

– Grand Central Mining Co., whose mill was between the Union Ditch and Fairbank.

– Hans M. Christiansen and his neighbors, brothers Augustus, Charles and Albert Noyes, who raised vegetables, grain and alfalfa near Fairbank.

– William F. Banning, Levi Scranton, Peter Moore, W.C. Greene, Joseph Hoefler, John W. Roberts and C.B. Kelton all of whom lived south of Crystal Springs. Kelton, Greene, Moore and Hoefler gave depositions in the case, which began during April 1888 – a year before Packard and Vickers bought the Moores' farm.

So Packard and Vickers went to court in 1889, asking that their deal with the Moores be rescinded and their $1,000 down payment returned, along with the promissory note. Second U.S. District Court Judge William H. Barnes refused to issue an injunction. He stated the Moores had negotiated in good faith, and were not defendants in Hill vs. Herrick but merely had given depositions. Packard paid court costs, then quickly concluded his deal with the Moores, who bought a place in Rucker Canyon in the Chiricahua Mountains' southern portion.[53]

Packard, as owner of property on the upper San Pedro, submitted his own deposition in Hill vs. Herrick on May 15, 1889. In it, he raised several points. Chief among them was that Boston & Arizona no longer operated its mill and had assigned its water right to farmer Robert T. Swan.

In June, Judge Barnes issued an opinion in Hill et al. vs. Herrick et al. Barnes listed the water each of the five defendants could have, and then left it to other agencies to prepare decrees enforcing his opinion. As for the Babocomari owners and those south, Barnes said their water usage did "not appear to have materially interfered with the uses of water below" and he placed no restrictions on them.[54] Packard, Greene and the others got all the water they needed to keep crops growing.

In early-day Cochise County, the San Pedro was more than a water source. It was a transportation route, linking Arizona and Sonora commercially and in other ways. An example of this was the John W. Hohstadt family.

They trailed the first cattle herd from California into the Southwest, arriving in Nogales in 1876, a year after setting out from San Luis Obispo, Calif. They gradually moved southeastward and in 1885 settled near Bacoachi, a village about 30 miles southeast of Cananea.[55]

Even this distance, however, didn't keep the Hohstadts safe from Apaches. In July 1885, John sent his wife and all but one of his children down the San Pedro to Tombstone. Hohstadt told *The Tombstone* he was glad he had because he and a son who'd stayed barely escaped with their lives when Apache raiders ransacked the ranch in August.[56]

The Apache threat was much diminished when Packard acquired his Sonoran ranch, but there were other dangers.

One was a lawless element that ranged along the border.

An example is the trouble William C. Land, a Tevis, Perrin, Land & Co. partner, had away from the Babocomari. Land took B.F. Hall to court, claiming Hall had put his brand on more than 100 cattle that belonged to Land.[57]

Packard dealt with another kind of theft. He took Andy J. Mehan to court, trying to retrieve a bay horse Packard said Mehan had taken. Mehan had previously faced an assault with a deadly weapon charge.[58]

The same as almost everyone else at the time, Packard carried a pistol. That he did so is clear from an incident reported in the Feb. 9, 1901 *Bisbee Review*.

"A crowd of cowboys came in [to Naco] Tuesday from the San Pedro River where they had been on a large roundup. ... Two of them were on the street when they saw the 'cattle king' of Arizona. [When] ... they started to throw rocks at him, he pulled his gun and threw down on the crowd and dared them to throw. The cowboys refused to be bluffed and made him dodge quite lively. He ... had to 'pack' his gun off. All the men playing were prominent cattlemen of Arizona and the gun play did not create much excitement."

Clearly, Packard and the others were indulging in high-spirited tomfoolery, but the fact he was quick to draw (even 20 years after Tombstone's rowdy days) speaks volumes.[59] Perhaps another reason Packard felt a need to carry was he was dealing in large sums of money as the result of his cattle-buying activities.

On Nov. 18, 1889, Packard Cattle Co. delivered in Benson "a large number of beef steers" to a California buyer.[60] At the time, two, three and four-year-old cattle could sell for $25 a head, and a medium-sized herd was 700 to 1,200 animals. This means Packard received $17-30,000 gross per shipment ($444,000-783,000 in 2013), and he made four shipments during November 1889.[61]

Obviously, not all these animals came from Packard's ranch. He was buying cattle in Mexico, crossing them into the United States, and shipping them to California or the Midwest – a tri-part business transaction that wasn't as simple as it first appears. Buying cattle in Mexico meant Packard gained the trust of fellow ranchers, both Mexican and American, and retained that trust through years of honest dealing.

This cattle herd, headed north after crossing the border in 1906, is being counted by its owner, Frank Moson, second rider from the left. The cattle are corriente-Hereford crosses. Perhaps the Hereford bull, on the herd's right-hand side, had been sold to Moson by Packard.

Bisbee Mining and Historical Museum

Packard succeeded as a Mexican cattle buyer because distance isolated Sonoran *haciendados* from the rest of their country. They developed a *norteño* spirit, one facet of which was an entrepreneurial attitude. For Sonoran ranchers, such as members of the Elías, Camou and Morales families, it was more profitable and easier to sell cattle to buyers such as Packard in the United States than to find a Mexican buyer and transport the cattle south.

Other Packard clients were Americans ranching in Mexico, such as the Hohstadts. The Americans produced part of the $2.25 million in livestock Mexico exported between 1881 and 1902.[62] That happened because long-time Mexican President Porfirio Diáz encouraged foreign investment and implemented liberal trade policies.

Despite these policies, crossing cattle required dealing with federal government bureaucracies of two countries, but on a local level. Both countries imposed taxes on cattle that crossed the border. In 1890, the American duty was $3 per head. The next year, with a change from Democratic to Republican administration, the duty jumped to $10 a head.[63]

In this period, Packard drove cattle to Benson's railhead, and then accompanied the cattle he was shipping. That way he kept an eye on the animals and avoided problems such as those described in a pair of suits filed by cattle buyer R.L. Benton against Southern Pacific. Benton alleged his cattle were ignored by the railroad, and received so little water and feed during their several-days journey that they lost much weight and thus value.[64]

During 1889-90, Packard developed a relationship with a California cattle buyer named Wright. In Kansas City, Mo., and Kansas state, Packard created long-lasting cattle-brokering connections. The same as other businessmen of the time, Packard generally avoided communication via expensive telegrams and instead relied upon letters, such as this example:

"Yours of Aug. 24th at hand[:] in reply will say your explanation of our matter is quite satisfactory and at your convenience you may place to my credit in the Phoenix National Bank $120, which will satisfy my demand, though should the other steer live and amount to anything, I will expect you to do what may ever right the matter.

"I will have more cattle for sale in October and I will be pleased to trade with you if you need more stock."[65]

The civility Packard displayed in this letter was put to the test in 1891. That year Packard, Greene and all their neighbors around Crystal Springs were summoned into court as defendants in actions filed by Jose Pedro Camou. He owned the San Rafael del Valle land grant, which took in Lewis Springs south to the vicinity of today's Hereford.

San Rafael, created in 1832 by the Mexican government and given to Rafael Elías, had passed into the hands of Guaymas, Son., resident Camou and other family members. The U.S. Court of Private Land Claims confirmed Camou's possession in 1891, after which he instituted a series of quiet title actions against squatters on the grant. They were Frank Valenzuela, Ramon Escalante, Simon P. Gallen, Hilaria Gomez, W.C. Greene, J.V. Vickers and B.A. Packard, Cornelius Harrington, H.W. Hasselgren, R.B. Clark (two cases), James Wolf, William F. Banning, Levi Scranton, Starks Sundam and Charles G. Johnson, Joseph Hoefler, Charles Anshutz, and A.M. and J.E. Hamm.[66]

Some defendants fought Camou in court; Hasselgren's case wasn't completely decided until 1911. Instead of contesting Camou's ownership, Packard and Vickers began negotiating with him. This resulted in an October 1891 agreement in which Packard Cattle Co. paid Camou for a quiet title so the company could continue to utilize its property.[67]

For Packard, as previously happened with the Knoxville/Stonewall/s, a favorable outcome in a legal matter was heralded by the birth of a child. Dorothea Lewis Packard was born July 23, 1890 in Tombstone.[68]

The Camou case was the next-to-last major court action in which Packard would be involved in his lifetime. But a bigger threat was looming, and 1893 proved to be one of the most difficult years in Packard's life.

Connections: The Life and Times of B. A. Packard

NOTES

1. Tweed: 1850 Census, Pensacola, Escambia County, Florida; 1880 Census Kings County (Brooklyn) New York City - Greater New York. Father: *The Tombstone* June 29, 1885 and *Nugget*, Aug. 24, 1886 and June 10, 1880.

2. Cochise County Deeds Book 4, pp. 586-89 and 685-87; Book 5, p.273-75. Apache raid: *Nugget*, Feb. 5, 1882.

3. "Colonel Packard Recalls...," *Dispatch*, Dec. 2, 1928.

4. Cochise County Deeds Book 7, pp. 608-9.

5. Limerick, pp. 127-9.

6. Axford, Joseph "Mack," *Around Western Campfires*. Tucson, Ariz.: University of Arizona Press, 1969, pp. 3-7.

7. Cochise County Brand Book No. 1, p. 426.

8. Bailey, *The Dragoon Mountains*, pp. 41-2.

9. Ibid, p. 62.

10. Father's claim (named the Cattaraugus): Cochise County Mining Locations Book 6, p. 635. Dozen claims: Mining Locations Book 5, pp. 504-519.

11. Tax list: "Supplement," *The Tombstone*, Feb. 13, 1886. Packard purchase: Record of Property (Chattel) Sale Book, p. 170, Arizona State Archives. Mill move: Bailey, Lynn R., *Tombstone: Too Tough To Die*. Tucson, Ariz.: Westernlore Press, 2004, p.183.

The ranch appears in various records under two names – Esmeralda and Emanuel. Since these names resemble each other when hand-written, confusion could develop. But the place's true name was Emanuel Ranch since Emanuel was Packard's friend. B.A. has no Esmeralda connection, other than it was the name of a musical performed in Tombstone in that era.

12. Power of Attorney Book 2, p. 103. Packard house: Cochise County Deeds Book 7, p. 657-8. The house and lots had appeared on delinquent tax list published *The Tombstone*, Feb. 13, 1886. Tweed house: *Epitaph*, June 10, 1886.

13. Cattle: "Local Notes," *Epitaph*, March 17, 1886. Inspector: *The Tombstone*, July 20, 1885, and *Record-Epitaph* ad, Sept. 6, 1885. Packard's territory was from Huachuca Mountains eastward to Cochise County's southeastern corner, a 60-mile swath of land.

14. Stebbins: "Obituary," *Epitaph*, July 11, 1889; and 1881, 1882, 1884, 1886 Cochise County voting registration. Mines: Misc. Record Book 1, p. 107-8; Civil Cases 733 and 1038. Toll road: Misc. Book 1, p. 54-61.

15. Wagoner, Jay J., *Arizona Territory 1863-1912, A Political History*. Tucson, Ariz.: University of Arizona Press, 1970, pp. 224-6. "Romance of Arizona's First Governor...," *Dispatch*, Jan. 14, 1931.

At the time of his appointment as Arizona governor, Zulick was imprisoned by Pilares mine laborers who intended to hold him until an absentee mine owner paid their wages. W.K. Meade, organizer of Zulick's escape, was a newly appointed U.S Marshal. M.T. Donovan, the man who actually went into Mexico to get Zulick, was a deputy marshal.

16. *The Tombstone*, Dec. 11, 1885.

17. "History of the Empire Ranch" provided by Empire Ranch Foundation.

18. Bailey, Lynn R., *We'll All Wear Silk Hats*. Tucson, Ariz.: Westernlore Press, 1994.

19. Letter and material sent to author by Nan White Orshefsky, Wainscott, N.Y., April 18, 1997.

20. Santiago, Dawn Moore, "Charles H. Bayless." *Arizona Journal of History*, Autumn 1994, p. 267-272. Charles lived in Tucson, where he became a University of Arizona regent and founded Tucson High School.

21. Birthplace: "J.V. Vickers," *Prospector*, Oct. 2, 1890. Same as Packard: *Nugget*, April 29, 1880 guest list in Cosmopolitan Hotel includes J.V. Vickers of New York. Sell: *Nugget*, Oct. 22, 1880. Office: *Nugget*, Aug. 5 and 12, 1880; and *Epitaph*, Aug. 11, 1880.

22. Expansion: *Epitaph* ad, April 15, 1886. Clapp: *Nugget*, Feb. 18 and Nov. 1, 1882. Alex Bayless: *Epitaph*, Sept. 11, 1885, and Sept. 29, 1886.

23. Bailey, *Silk Hats*, pp. 14-17, 26-27.

24. Ship price: *Epitaph*, March 16, 1885. Market price: *Epitaph*, Jan. 24, 1885.

25. Edward Vail's day book, University of Arizona Library Special Collections, details the drive. It enabled the Empire to escape the railroad's $7 a head charge. The drive began Jan. 31, 1890 with about 1,000 head. There were 10 hands (all but one had Mexican names), who were paid $15-30 ($1,860-$3,730 today) for the trip. Twenty-two horses (Vail listed all of them by name) returned to the Empire via rail after the drive.

26. *Tombstone Prospector*, Nov. 21, 1889. The *Star*, March 23, 1889, said the shipping charge from Deming was $2 a head, with ranchers getting $11-15 a head at market.

27. Myrick, David F., *Railroads of Arizona Vol. 1*. Berkeley, Calif.: Howell-North Books, 1975, pp.177-83 and 187.

28. Jordan, Terry C., *North American Cattle-Raising Frontiers*. Albuquerque, N.M.: University of New Mexico Press, 1993, p 231.

29. Ibid, p. 267.

The Tombstone, Jan. 2, 1886, reported members present at a Tombstone Stockgrowers meeting were Theo White, president; T.F. Hudson, J.V. Vickers, Jacob Everhardy, Joe Pascholy, E.O. McClure, W.C. Greene, Ed Roberts, William Bayless and Thomas Dunbar.

30. Vickers family: Bailey, *Silk Hats*, p. 15. Old Guard: Chafin, p. 310.

31. Injury: The *Prospector*, April 25, 1889, reported a cactus thorn lodged

between Greene's second and third fingers, causing an infection requiring opiates. Testimonial: *Prospector*, Nov. 14, 1889, quoted Greene, "I carried an accident policy for a long time and paid up regularly to J.V. Vickers, agent. I forfeited it, however, just about a month before I ran a cactus thorn into my hand, which laid me up for several months. The $15 a week would have come in very [illegible] while I had my arm in a sling."

32. Sonnichsen, C.L., *Colonel Greene and the Copper Skyrocket*. Tucson, Ariz.: University of Arizona Press, 1974, pp. 6-12, 23-4. Miner: "Reminiscences of Rafael Elias...,"*Bisbee Review*, July 29, 1934.

33. Ash Canyon: Chafin, p. 323. Parsons twice mentions riding to Ash Canyon. On Sept. 27, 1885 he worried about Indian reports so he "mounted Packard's horse and after several ineffectual attempts owing to deucedly contrariness of horse, got away. Reached [Emanuel's] ranch, thirty miles, shortly after dark." On Jan 29, 1886, Parsons "Got horse and rode to Ash Canyon to see Farishes. ... Quite a talk and smoke and exchange new[s], etc. Packard at ranch tonight."

Farish: Bailey, Lynn R., *Cochise County Stalwarts Vol. I*. Tucson, Ariz.: Westernlore Press, 2000, pp. 122-3.

34. Strawberry farm: *Epitaph*, June 6, 1886; 1886 Cochise County voting registration. Fund-raiser: *The Tombstone*, May 20, 1886. Principal: *The Tombstone*, Aug. 3, 1886. Marry: *The Tombstone*, Nov. 6, 1886. Oso Negro: *Epitaph*, Aug. 18, 1889. Marry and Oso Negro: St. Paul's Episcopal Church registers, Tombstone, Ariz.

35. Methodist ladies meet: *Epitaph*, Feb. 10, 1886; *The Tombstone*, April 13, 1887. Dunbar: "General News," *The Tombstone*, Dec. 15, 1885.

36. Articles of Incorporation, Book 1, pp. 368-73; Cochise County Superior Court Civil Case No. 1410.

37. "Inspector's Notice," *Epitaph*, March 3, 1887.

38. Cochise County Deeds, Book 1, pp. 477-79.

39. Cochise County Bill of Sales Book 2, pp. 394-5; and *Epitaph*, Dec. 3, 1887.

40. Sharp, Robert L., *Bob Sharp's Cattle Country*. Tucson, Ariz.: University of Arizona Press, 1985, p. 142.

41. Roland "Buster" Pyeatt interview recorded by Gene B. Pyeatt, July 5, 1977, Bakersfield, Calif. Provided to author by Gene Pyeatt Nov. 18, 1997.

42. Pyeatt interview. John Aston married Anna Pyeatt.

The Pyeatts' turkey track brand appears on p. 277 of Book No. 1 *Brands and Marks*, issued by the Arizona Livestock Sanitary Board of Arizona on July 13, 1908. It was later purchased by Whitbeck & Robbins, when it received the Turkey Track name.

43. Cochise County Incorporations Book 1, pp. 329-30.

44. Cochise County Deeds Book 10, pp. 416-17. Location: Cochise County Civil Case No. 1308. Impoundment size is based on photo of Gird Dam in

Cynthia F. Hayostek

Tellman, Barbara and Hadley, Diana, *Crossing Boundaries: An Environmental History of the Upper Sam Pedro River Watershed, Arizona and Sonora.* Tucson, Ariz.: Arizona State Museum et al., 2006, p. 41.

45. Cochise County Misc. Book 1, pp. 392-93.

46. Cochise County Deeds Book 10, pp. 415-16.

47. Cochise County Deeds Book 10, pp. 230-31. The cistern still exists. Thank you, Jack Ladd Sr., Naco, Ariz., for showing it to me, my children and my father on July 14, 1995.

48. "Railroad Time Tables," *Prospector,* Nov. 3, 1894.

49. "One Result," *Prospector,* May 23, 1889; Cochise County Superior Court Civil Case No. 1412.

50. Cochise County Superior Court Civil Case No. 1308.

51. The *Prospector,* Dec. 13, 1894, reported a fish caught in the San Pedro was 17½ inches long and weighed 3½ pounds.

52. Cochise County Superior Court Civil Case No. 1219.

53. "Packard vs. Moore," *Prospector,* May 24, 1889. "Moore Buys Ranch," *Prospector,* Dec. 6, 1890.

54. Cochise County Superior Court Civil Case No. 1308.

55. "Came With Father's Herd...," *Dispatch,* Jan. 19, 1930,. Although John Hohstadt ranched near Bacoachi, he registered to vote in Tombstone. In 1888, he gave that town as his residence. The Hohstadt presence on Ojo de Agua is mentioned in *Tombstone,* April 22, 1886.

56. "The Apaches," *The Tombstone,* Aug. 19, 1885.

57. Cochise County Superior Court Civil Case No. 1409.

58. Cochise County Superior Court Civil Case No. 91; Cochise County Criminal Calendar, Book 2, p. 1.

59. Further evidence that Packard toted a gun regularly is *Epitaph,* June 7, 1893, which reported his expensive pistol, stolen from the Half Moon Ranch in December 1892, had been recovered from a man arrested in Bisbee.

60. *Prospector,* Nov. 18, 1889 and July 19, 1890.

61. Cattle price: *Prospector,* June 21 and Aug. 13, 1890. Quantity based on Axford, pp. 6-7. Four shipments: *Prospector,* Nov. 26, 1889.

62. Machado, Manuel A. Jr., *The North Mexican Cattle Industry, 1910-1975.* College Station, Texas: Texas A&M University Press, 1981, introduction.

63. "It's A Go," Prospector, April 17, 1890.

64. To Benson: Axford, pp. 6-7. Benton suits: Cochise County Superior Court Civil Case Nos. 766 and 1017.

65. Photocopy of Sept 1, 1907 letter from B.A. Packard to C.D. Clark in author's possession.

Connections: The Life and Times of B. A. Packard

66. Cochise County Superior Court Civil Case Nos. 1594-1508, 1610, 1612.

67. Hasselgren: *International*, "Camou Wins Case...," June 28, 1911. Quiet title: Cochise County Misc. Book 4, pp. 770-773.

68. Date supplied by Ashley B. Packard, Lions Bay, B.C., Canada. The *Prospector*, July 23, 1890, includes: "Mrs. B.A. Packard was taken seriously ill this afternoon." Seriously ill was a Victorian euphemism for going into labor.

Cynthia F. Hayostek

1893

"It is difficulties that show what men are."
— Epictetus, 55-135 AD, Greek philosopher

As the San Pedro water rights court cases demonstrate, the amount of water flowing downriver diminished in the late 1880s and early 1890s. Some of this was due to increased usage, but another factor was several years of slight rainfall. The March 20 and April 11, 1886 issues of the *Epitaph* were just two of many mentioning grass scarcity. By 1890, the articles were about drought.

"The cattlemen in Southern Arizona have come to the conclusion to ship large numbers of their stock this fall so as to relieve the ranges...," reported the July 19, 1890 *Epitaph*. "If they will now take concerted action in regard to putting up windmills and sinking wells over the ranges, there will be very little complaint next summer about dying stock."

Unfortunate ranchers with no access to the San Pedro relied upon small streams or catchments that dried up during summer months. Since grass around water sources was the first to disappear, skinny cattle walking miles every day between water and feed became a common sight. If this enforced foraging and stress didn't kill a herd, a dried-up water source would.

Selling surplus cattle was the first of two steps many ranchers took to cope with the drought. Slaughter and Vickers led the way, but it was to little avail. The Feb. 22, 1891 *Epitaph* reported area cattle were rapidly falling off in flesh, and that Slaughter again was gathering cattle to sell.

The second step ranchers took, if they could afford it, was shipping cattle out of Arizona. The March 29, 1891 *Epitaph* told of the Babocomari Co. sending 2,000 head to Kansas. About the same time, the Erie began what turned out to be a permanent move to Ashland, Kan. By autumn 1891, Slaughter had shipped 2,000 steers to Kansas, leaving only 400 head on his San Bernardino Ranch.[1]

Packard joined Slaughter in shipping cattle to Kansas, thus joining a trend in which that state pastured many Cochise County herds. In May 1891, B.A. accompanied his livestock to Eureka, Kan. There, he pastured them for $1 a head before returning to Tombstone in June. Looking after his animals required a two-month stay in southeastern Kansas before the year was over.[2]

Other Cochise County ranchers joined the exodus; issues of the 1892 *Tombstone Prospector* are full of items about ranchers traveling, selling and shipping cattle. T.F. Hudson shipped cattle to Kansas and then Colorado. H.S. Boice bought Arizona cattle and sent them to New Mexico. The San Simon Cattle Co. of northern Cochise County headquartered in Abilene, Kan.[3]

June 1892 saw 20,000 head, including those of Fred Herrera and Ernest O. McClure, shipped out of Deming, N.M.; most went to Kansas. Frank Proctor, Pima County rancher and cattle inspector, said the Benson inspector checked 17,000 head during June, with most leaving for Montana.[4]

In early 1892, Packard looked over his livestock near Glenwood, Kan. He returned to Tombstone in May and took his family to the Half Moon. He found the San Pedro Valley stripped bare. Parts of the Sulphur Springs Valley retained some grass, but it too was gone by the end of the year.[5]

Vickers, managing the CCC, didn't wait for that to happen. He shipped 19 railroad carloads of CCC cattle from San Simon in June 1892. Packard helped Vickers later that year by selling five carloads of CCC cattle in Los Angeles, and some of his own. Packard then went to "Panhandle country" to secure pasture for more CCC cattle, which arrived in early December.[6]

During January 1893, the country's economy, which had been struggling to recover from a recession that began in 1890, suffered what's known as the 1893 Panic. This recession originated in improved technology and increased railroad access in the 1880s that helped farmers, especially Midwestern ones, produce and market bumper crops.

To procure the new technology, farmers went into debt. They borrowed money that had been deflating since the Civil War, but this weakness was largely hidden. When drought and other unfortunate weather conditions beset farmers, they found decreased prices resulting from their previous overproduction.

This difficulty was one of several causing the 1893 stock market panic. Business failures, including some banks, quickly amounted to $357 million, and unemployment surged to 10 percent and more. President Grover Cleveland persuaded Congress to annul the Silver Purchase Act, causing silver's price to drop 40 cents.

An agricultural business that didn't fail was the boneyard. The April 19, 1893 *Epitaph* reported carloads of bones shipped from Benson to St. Louis, where they brought 15 cents a ton ($4 in 2013). "They are gathered along the [San Pedro] River and are all that is left of the carcasses of cattle that have died in large numbers during the last two years," said the *Epitaph*.

In May, the newspaper told readers that Packard and George Metcalf left Willcox with five carloads of cattle bound for Kansas. Ella and the children departed a few days later, reuniting in Kansas City. B.A. stayed there, while Ella and the children traveled on to Chicago.[7]

That destination was immensely popular in 1893 because it was the site of the Columbian Exposition, marking the 400th anniversary of the Americas' discovery by Columbus. Ella and the children saw the Court of Honor, a cluster of neoclassic buildings which were, like everything else, illuminated with 90,000 incandescent and 5,000 arc lights.[8]

After enjoying the sights, Ella took the children to New York to visit their grandparents in Portville and Genesee. B.A. returned to Arizona. This arrangement of wife and children spending time in a cooler place while the husband worked in Arizona's hot season, was fashionable at the time. The Packards had done this the previous summer.

Ashley G. Packard's home in Portville, N.Y. was the backdrop for this photo taken late in 1891. Ashley G. is standing on the left. His wife, Virtue, is seated with granddaughter Dorothea in her lap. Ella Packard is standing on the right, behind her daughter Gertrude and son Ashley B. Packard.

Packard family photo

They filled their separation with letters written once or twice a week. The letters B.A. wrote were filled with Tombstone news, such as the illness of Greene's wife.[9] On May 13, 1893, Ella wrote her first letter from New York:

My Dear Boy,

I have only time for a few words for Father is going down [into town] after [my] trunk and if I hurry you may get this much sooner than if I waited till Mon. I could not write from Chicago as the brief time I remained there was spent at the Fair grounds and I found after boarding the Erie train at 2 p.m. that a message could not be sent to Kansas till we should reach Marion [Ohio] at 10:30 p.m.

With the exception of a dull headache, which is even now disappearing after a dose of salts and a good cup of tea, I feel quite as well as when I saw you last.

Arriving at Portville..., I found someone who could order a carriage ... and took our folks entirely by surprise as they did not look for us till next week... .

I was so sorry dear, not to see you again and could hardly hold back the tears, but thought probably it would be better to go be brave. Uncle William and Aunt Elsie are here and they send love. I will write at greater length in a few days.

With best love,
Yours devotedly,
Ella L. Packard

Ella's letter of greater length was written May 21, 1893.

My Dearest Boy,

I have been looking for a letter from you but begin to think you did not think it worthwhile to write from Kansas City, else I would have received it by this time. I live in hope of receiving one the coming week.

My throat has been very bad the last week, and the Dr. has been here three times. He has ordered for me one of those steam atomizers, and suppose it must be waiting for me at the Express [Freight] office now. He brought me the medicine yesterday to use with it. ...

The Dr. says my lungs are all right, but that I have a very bad throat and that I must have <u>rest</u>, <u>rest</u>, <u>rest</u>. My throat has been much worse here than at any time in Tombstone – so sore that it gives one almost constant pain and I would rather go without any thing to eat than to attempt to swallow.

I think the sudden change made me take cold, which of course caused high fever and of course made my throat so very sore. He seems to think I may fully recover in time if I attend faithfully to his instructions.

Many of the relatives have been to see me, and all wish to be remembered to Burdette. The children are well and having a good time. ...

School only keeps another week here so I am going to put Gertrude and Ash in school over at my father's, and they can attend school here as soon as it opens the 1st of Sept. I do not see what can be done for they cannot be allowed to "run wild." They have almost driven your mother crazy these few days they have been here, and it is not to be wondered at for it has been too rainy to play out of doors much.

There is much which I would like to write about but weariness compels me to stop. Hoping this may find you well and with dearest love,

I remain as ever,
Your affectionate wife,
Ella L. Packard

The reason B.A. had not written was, after he returned to Tombstone, he'd gone into Mexico with his San Pedro neighbors Greene, Kelton (who'd just finished a term as Cochise County Sheriff), and Charles F. Berger, as well as Arizona's Congressional delegate Marcus Smith. Not long afterward, rain broke the drought and the San Pedro River flooded. More rain followed and the San Pedro Valley began to recover.[10]

On June 26, 1893, Ella wrote:

> My Dear Husband,
> I was delighted this week past to receive two letters from you dated the 10th and 12th of June. Your father was over here [Genesee] Thursday and brought them.
> I was over there [Portville] yesterday as it was a very fine day and I had an appointment with Dr. Place. I am feeling much stronger than I did just a few days ago.
> [Ella relays some news of relatives and says] they started for home an hour or two before I started for home with my father and the roads were in excellent condition with little dust. ... They all inquired for you.
> Dorothea was quite sick with indigestion all last week and was so cross that I could not get this letter written earlier. I had the Dr. give her some medicine and she seems to be better today. The other children are feeling well and are out under the porch to play.
> In regards to Mr. Edwards taking care of the yard [in Tombstone]. He offered to take care of it for the fruit in it, but I expected to pay him something if the fruit didn't turn out well. I think you will be able to find him at the Wauxhunt house up on the corner almost any evening. ... I did not look for the water supply to be off entirely. I think you would do well to see him.
> I hope by this time you are having rains and that your affairs are going more smoothly. Drink only boiled water. I believe the low state of the water had something to do with my malaria which is troubling me. ...
> Strawberries are ripe but I have not been out to pick any. ... Write often.
>
> *Much devotedly yours,*
> *Ella*

Connections: The Life and Times of B. A. Packard

Ashley wrote his father a letter dated June 25, 1893.

> Dear Papa,
> I am having a good time here.
> I am going to school and the roads are full of mud and the hole country is full of green grass.
> The fourth of July we are going down to uncle Hornblowers to shoot our fireworks.
> It is raining today and we cannot get out.
> Mama is going to get me a third reader and I will be in the third reader. Gertrude and I want to know if you will give me a wheel [bicycle] to ride.
> Is there any fish in the [San Pedro] river now?
> The school boys are very rough and the teacher is a lazy one. She sits around doing nothing and when we go out at noon, she goes with us over to the saw mill.
>
> *Love to you,*
> *From your son,*
> *Ashley*

In July came four letters that would change everything for Packard. The first, written by his father, is dated July 7, 1893.

> Dear Son,
> I write to inform you of our health, which is fair and the children are well. Ella has consented to go to Buffalo a spell for treatment. She don't seem strong as we would like. She would have written before but waited to consult the doctors Place and Goodrich, and they thought it would be as well for her to go and put herself under regular treatment.
> She will write you tomorrow. It is a sudden conclusion or you would have been consulted. She starts Monday. Place will go with her and see that she has a good place. We will keep you informed as regards her and the children.

Cynthia F. Hayostek

Your father,

A.G. Packard

P.S. I wrote these lines as Ella was busy fixing her trunk and things to carry with her.

[In Ella's handwriting] Burdette My Darling, I have just received yours of the 30. Will answer tomorrow if I can. I am feeling quite well for me. Yours

The next letter was from Ella's sister, Carrie. It's postmarked July 12, 1893.

My Dear Brother:

Yesterday afternoon I went down home to help Ella what I could to get ready to start for Buffalo this morning. I had not seen her for eight days. She seemed about the same as when I saw her the week before, but did not complain of the fever as much.

I stayed late until after mother had returned from Olean where she had been to get some necessities for Ella, among them a lounging dress, which did not suit her at all. In a playful tone, I said I would just take her measure and send to you to get her one. She resented the word measure in such a manner it set me to thinking. Knowing her to put her best side out, I wondered if she has written you the exact truth about herself.

She has such will power, she will not give up. You know the malaria reduces one to skin and bones. I doubt if she weighs 80 lbs. For a few days, she has had a good appetite.

I have always had confidence in what Dr's say, especially Dr. Goodrich, but I cannot get rid of the idea that she has quick consumption. It is such an insidious disease and she has, to me, a peculiar look which makes me think so.

The Dr's claim not. I hope they are right. Something is certainly sapping her vitals. Ascertain correctly if possible and find out if she is getting relief at the hospital during the coming fortnight. If not, come East and take her to New York [City], or we shall not have her with us long.

Dr. Place goes with her this morning. He has been so slow in looking after her. I'm afraid it has been the means to endangering her chance for life.

Please let no one know I have written you. I may be unduly alarmed. With love and much concern for Ella,

I remain ever,

Your sister,
Carrie Howard

P.S. The children are well and will be looked after.

On July 13, 1893, Ella wrote B.A. from General Hospital in Buffalo. The letter is stained with tear drop splatters.

My Dear Husband:

I came up with Dr. Place to be treated 2 days ago and they have finished and given me the result, which is that I have lung tuberculosis and that I can treat myself as well at home as here in the hospital.

Dr. Rochester, the great specialist, prescribes all the medicine and of course I use it according to directions. Dr. Rochester of course can not even make a guess how long I may live, whether for years or for months. It was a great shock to me, although I had braced myself for it and stood it bravely.

My Darling, my great love for you rolls over me like a great flood. I know you love me, although I have caused you so many years of unhappiness [perhaps a reference to her reluctance to move to Arizona]. I had honestly planned to rest and try to make you happy more after your liking, but a divide has interposed. His will be done.

My heart is broken for my children, but they will be provided for in some way. It might be well for you to come home soon [to New York] to stay a little. I have improved greatly in strength the last 5 or 6 days. With little treatment, I can walk about but tire easily.

While till [sic] I found out whether I am going to improve – say in the course of a week or two. Bring all my dresses, ransack the bureaus. I think I have some trinkets in the upper drawer of the chiffonier (bureau) in dining room. Look in the little bedroom and take all the embroideries, red plush lambskin and in the closet, find 3 tablecloths, a lot of black fur tucked on the first shelf in the corner, and the clean clothes in the basket fold in the smallest [clothes] compress. My best shears [scissors] are on the 2nd shelf from the bottom at the very left hand, if I am not mistaken. Bring my Bible and the silverware, and Ashley's corduroy pants must be tucked in there somewhere. Don't let the Yussies have anything to do with anything.

You will do the best you can and I will apply treatment as soon as I can get the prescriptions filled. I am going down to Portville and will stay there with [Cousin] Min tonight.

I forgot to say that Dr. Rochester thinks I had better spend the winter in California if I am strong enough.

Devotedly yours,

Ella

On July 14, 1893 Dr. DeLancey Rochester wrote B.A. on letterhead stationery.

Dear Sir,

Three days ago, your wife consulted with me to examine her chest and throat and to advise her as to what was the matter with her and what she should do. At her request, I write to tell you also the result of my examination.

I find that her throat is not markedly involved, but that her left lung is seriously diseased. That is, I am sorry to say, she has consumption and that quite seriously.

In consequence of the lung trouble and the marked interference with nutrition, her heart too is showing a great deal of strain and will likely give way under it.

However it is possible that she may improve under the treatment that I have advised for her. If she does, she ought not to remain here through the winter but should return west to Los Angeles or Santa Barbara or one of the South Western states. I do not know much about places in Arizona, but the country round about Denver and Colorado Springs has an excellent climate.

While barring accidents – she is not in immediate danger, still I fear from the rapidity with which she has already run down that the case will be a rapid one in the further course.

I am sorry to have to write thus to you but I think that nothing is ever gained by hiding the truth in these matters from those who ought to know it.

I am, with sincere sympathy,

Very truly yours,

DeLancey Rochester

Packard went to New York as quickly as possible. Refusing to accept Rochester's analysis, B.A. spared no expense in battling Ella's disease. It was to no avail. She died Sept. 2, 1893 in the Packards' Portville home, seven weeks after her diagnosis.

The *Prospector* eulogized her as "a loving and devoted wife and affectionate and conscientious mother, a loyal daughter, a true and tried sister, a faithful friend and a trustful and devoted child of God."[11]

Ella's illness and death devastated B.A. Less than a month after her death, he went to Kansas and sold all his cattle there,[12] perhaps to pay her medical and funeral expenses. He left 10-year-old Gertrude, nine-year-old Ashley and three-year-old Dorothea with his parents.

In October, Packard returned to Tombstone and, in what appears to be a blind rush away from heartbreak, he continued on to Ojo de Agua. It had adequate grass and Packard decided not to sell any more cattle.[13]

Packard's hyperactivity during the next year indicates a person trying to cope with grief. He left his children in New York, perhaps Ella felt they'd receive a better education there. Gertrude helped her grandparents with rearing Dorothea, and finished primary school in New York with Ashley. As B.A. had when Ella was living in New York, he visited several times a year.

In Arizona, Packard had much to occupy him. The drought changed the way ranchers did business. They dug more wells and put up windmills. They stopped shipping 3 to 5-year-old animals raised solely on grass, and began sending out 1 to 2-year-olds, which were fed to maturity in stockyards.

Hand-in-hand with this was acquisition of cattle breeds, such as Herefords, that gained weight rapidly. To this end, Packard helped found the Kansas City Livestock Show, and began attending it annually to purchase registered stock.[14]

In the Sept. 2, 1893 *Prospector*, Greene estimated Cochise County cattle loss at 50 percent. He responded by adjusting his techniques and diversifying, which included raising hogs.[15] Packard and other agriculturalists undertook many of the things Greene did but drew the line at raising pigs.

Another thing Greene did was buy a hay press (baler) in order to obtain a higher price while fulfilling a contract to provide hay to Fort Huachuca. His hay press allowed him to sell baled hay for $14 per ton instead of $13.50 per loose ton.[16]

The hay contract probably assisted Greene in making his own trip to the Columbian Exposition. Greene's growing prosperity enabled him to keep an insurance policy with Vickers. When Greene's barn, with 100 tons of hay in it, burned down in mid-1893, the loss wasn't a complete one.[17]

Connections: The Life and Times of B. A. Packard

Greene bought thousands of cattle at "distress sale" prices, and shipped them to California, where they were fed barley and alfalfa until ready to market. Packard did the same thing, but also fed cattle on the Half Moon before trailing them to the Benson railhead.[18]

The 1890-93 drought forced many Cochise County ranchers to send their cattle out of state. It was an 1890s demonstration of what today is called grass banking, and a reason some experts say 1800s ranchers didn't cause as much environmental damage to the San Pedro Valley as is commonly thought.[19]

The ranchers who didn't have enough savings to ship their cattle out suffered the 50 percent or more die-off Greene mentioned. Because these small ranchers sold surplus animals early during the drought, the die-off was amongst their breeding stock. This meant small ranchers were unable to recover quickly once the drought eased, and were forced to make arrangements with prosperous ranchers or large firms.

"The spring following those unusual drought years," recalled Packard, "I bought seven brands owned on the San Pedro River; two of those brands belonged to Bisbee gamblers and one belonged to a widow in Tombstone. ... It was agreed that my foreman, Henry Aston, should brand the cattle at 75 cents per head, so I really paid only $5.25 per head for the cattle. Today the price of the cattle, on a like delivery, would not be less than $35 per head."[20]

Some ranchers lost their property. This likely happened to Packard and Greene's San Pedro neighbor, Anshutz. In 1899, he no longer worked his San Pedro River land, but instead was laboring in a Bisbee mine where he was killed in an explosion that fellow miners suspected Anshutz deliberately set so as to commit suicide.[21]

Other Packard connections recovered by supplementing their income through political jobs. In 1894, Hugh Conlon, a manager for the Shattucks and others, and Edward M. Dunbar, Thomas Dunbar's stepson, worked as Cochise County voting registration officers. Conlon served Taylor's Ranch, Dunbar in Tres Alamos; and Packard in Hereford.[22]

Another way Packard came to the supervisors' attention was when he, Vickers and Greene in 1893 received the supervisors' permission to build fences across a road along the San Pedro. The supervisors built a new road to replace the fenced-off one, but it forced area residents to go 10 miles out of their way. In 1894, the three agriculturists and other Hereford area residents appeared before the supervisors asking that the old road be restored.[23]

Vickers was already involved in county politics, having been appointed Cochise County Treasurer in 1888. Putting his accounting skills to use, Vickers finished out the term and then, perhaps encouraged by Stebbins, ran for Territorial Council in 1890.

The Council was the equivalent of today's state senate and, the same as the House of Representatives, met every other year. Elected as Cochise County's sole Council member, Vickers attended the 16th Territorial Legislative Assembly in Phoenix in 1891. Vickers thus participated in what was the most active territorial assembly, which passed more than 100 bills.

Among them were adoption of the secret ballot, requirements that calves be branded before selling and all cattle inspected before shipping, creation of Yavapai County, and efforts to write a constitution in preparation for possible statehood.[24]

Vickers' experiences undoubtedly propelled Packard into the next phase of his life – that of a public servant. In 1894, B.A. ran for political office.

NOTES

1. Erie: Bailey, *Silk Hats*, pp. 132-33. 1900: *Prospector*, April 1, 1892. Slaughter: *Epitaph*, Oct. 11, 1891.

2. Kansas: Wood, Charles L., *Journal of the West*, January 1977, pp. 16-28. Ship Kansas: *Epitaph*, May 31, 1891. $1 per head: *Epitaph*, May 10, 1891. Extended stay: *Epitaph*, Sept. 6 and Nov. 15, 1891.

Connections: The Life and Times of B. A. Packard

That Packard went to Eureka may have been the influence of Slaughter, who had dealings with G.S. Baker of Eureka in 1891.

3. Hudson: *Prospector*, Feb. 16, 1892. Boice: *Prospector*, Feb. 27, 1892. San Simon: *Prospector*, March 1, 1892.

4. Deming: *Prospector*, July 6, 1892. Herrera: *Prospector*, May 7, 1892. Proctor: *Prospector*, June 29, 1892. In addition to cattle, Herrera and McClure had a general store in Charleston.

5. Glenwood: *Prospector*, April 29, 1892. Returned: *Prospector*, May 16, 1892. To ranch: *Prospector*, May 19, 1892. Conditions: *Prospector*, June 15, 1892.

6. 19 carloads: *Prospector*, June 23, 1892. Packard help: Prospector, Nov. 5, 1892. Panhandle: Prospector, Nov. 15 and Dec. 5, 1892.

7. Kansas-Chicago trip: *Epitaph*, May 3, 7 and June 3, 1893.

8. Klein, Muray, *The Power Makers*. New York, NY: Bloomsbury Press, 2008, pp. 301-6.

9. This letter, and all others quoted in this chapter, are in possession of Watkins.

10. Mexico trip: *Epitaph*, June 25 and 28, 1893. Flood: *Prospector*, July 5, 1983 *Prospector*. Rain, recovery: *Prospector*, July 17 and 19, 1893.

11. "In Memoriam," *Prospector*, Sept. 15, 1893. "Portville," *Olean Weekly Democrat*, Sept. 8, 1893.

12. Sell all: *Prospector*, Oct. 3, 1891.

13. Ojo trip: *Prospector*, Oct. 26, 1892.

14. Wagoner, Jay J., *Journal of Arizona History*, Vol. II, p. 23-7; Wood, Charles L. *Journal of the West*, January 1977, p. 16-28. Bank stock: "Visited Great Stock Show," *International*, Nov. 27, 1922. Found show: "Packard on Tour...," *Dispatch*, Nov. 3, 1931.

15. The 1890, 1891 and 1892 Cochise County tax assessment rolls show 50 hogs on Greene's San Pedro property.

16. Contract: *Prospector*, July 28, 1893. Press: 1894 Cochise County tax assessment roll. Hay price: *Prospector*, Sept. 20, 1893.

17. Trip: Prospector, Oct. 30, 1893. Burn: *Prospector*, Aug. 5, 1893. Insurance: *Prospector*, Aug. 10, 1893.

18. Greene cattle: *Prospector*, Dec. 31, 1893, mentions 1,700 head and Jan. 25, 1894, 1,200 head. Packard cattle: *Prospector*, Jan. 8, 1894; 1895 Cochise County Tax Assessment Rolls; Axford, pp. 6-7.

19. That ranchers shipped tens of thousands of cattle out of Cochise County during the 1890s drought is one reason environmental damage was minimal. Claims of overstocking after the drought must be considered in light of Greene and Packard's techniques. They had many head, but fed them alfalfa and the animals were on the land for a short period of time.

Cynthia F. Hayostek

Historian and former rancher Diana Hadley, in "Cattle and Drought on the San Pedro River," a 2003 Arizona Historical Society Convention presentation, made a case the worst southern Arizona drought occurred during 1954-58 and it was the one that drastically changed the San Pedro landscape.

20. "Cattlemen of State ...," International, March 5, 1915.

21. Cochise County Coroner's Inquest No. 417.

22. Conlon: *Prospector*, April 20 and Sept. 24, 1892; *Epitaph*, June 21, 1894. Registration: *Prospector*, April 17, 1894.

23. *Prospector*, July 23 and 28, 1894.

24. Wagoner, Jay J., *Arizona Territory 1863-1912, A Political History*. Tucson, Ariz.: University of Arizona Press, 1970, pp. 287-9 and 520. www.cochise.az.gov/cochise_treasurer; accessed Jan. 23, 2007.

Politics and Greene

"There is no gambling like politics."
— Benjamin Disraeli, 1804-188, British Prime Minister

While 1893 was a year of tragic difficulty for Packard, it was the beginning of tremendous fortune for Greene. That year, he planted alfalfa and barley on 500 acres – the largest cultivated tract in Cochise County. Making this possible was Greene's dam, a mile or so down the San Pedro from today's Hereford.$_1$

In 1894, Greene sold 4,000 bushels of barley "at the machine" for $1.40 per 100 pounds, or $91 per acre. A portion of Greene's crop yielded 65⅔ sacks per acre.$_2$ Thus, Greene's earnings could have been $45,000 ($1.2 million in 2013). He must have deliberated where to invest this windfall and, given his mining background, considered that first.

Packard continued selling and buying cattle, some for as little as 24 cents a head. These drought-ravaged animals recovered on the Half Moon, which Packard expanded to 600 acres by leasing "Sime" Gallen's property. The cattle were shipped to California for further fattening. Sometimes, Packard and Greene traveled to California together while cattle dealing.$_3$

Undoubtedly feeling bereft without Ella or his children, B.A. spent little time in the Tombstone house. Early in 1894, he bought another Tombstone dwelling, and used portions of it to improve the Half Moon house. In 1895, he moved his Tombstone furniture to the ranch.

Late in 1894, he started shipping cattle from Osborn Station, and began spending more time in Bisbee. He stayed in Bisbee's best hotel of the time, the Bessemer, which was run by Mary Crossey and her loud parrot.$_4$

While Packard had a personal reason for this change, it turned out to be an astute political move. That's because growing copper demand had made Bisbee, by 1890, into Arizona's fifth-largest city with 1,500 residents.

Tombstone, on the other hand, had lost population. Just a few hundred people lived there following repeal of the Sherman Silver Act, which caused silver's price to plummet from $1.05 an ounce in 1893 to 65 cents in 1895. Beginning that year, an exodus to the boomtown of Pearce in the Sulphur Springs Valley exacerbated Tombstone's population decline.

The bimetallism alliance (which promoted backing American currency by a silver as well as gold standard) was a contentious topic in American politics for almost two decades. It was a major issue for the populist movement, and an important factor in the rise of Bryan, a Midwesterner. His "Cross of Gold" speech, denouncing gold as the sole standard, was the highlight of his 1896 Presidential bid.

Packard, as a former Tombstone mine owner, undoubtedly made free silver part of his campaign speech repertoire when he ran for Territorial Council in 1894. Greene nominated Packard at the Cochise County Democratic convention held in Bisbee, said the Oct. 10, 1894 *Prospector*. Packard campaigned around Cochise County the next four weeks against Willcox resident Charles W. Pugh.

Packard won the election by 35 votes. Pugh carried northern Cochise County, while Packard dominated the San Pedro Valley. The difference was Bisbee, where Packard garnered 174 votes to Pugh's 139 – a difference of 35 votes. Vickers won by more than twice that margin in his bid for Cochise County Treasurer.[5]

On Jan. 21, 1895, Packard was in Phoenix for the Arizona Assembly opening.[6] During the 18th Legislative Assembly, Packard received appointments to the Council's ways and means, corporation, judiciary, roads and ferries, and claims committees – the last as chairman.[7]

He introduced 10 bills; two, regulating the livestock industry, got the governor's signature. One created a fee of 25 cents per head for inspecting slaughtered cattle. The other amended an act previously passed "to protect interests of livestock producers" by requiring railroad section foremen to record all livestock killed by trains.

Another livestock bill gaining Packard's favor concerned cattle theft. While fighting a losing battle to pass Council Bill 49, Packard noted it cleared the House because, he said humorously, the House contained more cattlemen and no lawyers.$_8$

B.A. Packard, Territorial Councilman, 1895.

Arizona State Archives photo

Creation of two new counties was a central issue for the 18th Council. Following a filibuster, legislators split Navajo County off from Apache County on the session's last day. An effort to create Miles County (named for the famous general) from portions of Cochise and Graham counties was defeated.

That Packard listened to his constituents is clear from his introduction of a bill that would have made it a felony for someone other than a physician to administer chloroform or use hypnotism. Packard said a Cochise County physician had recommended introduction of the bill.

That physician was Dr. Frederick A. Sweet, the Copper Queen's chief surgeon in Bisbee. Sweet was also chairman of Cochise County's Democratic Committee, and thus well acquainted with Packard. Their friendship undoubtedly began when Packard started spending more time in Bisbee.

While in Phoenix at the Assembly, Packard renewed connections with Dunbar and Tweed, who'd both left Tombstone for Phoenix in 1889. Dunbar had become editor of the *Phoenix Gazette* and then the *Phoenix Democrat*, while Tweed prospered by selling Phoenix real estate.[9]

All-day train trips to Cochise County for ranch business and back to Phoenix for legislative sessions drained Packard.[10] After the Assembly's end, the March 29, 1895 *Prospector* said Packard, "whose strict attention to duty at the recent session of the legislature caused his health to be temporarily impaired, took his departure for Los Angeles where he expects the sea breeze to bring him around to normal condition."

On April 15, 1895, the *Prospector* reported, "B.A. Packard of Tombstone, one of the sterling democrats that leavened the 18th legislature, has spent several days in Phoenix. He will in a short time take a trip to New York to visit his little children. No one has made more friends in Phoenix than has Mr. Packard during the past few months."

When Packard returned from New York two months later, he found Greene deeply involved in a Sonoran gold mining venture. It was a placer operation called San Domingo on the Altar River, southwest of Nogales. In April 1895, Greene had 40 men working gravel beds 10-feet deep along an 11-mile stretch of the Altar.[11]

Greene encountered a difficulty late in 1895 when a Mexican Army officer arrived in the camp

William C. Greene
Library of Congress

seeking recruits. Greene "objected to his men being taken. That night the officer and a party of soldiers returned to his camp and told him he was wanted before the judge. He said he wouldn't go. In a minute, several Winchesters were stuck in his face and he immediately signified his intention to go. After lying in jail one day, he was released on a telegram from [Sonoran] Governor [Ramon] Corral."[12]

Greene's San Domingo venture was worth the jail time. In January 1896, he displayed around Nogales a coffee-cup-sized rock that contained approximately 14 ounces gold. A more usual find were nuggets the size of $5 gold pieces.[13]

This visible proof of San Domingo's richness convinced a British company with California interests to examine the property. It sent "noted mining expert Frank Reed of Jordan & Reed of San Francisco, who spent two months in" San Domingo. In June 1896, the English firm bought San Domingo for $400,000 ($11.4 million in 2013).

About the same time, Greene "closed a deal with San Francisco capitalists for the erection immediately of a 100-stamp mill on his Chivato mining property in the Altar District for an interest in the mine, and shipping of machinery has already begun."[14]

While Greene considered where to invest this second windfall, Packard continued buying and selling cattle. In 1895, there was plenty of rainfall, most cattle prices soared, and prosperity returned to the San Pedro Valley.

One, two and three-year-old corriente steers sold for $3, $6 and $9 each. Larger breeds brought $11, $13.50 and $16.50 for the same ages. This prosperousness extended to Charles A. Overlock, newly-arrived Tombstone butcher, who sold hides (with tail) for 11.5 cents each – an increase from six cents just a short time before – and to Packard's San Pedro neighbor James Burnett. He obtained a contract to provide beef to Fort Huachuca at $5.95 per pound, and then opened a store in Pearce.[15]

Packard bought cattle and fattened them on alfalfa pastures he'd discovered while at the Assembly. He gained control of land in Kyrene, southeast of Phoenix and south of Tempe, from Alfred Peters and George Taylor. After the 1895 Assembly concluded, but before he left for New York, Packard shipped 10 railroad cars of cattle from Kyrene to Denver.[16]

Increasingly during the late 1890s, Packard dealt in the Sulphur Springs Valley. Its abundant grass hosted cattle owned by Vickers and White's CCC, the Shattucks' Erie and smaller operations. One such was the Swisshelm Cattle Co., of which William Lutley was principal member.

English-born Lutley arrived in 1881 Tombstone, where he took up freighting. He switched to ranching in 1884 and developed links to the Shattucks and their connections: John Meadows, Conlon, James C. McNair, William H. Neel and Joe Hood.[17]

The southernmost Sulphur Springs Valley provided access to the Sonoran cattle ranges of the Hohstadt brothers and a relative, Harlow M. Teachout, in Sonora's Ajo Mountains. They and their neighbors crossed so many head of cattle for shipping out of Osborn Station that the Mexican government moved its customs house in 1895. Ochoaville, on the San Pedro River, was abandoned in favor of La Morita, a Mexican ranch near a distinctively shaped rock formation a few miles south of Osborn Station.[18]

In late 1895, 20,000 Sonoran cattle crossed between La Morita and Osborn Station. Packard imported 1,000 of these on Nov. 16, while fellow stockman William Land did the same. On Nov. 28, Packard "started ... about 3,000 head of cattle, which he will drive overland to Phoenix; half of that number will be put on pasture in the Salt River Valley, and the balance will be taken to Montana and put on pasture there."[19]

The Osborn Station stock pens became important during 1895 for another reason. Cattle were inspected there to check for cattle fever ticks, which carried a parasitic protozoan that caused bovine babesiosis. Known in the 1890s as Texas fever,

B.A. Packard joked around on top of the Osborn station cattle pens in 1897. The cattle in the pens had been inspected for ticks and were to be shipped out on the Arizona & Southeastern Railroad.

Packard Family photo

bovine babesiosis caused high mortality among northern U.S. cattle, while animals from the southern U.S. and Mexico displayed some immunity.

The U.S. Department of Agriculture fought Texas fever by limiting shipping to winter months and insisting upon manual inspection, with cattle either declared tick free or dipped in a liquid chemical to kill the insects. The cattle dip at Osborn Station was why Packard could send cattle to Montana.[20]

In addition to the Osborn Station pens, Cochise County's economy received another boost when Meyer Guggenheim & Sons purchased the Pilares copper mines. The New York firm built an ore processing operation in Nacozari, west of Pilares. Freight for this project left Osborn Station in wagons, cleared Mexican Customs at La Morita, and moved along the Ajos' west side before crossing the mountains through which the Hohstadt and Teachout cattle ranged.

All this economic development likely was one factor that encouraged Packard to accept another nomination from the Cochise County Democratic Party for the county's Council seat. Packard's opponent, Bisbee miner W.P. Long, was almost an unknown, and the election results reflected this. Long received 297 votes, and Packard 664 – more than even Smith, Arizona's popular Congressional delegate.[21]

"B.A. Packard, who is again returned to the legislative Council from this county by a handsome majority," said the *Prospector* in December, "has been most of the time during the past two months in the east looking after his large cattle interests in Kansas and the Indian Territory [Oklahoma], having during the season shipped numerous trainloads of cattle from the ranges in Cochise County and elsewhere to pasturage and close to market. ...

"Mr. Packard has given considerable attention to graded cattle and with his return has shipped 23 head of Hereford bulls for the ranges here. The animals are fine specimens of bovine perfection and will soon be roaming over the Hereford range on the river. Mr. Packard expects to continually add to his graded herd and finds it a profitable investment."[22]

Throughout 1896, Packard deepened his connections with Bill Land, who in the late 1890s managed the Kern County Land Co. holdings in Cochise County. In 1890 at age 55, Land married 25-year-old Harriet Catchim and they had a daughter.

Edward, Land's son from his first marriage, had read for law in Tombstone and opened an office in Bisbee. Packard brokered Land cattle and also for the Hohstadts, Teachout and Greene, thus staying "almost continuously on the go with his large cattle interests."[23]

Sometime during the second half of 1896, Packard must have talked with Greene about investing his San Domingo profits. The result was that in December 1896, Greene leased the Cananea copper mines from the widowed Elena Pesquiera.[24]

Packard, through his previous business deals with her in which he leased Ojo de Agua, may have provided Greene with this connection. But Packard certainly didn't provide any money to Greene. Nor did anyone else because Greene had plenty of cash after selling San Domingo. This fact, however, has been overlooked by everyone, including Greene's relatives and his biographer.[25]

While Greene took the preliminary steps toward assembling financial backers to develop Cananea, Packard went to New York in December for his father's funeral, and to spend the holidays with his children. Wishing to stay in New York as long as possible, Packard left there at the last possible minute and, because of "miserable railroad facilities," arrived several days after the start of Arizona's 19th Assembly session.[26]

Making up for his late arrival, Packard served on five committees. He was chairman of the busy territorial affairs committee, and a member of the mines and mining, ways and means, enrolled and engrossed bills, and claims committees. With these assignments, Packard played a large and varied role in the 19th Assembly.[27]

Around the turn of the 20th Century, Arizona had only 12 counties; each had one representative in the Council chamber. That made sitting at a Council desk an exclusive experience. Future Arizona governor G.W.P. Hunt is at the middle desk on the right side. Packard is the second legislator from the right.

Arizona State Archives photo

Packard voted for bills to fund the University of Arizona and construct Arizona's capitol building, still used today. He played a key role in the demise of an objectionable mining bill. Another crucial Packard vote halted moving the state prison from Yuma to Prescott. During that debate, the *Phoenix Republican* mentioned Packard was "in his glory" with a new spring suit.[28]

Dunbar also teased Packard in the pages of the *Gazette*, as only a friend could. Dunbar said Packard stayed busy buying "chewing gum for the girls." Packard's social life attracted others' attention. Included in a recap of bloopers made by legislators during the 19th Assembly was Packard's "I have a date, Mr. President."[29]

The effort begun in the 18th Assembly to create a new county from parts of Cochise and Graham counties, with the seat in Willcox, continued during the 19th Assembly. James J. Riggs and William Speed, two of Cochise's three representatives, called Willcox home. Speed, one of only two Republicans in the House, introduced the bill to create Chiricahua County.

In the Council, Packard strongly opposed the bill. He voiced concern that Chiricahua County would be hampered by excessive indebtedness and its tax base would be inadequate. He specifically mentioned opposition by Ben Williams, CQ Mine superintendent in Bisbee – another example of Packard listening to his constituents. The Chiricahua County creation bill died in the session's final days.[30]

Packard played a major part in passage of CB-40, which revised and codified Arizona's brand laws. Instead of referring CB-40 to committee, the Council as a whole considered the bill over several days, with Packard in the chairman's seat much of that time. The Council felt Packard's input was so important that it decided to run late one evening so he could speak about the bill. It required brand registration with the state instead of counties, thus creating the Arizona Livestock Sanitary Commission.[31]

During the 19th Assembly, Packard stayed in the Adams Hotel, owned by John C. Adams. A successful Chicago attorney until he moved to Phoenix, Adams bet his new home town, which had perhaps 4,000 residents, was ready for a first-class hotel.

The Adams, dedicated early in 1897, consisted of 200 rooms in several stories, with each room opening onto a balcony. On the ground floor were meeting rooms and a bar, to which so many politicians gravitated it was dubbed the "third legislative branch."[32]

"They had an elegant bar in the old Adams Hotel," recalled Packard years later, "and they served good whiskey there. As a consequence, much of the law making in the Territorial days ... was perfected in front of the bar in the Adams Hotel. I ... attended many sessions there myself, both as a legislator and as a private citizen."[33]

The original Adams Hotel in downtown Phoenix, ca. 1900. In May 1910 Phoenix's Hotel Adams burned to the ground.

Keith Davis collection

In 1897, much talk along the Adams bar concerned Gov. Myron H. McCord. He'd begun his Arizona political career in 1895 with an appointment to the Arizona Board of Control, which oversaw the territorial prison, insane asylum and reform school. McCord served on the board until he became governor in 1896.

While on the board, McCord signed a contract with the State of Arizona Improvement Co., organized by Eugene S. Ives to construct an irrigation canal near Yuma. Ives was an attorney who'd reportedly been a denizen of New York's Tammany Hall political machine before moving to Arizona. McCord signed Ives' Tammany-like contract, which paid prison laborers 70 cents a day – not in cash but in "water rights." This meant "the territory could purchase water at the regular rates to irrigate any lands in the vicinity it might possess when and if the canal was finished."[34]

During the 19th Assembly, a joint investigating committee focused on McCord's role in this dubious contract. McCord, however, escaped censure and remained governor until 1898. He resigned then to become a colonel in Arizona's First Territorial Infantry, created during the Spanish-American War. Ives showed no such patriotic fervor, but did remain part of Arizona's political scene.[35]

After the 19th Assembly ended, Packard returned to his cattle dealings. These were interrupted by a tragic event in Greene's life. On June 24, 1897, Greene's nine-year-old daughter, Ella, and her friend, Katie Corcoran, drowned in the San Pedro.

Katie had come from Tombstone to stay with Ella and seven-year-old Eva on the ranch, and they decided to go wading in the river. Racing there, Katie beat the sisters, splashed into what had been a shallow, sandy area, and dropped from sight. Ella, knowing her friend couldn't swim, jumped in after her. Ella screamed at her sister, "Eva, go back, go back!" and Eva ran to the house for help, which arrived too late.

The girls' funeral, held in the Bessemer parlor June 26, drew an overflow crowd, which learned the girls had drowned in a riverbed hole scooped out by rapid water flow caused when Greene's dam broke. A June 30 ad in the *Prospector* revealed what Greene thought happened: "I will pay $1,000 reward for proofs of the party or parties, who blew out my dam at my ranch on the night of June 24, thereby causing the death of my little daughter and Katie Corcoran."

Greene soon made it clear who he thought the party was. On July 1, he shot James Burnett to death outside the OK Corral, handed his pistol to Tombstone's Chief of Police, and declared, "Vengeance is mine." From jail, Greene told a reporter, "I have no statement to make other than that man was the cause of my child being drowned."

Three men proffered to post Greene's $20,000 bail. Packard and Tombstone merchant Sam M. Barrow both said they'd put up $10,000, but it was Greene's brother-in-law Ed Roberts who bailed Greene out. Upon his release, Greene left for Nogales in order, the July 8 *Prospector* said, "to perfect the transfer of the mining property recently sold to California parties by him."[36]

The U.S. District Court met only twice a year then, and so murder charges against Greene were not heard until December. The jury took just 10 minutes to acquit him.

Despite this quick decision, the case remains mysterious. Greene declared the dam was blown up, but was it? Greene insisted that Burnett was to blame, but was he?

When considering these questions, it's important to understand the dam's construction. Today, dam implies high-rise block and cement, but that's not how dams were built on the San Pedro in the last quarter of the 19th century.

The *Prospector* described all dams on the San Pedro as "built of brush and earth with some stone, if stone can be had[. S]ome are built by filling sacks with sand and laying them across the stream, thus throwing the water from the main current to the head of the irrigating channel."[37]

An 1880s photo of Richard Gird's San Pedro dam shows it was approximately four feet tall.[38] Greene's dam probably wasn't that tall, and it certainly wasn't permanent. It washed out twice during 1896.[39]

Greene's house was slightly below the dam. That's certain because no one noticed the pond behind the dam vanished during the darkness of June 23-4. No one on the ranch the morning of June 24 mentioned the pond's disappearance.[40]

Greene was in Nogales, and his wife didn't detect anything amiss. If Ella had, it's unlikely she would have let her daughters and Katie go to the river. Perhaps a slight rise or vegetation blocked the girls' view, or probably because they were racing each other, they didn't notice the dam was damaged.

If, as Greene maintained, someone "blew out my dam," why did no one hear an explosion? The dam was close enough to Greene's house that, even if an explosion occurred at night, the noise would have awakened sleepers. Greene said he found an exploded cap and fuse at the dam site, but he made this claim *after* he shot Burnett.[41]

Given the dam's rickety construction, it seems more likely that it gave way rather than was blown up. Did someone "help" the washout occur by removing small but crucial portions of the dam – some rocks here, shovelfuls of dirt there? Perhaps, but it's unlikely Burnett did this, despite his unsavory reputation, which was based partly upon the shady way he ran Charleston's justice of the peace court in the 1880s.[42]

During Greene's trial, Tombstone lawman Fred Dodge testified that Burnett once tried to kill him. Two dozen people, including Packard, swore to Greene's good character or that they'd heard Burnett threaten Greene. But no one specified the reason for this ill feeling, or said that Burnett acted upon his threats. For example, George Gallen, Sime Gallen's son, testified he heard Burnett threaten Greene on June 29 in Burnett's Pearce store. But George never said, nor did anyone else, that they'd seen Burnett in the San Pedro Valley around the time the dam broke.[43]

Burnett could have left Pearce and traveled to Greene's property. If he'd ridden or gone in a buggy, it would have taken at least eight hours one way to travel between Pearce and Hereford. No one testified that Burnett wasn't in his store over a two-day period. Burnett could have ridden to Willcox, boarded the Southern Pacific Railroad, changed trains in Benson, and then ridden from Packard Station to Hereford, but no one testified they saw Burnett on a train or in a station.

The 1897 Cochise County tax rolls show Burnett had almost no interest in the upper San Pedro Valley when he died. Ten years earlier, he had a ranch near Fort Huachuca on which Hilaria Gomez ran 100 cattle. But by 1897, Burnett's only property in the San Pedro Valley was Crystal Springs.

In 1897, the widowed Gomez had 250 head of cattle on her own ranch, around Crystal Springs. Burnett seems to have left management of the springs to Gomez, while he took advantage of Pearce's boom with his store.[44]

Since Burnett paid little attention to Crystal Springs, it's not likely he'd bother damaging Greene's property, despite their well-known animosity. There were, however, some area residents who benefited from the dam's collapse and who may have wanted to cause Greene grief.

In 1896, Greene leased a portion of his ranch to Ah Lum Co., consisting of Ah On, I On, Tum On Sam, Ah Quay and Sam On. These Chinese men agreed to pay Greene $1,260 yearly rent for land on which they grew vegetables, but they only managed to pay $568. In a suit Greene filed to get the rest of the rent, he claimed Ah Lum also owned him $50 for a horse.[45]

Ah Lum needed a horse to pull a wagon it purchased from Emanuel. He had recovered from the financial difficulties Packard helped him with, started a wagon and carriage business, and gotten a job as Clerk of Superior Court.

In 1896, Emanuel sold Ah Lum a wagon for $200. The wagon was constantly in Emanuel's shop, and soon the repair bill totaled over $250. Ah Lum paid part of what it owed, but

Emanuel sued to get the rest. He sold the debt to Greene before the case was decided in court.[46]

Ah Lum thus owed Greene more than $700, and so rented from Gomez in 1897. This got Ah Lum off Greene's land but eliminated the company's easy access to irrigation water. Ah Lum had no way to pay its debt since growing vegetables during the hottest, driest portion of the year was difficult without the water impounded behind Greene's dam.

Perhaps this compelled Ah Lum's members to remove a few rocks or shovelfuls of dirt from Greene's dam in an attempt to increase the water flowing down the San Pedro to Ah Lum's cropland. Since this most certainly would have been done at night, the Chinese farmers would not have known that the surging water created the riverbed hole in which Ella and Katie drowned.

Ah Lum's members, however, quickly learned what happened. When Greene visited them June 28, they presented an explanation that shunted blame onto Burnett. Ah On said, according to Greene, that Burnett told them that "if they need[ed] any water to blow my dam out, and if I did anything he [Burnett] would kill me."[47]

This deflection did not get Ah Lum off the hook. Greene got a writ of attachment on Ah Lum's property, which required Cochise County Sheriff Scott White to go to the Gomez ranch and take possession of Ah Lum's "wagons, horses, mules, harness and growing crop."[48]

On July 1, Ah Lum submitted a notice to the First Judicial Court that it didn't "accept the bond on attachment filed."[49] This notice could be the reason Greene went to Tombstone that day, resulting in the chance encounter that ended with Greene shooting Burnett dead.

When the jury found Greene not guilty, the courtroom crowd joined Mrs. Greene in rejoicing.[50] Clearly, San Pedro Valley residents thought highly of Greene and few mourned Burnett's passing. Many people had testified to Greene's good character and Burnett's "vindictive and revengeful" one.[51]

Greene's December 1897 exoneration let him begin laying groundwork for Cobre Grande Copper Co. – Greene's initial attempt to exploit Cananea's copper ore. He did not, however, devote all his time to the firm until after the death of his wife, Ella, from cancer in December 1899. Packard undoubtedly consoled Greene by drawing upon his own experience of losing a wife to disease.

Packard spent 1898 working his ranches, sometimes hand-in-hand with Greene. In the spring, Packard and Greene, along with an Aston brother and Bisbee cattleman G.A. Spindle, sold 5,000 cattle for $17 a head to Kansas City buyers. Packard and Greene leased some of their San Pedro property to neighbor Levi Scranton, who then became a major alfalfa supplier to Bisbee.[52]

Packard went to his Kyrene ranch regularly, and spent the 1898 summer in New York with his children. While he was gone, Cochise County's Democrats held their nominating convention. Although the *Epitaph* promoted another Council term for Packard, he must have left strict instructions not to nominate him because CQ employee Charles C. Warner got the nod and won the election.[53]

Packard's major undertaking during 1898 was putting up fence. Although the Erie built a 50-mile drift fence through the southern Sulphur Springs Valley in 1897,[54] Packard contemplated barbed wire before that. The Erie fence segregated its cattle from Mexican livestock, but clearly Packard intended a larger purpose with his fence.

"During the spring of this year," reported the July 21, 1898 *Prospector*, Packard "had 74 miles of barbed wire fence constructed on the Camou grant, just below the line, which grant he holds under lease, with the privilege of purchase. Within a few days, he has turned into this immense pasture 1,500 head of cattle in addition to a large herd already there, and last Friday he contracted for 2,500 head more to be delivered in the fall. Mr. Packard some time ago came to the conclusion that the only satisfactory way of handling and raising cattle in the range country is to have them under fence, and he is now in a position to control his range and regulate the breeding of his herd."

This last phrase meant Packard was upgrading his herd with the 23 Hereford bulls he'd bought, and the fence kept out non-Hereford bulls. The enormity of fencing hundreds of thousands of acres is conveyed by a Feb. 12, 1899 *Bisbee Weekly Orb* article that covered Packard's next fencing project.

"The Turkey Track Cattle company is busily engaged in fencing the San Jose ranch property of the company located in Old Mexico. They will use about 40 tons of barbed wire in this work and when completed will have in this one tract 150,000 acres enclosed with a 4-wire fence.

"This adjoins another tract of 100,000 acres, the property of the Packard Cattle company, thus giving the two companies 250,000 acres of the best grazing land in northern Sonora, all under fence, on which to keep their large herds of cattle. The Turkey Track company is composed of Walter Vail, J.V. Vickers, B.A. Packard and Mr. [E.J.] Gates."[55]

The four men associated themselves under the Turkey Track name, but did not incorporate or even use a turkey footprint brand. At first, the Turkey Track used Packard's half moon brand. Two years later, when Greene incorporated a cattle company in Arizona, he involved Packard and Gates and used the Turkey Track name.[56]

During the summer of 1899, while Packard was in New York for his months-long stay with his children, he undertook arrangements for their educations. Gertrude attended school in the East while Ashley went to Shattuck, an Episcopalian, boys' boarding school with military emphasis in Faribault, Minn.

In late September 1899, Packard returned to Bisbee. Stepping off the train with him were Greene, George Mitchell and George Treadwell.[57] Mitchell had invented the Mitchell Economic Hot-blast Furnace; Treadwell was a mining engineer and promoter. The three men were headed toward Cananea, where they took the preliminary steps to create what became, with amazing rapidity, a multi-million-dollar copper operation initially known as Cobre Grande. Packard too soon rode into Mexico, but for a different reason.

While he was still in New York, there'd been a fracas on his ranch. Gavino Villa was shot in the leg and his assailant escaped into Mexico. It was one of several shooting incidents along the border around that time. After a Sept. 17 fight between "cowboys and Mexicans" wounded two, Packard joined a group headed for La Morita to meet with Col. Emil Kosterlitzky and Juan Fenochio, top officers of Mexico's *rurales*, in an effort to prevent further trouble. Less than a month later, the Mexican government announced plans to move its customs house from La Morita to Naco, Son.[58]

Tim Taft, seated right, was the driver of this rough-and-ready stagecoach paused in front of the Mexican Customs building at La Morita Ranch, three miles south of the American customs building that was five miles east of today's Naco. Taft's "stagecoach" is really a modified wagon that hauled freight and people from La Morita through the Ajo Mountains to Nacozari. This building was abandoned in 1900 when customs operations of both countries moved to Naco.

Bisbee Mining and Historical Museum

There was also a Naco, Ariz., which sprang up after Phelps Dodge Corp. (PD) bought the Guggenheim interests in Nacozari, and let it be known that a railroad would go there. The first step in this was building four miles of Arizona & Southeastern Railroad (A&SE) track from Deer Point, in the southwesternmost Mule Mountains, to what became Naco Junction.

During the summer of 1898, Naco, Ariz., took shape. Packard said that when engineers were laying out the four-mile line, they asked him for name suggestions. He said Naco since it was the first four letters of Nacozari.[59] A railroad to Nacozari was never built from Naco, but in 1900 one went to Cananea, which contributed greatly to that town's growth and Greene's fortune.

Packard continued brokering and shipping cattle. In May 1899, the Bisbee *Weekly Orb* reported "while a part of the herd of two thousand cattle belonging to the Turkey Track company were being loaded for shipment to Kansas, Deputy Collector of Customs Welch stepped up to Mr. Packard and informed him that his cattle were under seizure by the U.S. government. ...

"The ground upon which the cattle were seized is a mystery to everyone, as the cattle were all rounded up on the ranges of the Turkey Track company on this side of the line, and were not subject to duty. The custom house officers claim that the cattle were seized so as to make a test case as to whether a cattle company has the right to run the same brand on their cattle on both sides of the line, the ranges of the Turkey Track company being on both sides and one brand used."

The *Orb* noted Packard was "out the time and expense of rounding up the cattle, [and] the expense of bringing the cars for shipment." Customs officials held the cattle overnight, then offered them to Packard. He refused to accept them, so officials released the cattle, which wandered off.[60]

Early in 1900, Packard "and his partner, J.V. Vickers, ... closed a trade with Senor Camou of Guaymas, whereby Mr.

Camou transferred to Packard & Co. 112,000 acres of fine land in Sonora and 1,890 acres in Arizona." This was Ojo de Agua and a portion of the San Rafael grant.

"Mr. Packard returned from Phoenix yesterday," reported the Bisbee *Daily Orb*. "From him we learn that ... the quantity of land in Arizona purchased by the Packard Cattle Co. is incorrectly stated.... Packard and Vickers ... purchased from Camou Brothers all of the land embraced in the San Rafael del Valle grant confirmed by the United States Supreme Court. It will require a survey ... but it is believed the number will reach 18,000."[61]

Dr. Frederick A. Sweet
St. John's Sweet Memorial Church

Also in 1900, Packard revived his political activities. On his way to New York for his annual visit, he stopped in Kansas City, likely for cattle business, and for the Democratic Party's national convention, in which he played a role. He was among those carrying the news to Bryan of his second Presidential nomination. When Packard returned from New York, he went to Arizona's Democratic convention, a contentious event bedeviled by credentialing disputes which he and Sweet helped solve.[62]

Cochise County's Democrats began their convention in October with a Bisbee meeting, complete with the CQ Band. Named county chairman, Packard introduced various speakers, including Ives. Convention attendees again nominated Charlie Warner for Cochise County's Council seat, and again he won.[63]

The pattern of Packard's life continued as a new century began. He remained a major cattle broker, dealing in as many as 7,000 head per transaction.[64] The founding of Douglas early in 1901 on the international border in the middle of the Sulphur Springs Valley expanded Packard's field of operations.

Packard, however, spent more time visiting Tucson than Douglas. The reason for this was Carlota "Lottie" (Wood) Holbrook, who married Packard "at a late hour" on June 26, 1902 in the parsonage of Tucson's Methodist Church. It was so late that pioneer Tucson merchant Emanuel Drachman had to be awakened to act as Packard's best man.

"No one had been apprised of matrimonial plans when Mr. Packard left for Tucson," reported the June 27, 1902 *Bisbee Review*. "When his friends here saw him escort a lady to the [still-new Copper Queen] hotel, even that caused no suspicion. It was not long, however, until the fact of the marriage was announced. Then his friends were [so] surprised [that] they laughed; then they clapped 'Old Pack' on the back... ."

It says much for her social acumen that less than a week after her arrival in Bisbee, Packard's bride was a hostess at a formal reception for Arizona Gov. Alexander O. Brodie and his wife during Bisbee's Fourth of July celebration. The festivities included a drilling contest, carnival and colored electric light display.

At the carnival, "the snake charmer who does business adjoining the wild man Zambezi misjudged a bad snake last night and but for the prompt arrival of night Officer Thomas, there would have been one less attraction on the midway.

"The snake charmer advertises to bite a snake into two pieces just back of the ears. At the performance last evening, the snake's head became lodged in the throat of the performer, and for a time it looked as if the undertaker's services would be needed. Charlie Thomas finally fished out the snake's head with a piece of bailing wire and the show proceeded as usual."[65]

Connections: The Life and Times of B. A. Packard

This juxtaposition of society reception and choking carnival performer was something Lottie Packard could appreciate. Born May 31, 1875 in Kansas City, Mo., she was the daughter of Robert C. and Virginia (Reynolds) Wood. Her father went through Tucson in 1854 on his way to California, where he lived until 1860. He returned to Missouri then, raised Wood's Battalion and led it throughout the Civil War.

He married Virginia Reynolds, a Kentucky general's daughter, and they had five children. Not long after the war, the family moved to Tucson. It's said the first iron stove in town was one Wood freighted in for his wife.$_{66}$

Daughter Lottie, also called "Dixie," attended Tucson schools and earned a teaching certificate after studies at the University of Arizona. On April 20, 1892, she married Albert A. Holbrook, a New Hampshire native who arrived in Tucson about 1890 and ranched with an uncle. After his marriage, Albert worked for Gardner & Worthen, a machine shop. He died June 17, 1895 of diphtheria.$_{67}$

Sharing the loss of spouses was one thing that lessened the age gap between 55-year-old B.A. and 28-year-old Dixie. Others were a well-developed sense of humor and a shared zest for life, which manifested itself in the couple's lifestyle.

The first of many trips they took together was to Chicago, the Great Lakes and then New York as a honeymoon and for B.A.'s annual visit. Gertrude was on summer break from her piano studies at the New England Conservatory of Music. Dixie also met Ashley, who'd enter Stanford University the next year, and Dorothea, who displayed much musical talent and a fine singing voice even at age 12.$_{68}$

When the Packards returned to Cochise County, B.A. resumed cattle dealing and Democratic politicking. Both often involved poker games. Burton C. Mossman, veteran cattleman and first Arizona Rangers captain, recalled in his biography a game in El Paso's Sheldon Hotel. Present were Packard, Pat Garrett, ex-Lincoln County Sheriff; and A.B. Fall, Greene's attorney at the time, who later became a U.S. Senator and Secretary of the Interior.

Mossman could do no wrong and chased everyone out of the game, including Packard, who'd previously beaten Mossman with ease. Mossman decided to rub Packard's nose in his loss by sending a roomful of flowers to Dixie.

According to Mossman, an overwhelmed Dixie told her husband, "I never knew you to buy flowers for me before."

"Guess I paid for 'em, all right," replied B.A. with a grin. "It's that goddamned Mossman."[69]

As chairman of Cochise County's Democratic Party, Packard presided over both the Bisbee and county caucuses in 1902. Bill Land nominated his friend for Territorial Council at the latter event.[70]

Because he was in California securing cattle pasture in response to another string of dry years, Packard didn't campaign much. Nonetheless, the *Bisbee Review* strongly endorsed Packard, and he defeated Republican candidate George S. Shibley, a Bisbee railroader, in every county precinct but two.[71]

Even before the Assembly began, there was talk of Packard as Council chairman. Four other Councilmen said they'd vote for Packard, but Yuma Councilman Ives was not one of them. Packard had cultivated a relationship with Ives by hiring him to do some legal work, but Ives ignored this and other gestures while riding roughshod toward the Council presidency.[72]

Perhaps the most far-reaching of the 99 bills passed during the 22nd Assembly was a compulsory eight-hour work day for underground miners. This was something Packard had implemented in his own mines 20 years before, and so he strongly backed the bill as a member of the mines and mining committee. Harry B. Rice, Graham County's Councilman who lived in Morenci, joined Packard in supporting the bill.[73]

Rice was one of several legislators who joined Packard in a bipartisan coalition that had some legislative influence, despite Ives' blatant attempt to sideline Packard. Joining Rice and Packard were Republicans Joseph H. Kibbey,

Maricopa County Councilman; John H. Page, Cochise County Representative; and Democrat Noah W. Bernard, Pima County Representative.[74]

Ives appointed Packard to the printing, agriculture, and counties and county boundaries committees. None played a direct role in any major legislation passed by the 22nd Assembly. This included limiting railroad workers to no more than 16 consecutive hours of work, curbing company store methods, establishing uniform licensing of physicians and dentists, and improving the insane asylum and juvenile reform school.

The Council's progressive bent included passage of two controversial measures, neither of which Packard voted for. The first, establishing women's suffrage, received Gov. Brodie's veto. The second, in which Ives was deeply involved, asked Congress for statehood with New Mexico. The Assembly sent the joint statehood resolution to the U.S. Congress without the okay of the Arizona House, which repudiated it. Still, it took the determined efforts of Arizona's Congressional Delegate Smith to halt consideration of joint statehood.[75]

At the Assembly's end, Brodie nominated Packard, Rice and two Republicans to a committee tasked with organizing Arizona's display at the Louisiana Purchase Exposition, better known as the 1904 St. Louis World's Fair. Ives launched a two-hour tirade attacking Packard, said the March 19, 1903 *Bisbee Daily Review*, "on the silly pretext that he was not a Democrat." Disregarding Ives, the Council confirmed Packard 8-3, with Packard not voting.

The March 19, 1903 *Phoenix Republican* said the reason for Ives' attack was Packard refused to let Ives tell him what to do. The *Bisbee Daily Review* echoed this, saying Packard declined to "be led around by the nose by any one ... and because he refused to be led ... is the reason which prompted the attack on him by Mr. Ives."

The *Review* assessed Packard's 20 years of work with the Democratic Party in Arizona, adding the understatement that Ives "will find but few who agree with him in opposing the confirmation on the ground that B.A. Packard was not a Democrat." Packard said nothing publicly about Ives' behavior but never again had anything to do with him.[76]

Extended trips with Dixie to Mexico City and Europe didn't interfere with Packard organizing Arizona's World's Fair exhibits and being fair commission treasurer. Packard delegated wisely; among his assistants was his poker-playing buddy, Bob Leatherwood. The Arizona exhibit is remembered as featuring a massive ore slab from the Copper Queen Mine, and a profusely illustrated booklet extolling Arizona's many virtues. The Fair attracted almost 20 million visitors, including Packard, who shook hands with Geronimo in the latter's display.[77]

About this time, Packard combined his affection for fairs with an old love – horse racing. In this, he was matched by Greene, whose Cananea Copper Company's meteoric stock market rise enabled him to have a private railroad car and trotting horse stable. When Greene and Packard played poker in Greene's railroad car, "Verde," the stakes included their race horses.

The Feb. 25, 1902 *Review* declared Packard to be the "proud owner of a beautiful trotter purchased in Phoenix" that won races held there on Washington's birthday. On May 4, the *Review* said, Cobre Grande, "one of Greene's string in Phoenix," recently lowered the state record by trotting a mile in 2:13¼. Five days later, the *Review* noted Cobre Grande was owned by Packard, and the stallion had covered a quarter-mile in .30½.

Obviously, whoever won the latest poker game was the man who owned Cobre Grande. Despite his ownership changes, Cobre Grande received consistent schooling because Packard and Greene shared the same trainer, George V. Klotzbach. He was an Iowan who bought Cobre Grande to the Salt River Valley and then took him to race in summertime New York under Greene's colors.[78]

The Phoenix stable where Packard and Greene kept their horses was also where John Adams had his race horses. Another who kept horses there was Thomas E. Pollack, a Flagstaff resident. Pollack ran large numbers of sheep and cattle in northern Arizona, and had interests in banking, New Mexico coal mines and a timber company with a sawmill in McNary, Ariz.[79]

Late in 1904, Adams invited some friends to dinner in his hotel. He told them that he, Packard and Pollack were organizing "a driving club" as a nonprofit corporation. They'd put up $5,000 each to "build and equip a first class race track and fair ground for the city of Phoenix," replacing grounds destroyed in an 1891 Salt River flood. Adams invited his guests to join the trio; his appeal raised $60,000.

The three friends paid $9,200 for 80 acres 1½ miles out of town on the northwestern end of Grand Avenue. They announced their intent to hold a yearly race meet there with "exhibits of all kinds from all over the territory." Once the fair was established, the trio planned to offer the event to the legislature.[80]

To this end, Packard stayed politically active. When the joint statehood specter raised its head again in 1905, Packard was one of many attending a special meeting in Arizona's Capitol building. Packard, along with Smith and another Democrat, represented their party in a joint meeting with three Republicans, all voicing Arizona's opposition to statehood with New Mexico. A more formal group, headed by Adams and including Packard, Phelps Dodge's Walter Douglas, Smith, and Tucson railroad magnate Epes Randolph, helped quash the issue.[81]

Beginning when Packard returned from his annual New York trip in 1905, he promoted the Phoenix race meet. The driving association built a covered grandstand and two tracks and enclosed them all with a wooden fence, thus attracting over 30 race horses stabled on site. Packard emphasized the

Cynthia F. Hayostek

In 1907, this post card helped promote the appearance of legendary harness racer Dan Patch at the third annual Arizona Territorial Fair. Packard and his friends, John Adams and Tom Pollack, who'd established the fair in 1905, ran it for another five years before relinquishing management to Arizona's territorial government.

Author's Collection

$13,000 in prize money for 20 races would come from the private sector – not the territorial government.₈₂

In autumn 1905, Cobre Grande, undefeated in New York that summer, returned to Phoenix. Coming with Cobre Grande was Greene's mare, Florence Wilton, who'd trotted a mile in 2:07. Adams raced a stallion named Custer, who'd paced a half mile in 1:01.

The Bisbee Stakes, for a $1,000 purse raised by Bisbee merchants, drew 12 entrants from California, New Mexico and New York. Another pacing race, the Clifton-Morenci Stakes, attracted 14 horses, with some from Iowa and four owned by Greene.₈₃

Many Cochise County people, including a large Bisbee delegation, attended the first fair on Dec. 4-9, 1905. They were led by Packard, who was Cochise County's member on the Territorial Fair Association.[84]

In 1907, the famous trotter Dan Patch was on exhibit. This, plus a cattlemen's convention in the Adams Hotel and various exhibits, helped the Fair turn a profit of $3,000 ($76,000 in 2013).[85]

In 1909, the operating agreement between the driving club and Territory grabbed Republican Gov. Kibbey's attention. Political antagonism between Kibbey and the Democratic-dominated Assembly had already contributed to the Arizona Rangers' demise. So when Kibbey called for Adams and Packard's resignation from the Fair commission, Adams appealed to the Assembly, "which joyously took up the fight."[86]

The Assembly investigated the driving club and cleared both men of any wrong-doing. Kibbey, however, wasn't satisfied and began his own investigation. Adams resigned in disgust, but Packard refused to be bullied and stayed on the commission.

In 1910, new Gov. Richard E. Sloan reappointed Adams to the commission. Packard resigned a few months later, declaring five years' devotion to the Fair was enough.[87] Kibbey's attack, along with Ives' vitriolic behavior, so soured Packard on political activity that he never again sought office.

In 1910, Cochise County Democrats nominated Packard to be a delegate to Arizona's Constitutional Convention.[88] This demonstrated the obvious regard county residents had for Packard, but he let it be known that he'd rather have a behind-the-scenes role, and 10 other Cochise County men helped write Arizona's progressive Constitution.

It's thus ironic that Packard was propelled into the next phase of his life by connections he made while he was a politician. Chief amongst these was Pollack, but other connections dated back 15 years and included a business associate of the by-then millionaire Greene.

Cynthia F. Hayostek

NOTES

1. *Epitaph,* May 21, 1893.

2. *Epitaph,* June 30, 1894.

3. 24 cents: *Prospector,* Nov. 24, 1893. Gallen lease: *Prospector,* Aug. 21, 1894. Recovery: *Prospector,* Jan. 8, 1894. California and Greene: *Prospector,* Jan. 17, 25 and 31, 1894.

4. Buy house: *Prospector,* March 26, 1894. Furniture: Prospector, May 4, 1895. Bisbee shipping: *Prospector,* Nov. 8 and Dec. 11, 1894. Bessemer: *Prospector,* Aug. 25, 1896.

5. "Election Table" and "Official Report," *Prospector,* Nov. 22, 1894.

6. Wagoner, Jay J., *Arizona Territory,* pp. 319-321.

7. Kelly, George H., *Legislative History 1864-1912.* Phoenix, Ariz.: Manufacturing Stationers, 1926, p. 174.

8. *Phoenix Republican,* Feb. 27, 1894.

9. "Editor, Dunbar's Weekly...," *International,* Feb. 11, 1921. Tweeds: *Prospector,* March 15, 1892.

10. Railroad timetables: Prospector, March 16, 1897. Travel between Bisbee and Phoenix required changing trains and lines three times. The Arizona & Southeastern went from Bisbee, through Packard Station, to Benson. The Southern Pacific went from Benson to Maricopa, and the Maricopa & Phoenix to the capital via Sacaton, Kyrene and Tempe.

11. Two months: *Prospector,* June 21, 1895. Greene: *Prospector,* "Mines and Mining," April 19, 1895.

12. *Prospector,* Nov. 19, 1895.

13. Cup: "Bisbee Dept.," Prospector, Jan. 20, 1896. General: "Work is Being Done...," *Prospector,* April 15, 1895.

14. "A Big Bond," *Prospector,* June 24, 1896.

15. Corriente: *Prospector,* Sept. 12, 1895. Larger: *Prospector,* Oct. 17, 1895. Overlock: *Prospector,* May 3, 1895. Burnett: *Prospector,* April 22, 1895.

16. *Prospector,* April 15, 1895.

17. "A Stock Country," *Prospector,* June 5, 1895. "William Lutley: The Laird...," *Bisbee Review,* Aug. 19, 1934.

18. *Prospector,* Nov. 6, 1895, reported La Morita's construction as almost finished. The Nov. 7, 1895 issue mentioned the large number of adobe bricks made there. The Nov. 12, 1895 issue said William King, "formerly the hustling Benson hotel man," and his wife were opening a hotel "at the new custom station on the line below Bisbee." In his book, *Billy King's Tombstone,* King

relates some tales of La Morita.

19. 20,000: *Prospector*, Oct. 28, 1895. Land: *Prospector*, Nov. 16, 19 and 20, 1895. Drive: *Prospector*, Nov. 29, 1895. This drive likely is one mentioned by Axford on p. 7 in *Around Western Campfires*.

20. "Cattle Fever Tick...," www.aphis.usda.gov; "Conquering Cattle Tick Fever," www.ars.usda.gov. Both accessed April 5, 2011.

21. Nomination: Prospector, Oct. 6, 1896. Opponent: *Prospector*, Oct. 9, 1896; 1896 Cochise County voting registration. Totals: Cochise County Board of Supervisors minutes, Nov. 16, 1896; *Bisbee Weekly Orb*, Oct. 23, 1898.

22. "The Hereford Range," *Prospector*, Dec. 12, 1896.

23. Bill Land: 1880 and 1900 U.S. Census; Eldridge-Estes-Timmons-Hall Family Tree on Ancestry.com, accessed April 6, 2011. Ed Land: 1894 Cochise County voting registration; Cochise County Roll of Attorneys; *Prospector*, Oct. 12, 1896. On the go: Prospector, May 2, 1896.

24. Roberts, Virginia Culin, "The Mosons And The Martins, Pioneer Ranchers of Arizona and Sonora." *Arizona Journal of History*, Autumn 2004, p. 28.

25. Greene's two windfalls apparently were unknown to Greene's biographer and even his descendants.

C.L. Sonnichsen in *Col. Greene and the Copper Skyrocket* calls Dane Coolidge a teller of tall tales and improvisations, but nonetheless repeats Coolidge's tale that Greene borrowed money from Packard to blast his copper skyrocket on its way.

Virginia C. Roberts in "The Mosons and Martins" (footnote 22) has a different take, but she too didn't give Greene any credit for being a Horatio Alger. Roberts said Greene got Cananea seed money from first wife Ella (Roberts) Moson Greene. Roberts quotes Ella's daughter, Virginia (Moson) Sneed, as personally giving her stepfather Ella's money with which he bought Cananea.

Roberts' citation, however, is a deposition Virginia gave when she was in her 80s during an extremely contentious, bitter and prolonged court battle over the estate of Greene's second wife, Mary. Virginia was trying to claim part of her stepmother's estate, and saying that her birth mother provided the basis for Greene's fortune was how she did that.

Sonnichsen stumbled across a reference to Greene's gold mine but dismissed it. For *Col. Greene and the Copper Skyrocket*, Sonnichsen interviewed Sam M. Barrow Jr., whose father put up bond money for Greene when he faced a murder charge (footnote 36). Barrow Jr. said Greene had "gold mining claims that started him to financial security." Sonnichsen found Cochise County mining claims in the name of Barrow Sr., but none in Greene's name, and apparently searched no further.

Sonnichsen wrote about the Greene Consolidated Gold Co. (p. 26 *Copper Skyrocket*) and that Greene worked the San Domingo property in 1893, but didn't associate this with Barrow's account.

26. Father's death: *Prospector*, Dec. 26, 1896. Miserable: McClintock, James H., *Arizona's Nineteenth Legislature*. Phoenix, Ariz.: 1897, p. 6.

27. Kelly, p. 178.

28. Republican, Feb. 20, 21 and March 11, 1895.

29. Dunbar tease: *Prospector*, Feb. 3, 1897. Bloopers: "Shades of the 19th," *Prospector*, April 10, 1897. Two other listed malapropisms, both made by Graham County Rep. J.K. Rogers, were: "I don't like to monopulate all the time" and "Our county will take care of its own indignant poor."

30. *Republican*, Feb. 24 and March 17, 1895.

31. CB-40: *Prospector*, Feb. 11, 1897. Whole and chair: Prospector, Feb. 11, 1897. Brand registration: *Prospector*, April 9, 1897.

32. Dedication: *Prospector*, Jan. 22, 1897. Layout: Peplow, Edward H. Jr., "Memories of the Old Adams," *Phoenix Magazine*, May 1975. Third house: "Hon. B.A. Packard Is Home ...," *International*, March 15, 1915.

33. "Colonel Packard Was Representative...," *Dispatch*, Aug. 24, 1932.

34. Wagoner, p. 336. Ives' Tammany roots are mentioned in Prospector, Feb. 3, 1896, and *Orb*, Dec. 22, 1900.

35. Wagoner, p. 345.

36. Sonnichsen, pp. 32-7.

37. "Cochise County," *Prospector*, May 10, 1895. This description confirmed by Cochise County Superior Court Civil Case No. 1308.

38. Tellman and Hadley, *Crossing Boundaries*, p. 41.

39. Washouts: Prospector, July 29 and Oct. 26, 1896. Both articles specifically mention Chinese farmers on Greene's property.

40. Roberts in "The Mosons and The Martins" has Virginia (Moson) Sneed implying she and the girls' governess inspected the site before the girls went to the river. But there's no mention of the pond's disappearance.

41. In "The Mosons and The Martins," Roberts quotes Virginia (Moson) Sneed: "We went right into Tombstone and found out where the powder was bought." If Greene found where the powder was purchased, surely he asked who bought it. But Virginia doesn't name anyone. Cap and fuse: *Tucson Citizen*, July 3, 1897.

42. Sonnichsen, pp. 29-30.

43. Ibid.

44. 1888, 1889, 1896, 1897, 1898, 1899, 1900 Cochise County Tax Assessments.

45. Cochise County Superior Court Civil Case No. 1969.

46. Cochise County Bill of Sale Book 2, pp. 204-5; Cochise County Superior Court Civil Case No. 1970.

47. "Court Matters," Prospector, Dec. 17, 1897.

48. Register of Actions and Fees Book 5, pp. 317-18.

49. Cochise County Superior Court Civil Case No. 1969.

50. "The Greene Case," *Prospector*, Dec. 20, 1897.

51. "Court Matters," Prospector, Dec. 18, 1897*Prospector.*

52. Sell 5,000: *Prospector*, March 27, 1898, *Prospector.* Scranton lease: Weekly Orb, July 3, 1898.

53. Kyrene trips: *Prospector*, April 10 and May 29, 1898. New York: *Prospector*, July 3 and Sept. 4, 1898. Newspaper promoted: *Epitaph*, June 12 and July 8, 1898. Warner: Wagoner, p. 524.

54. *Prospector*, Jan. 30, Feb. 3 and Aug. 25, 1897.

55. *Weekly Orb*, Feb. 12, 1899.

56. Name: *Weekly Orb*, Jan. 8, 1899. Brand: *Brands and Marks*, Book 1, Livestock Sanitary Board of Arizona, p. 244.

The first incorporated Turkey Track Cattle Co. had Greene and three New Yorkers as its incorporators on July 17, 1901. Headquartered in Manhattan, the corporation's stated purpose was livestock and real estate dealings. (Cochise County Incorporation Book 2, pp. 259-62.)

On Aug. 24, 1904, Greene, Packard and Gates incorporated the Turkey Track Cattle Co. in Cochise County. Headquartered in Naco, its stated aims were oil and mine exploration, real estate development and livestock. (Cochise County Incorporation Book 3, pp. 228-32.)

Greene incorporated Greene Cattle Co. with in-laws Frank B. Moson and Ben F. Sneed on April 20, 1901. GCC concentrated on livestock and real estate. (Cochise County Incorporation Book No. 1, pp. 604-7.)

57. *Weekly Orb*, Sept. 24, 1899.

58. *Weekly Orb*, Aug. 8, 1899; *Daily Orb*, Sept. 17, 26 and Oct. 3, 1899. Other attendees were Mexican Consul Max Gavito, railroad superintendent William A. Harvey, Greene, Sheriff White and Phelps Dodge superintendent Ben Williams.

59. Myrick, p. 194.

60. *Weekly Orb*, "Cattle Seized," May 7, 1899.

61. *Daily Orb*, "The San Rafael Grant Purchase," Jan. 24, 1900.

62. Convention: "Hon. B.A. Packard," *Cochise Review*, July 2, 1900. Carry: "Local Notes," Review, Aug. 27, 1900. Dispute: "Local Briefs," *Review*, Sept. 18, 1900.

63. *Review*, Oct. 10 and 11, 1900.

64. Among Packard's large transactions were 22 carloads with Vickers from Naco, *Orb*, May 30, 1900; 700 head from Naco, *Review*, Dec. 23, 1900; another 700 with Walter Vail at $31 per head, *Review*, Jan. 17, 1901; and 7,000 head from Douglas, Review, May 4, 1902.

65. "News of the Town" and "Personals," *Review*, July 4, 1902

66. Family: *Star*, "Pioneer Dies," Oct. 13, 1902. Mining: *Epitaph*, July 17 and 27, 1880 and Aug. 6, 1880. Ranch: *Epitaph*, Feb. 4, 1880.

67. "Happy Nuptials," *Star*, April 21, 1892; Pima County Marriages, Book 1, p. 214. Death: *Star*, "A.A. Holbrook Dead," June 18, 1895.

68. Interview with Dorothea Watkins, Phoenix, Ariz., May 10, 1996.

69. Hunt, Frazier, *Cap Mossman*. New York: Hastings House, 1951, pp. 260-1.

70. Review, Aug. 9, 13, 21 and 26, 1902. Shibley: 1898 Cochise County voting registration.

71. Dry years: "Arizona drought...," *Star*, June 3, 1996. Endorse: *Review*, Aug. 28, Oct. 22 and Nov. 6, 1892.

72. Talk: *Review*, Jan. 10, 1903. Legal work: Eugene S. Ives file, University of Arizona Special Collections Library, shows Ives handled several legal matters for Packard during 1901-03. Ives won: Wagoner, p. 526.

73. Wagoner, pp. 364-5.

74. Harry B. Rice letter to Dixie Packard, dated March 19, 1935. Letter in possession of Watkins.

75. Wagoner, pp. 403-411.

76. Assessed: "Senator Ives' Attack...," *Review*, March 20, 1905. Nothing publicly: "Packard Comes From Phoenix," *Review*, March 22, 1903.

77. Treasurer: "Exhibits at World's Fair," Review, April 19, 1903. Trips: *Review*, April 1 and Sept. 20, 1903. Booklet: "Arizona – It's [sic] True Condition, Resources, Wealth...," *Bisbee Daily Review* job department, 1904. Geronimo: Adams, Alexander B., *Geronimo – A Biography*. New York: G.P. Putnam Sons, 1971, p. 313.

78. "Cananea News," *Review*, June 8, 1902; *Phoenix Enterprise*, March 29, 1904.

79. Connors, Jo, *Who's Who in Arizona*, Vol. 1. Tucson, Ariz.: Arizona Daily Star job department, 1913, p. 754.

80. "Territorial Fair Association," *Review*, Nov. 3, 1904. "126 Years of Fair Fun!" www.azstatefair.com/about/ourstory.aspx, accessed May 30, 2011. "Colonel Packard Calls ...," *Dispatch*, Oct. 27, 1930.

81. "Forcibly Declares...," *Review*, May 28, 1905; "Raising The Sinews," *Review*, June 21, 1905.

82. "Sweet Marie...," *Review*, Oct. 5, 1905.

83. *Review*, Nov. 18 and Dec. 15, 1905.

84. *Review*, April 18, Dec. 26 and 28, 1905; Jan. 2, 4 and 6, 1906.

85. *Review*, Nov. 9, 15 and 20, 1907.

86. McClintock, *Arizona, Vol. II*, p. 358.

87. "Packard Is To Retire," International, April 5, 1910.

88. "Four Come Out For Delegate," *International*, Oct. 10, 1910. Two other reasons Packard didn't become a delegate were he was on an Oriental cruise when the Democratic caucus was held and he opposed a plank advocating recall of judges.

Cynthia F. Hayostek

Banker

"Banks, properly established and conducted, are highly useful to the business of the country, and will doubtless continue to exist in the States so long as they conform to their laws and are found to be safe and beneficial."
– Martin Van Buren, 1782-1862, eighth President of the United States

Greene was one of several men with Packard connections who amassed fortunes in southern Cochise County as the 19th century turned into the 20th. Another was John B. Angius, an emigrant from the Balkan Peninsula to Cochise County.

Angius grew up in the Austrian-Hungarian Empire. The same as many others, he emigrated to the New World, arriving in Virginia City, Nev., in 1874 at age 16. In 1881, he moved to Tombstone, where he opened a mercantile store. Through hard work, he accumulated property and moved to Bisbee in 1889.[1]

One of Angius' endeavors was a wood-cutting business. Early in 1895, his crew was cutting trees in the Mule Mountains east of Packard Station and putting the wood on the train to Bisbee. This activity renewed the acquaintance between Angius and Packard – who must have known each other in Tombstone – and it was a connection they maintained in Bisbee.[2]

In 1897, Angius built a two-story structure on Bisbee's Main Street, establishing a grocery store in the bottom floor and a hotel in the top. He painted his Angius Building "a darkly, deeply, beautiful red."[3]

The grocery store functioned as an informal bank, as did the Copper Queen Mercantile Store. That was because the stores had safes, and miners and ranchers found them convenient places to exchange vouchers or make deposits. Packard deposited $500 in the CQ safe in 1898.[4]

In 1900, CQ principals James S. Douglas, William H. Brophy, Ben Williams and Michael Cunningham gathered $50,000 ($9.7 million in 2013) to capitalize the Bank of Bisbee. Unable to find a suitable building, the CQ men approached Angius and so the Bank of Bisbee opened Feb. 19, 1900 in his store. The next year, Angius, Packard, Lemuel Shattuck, Brophy and Bisbee merchant Otto Geisenhoffer (who'd been involved with the Vizina in 1881 Tombstone), all signed bonds that helped solidify the bank's status. Packard and Angius became bank directors.[5]

In 1901, the bank directors engaged Eastern architects to design a building at 1 Main Street; by February 1902 construction was complete. In 1906, the highly regarded El Paso architect Henry C. Trost produced plans expanding the bank on its west side, a project finished in 1907.[6]

During this time, both Angius and Packard continued their normal business. For Angius that included election in 1902 to Bisbee's first city council. For Packard, it was continued ranch management and cattle brokering, which involved much train travel, especially to California. To facilitate this, he rented a house in Naco after he married Dixie in 1902.

Naco replaced Pearce as Cochise County's boomtown when both American and Mexican Customs announced they'd open offices there late in 1899.[7] Naco was lively, as the *Cochise Review* noted on July 20, 1900. "An impromptu dance was held here Wednesday evening. The affair was enjoyed by all. Naco is noted for its entertaining qualities and scarcely a week goes by without a social event or two."

Social events of a less genteel sort were what many other Naco residents wanted. Before completion of Greene's Cananea, Yaqui River & Pacific Railroad (CY&P) between Naco and Cananea, hundreds of teamsters drove spans of as many as 30 oxen or 20 equines hauling goods between the two towns. Saloons these teamsters frequented included the Comet, Fashion, Cow Yard, Palace, Rip Snorter, Warm Member and Jim Twister. There was also the resort of "Madame Rose Bonheur de Stewert ... doing an extensive and growing business in her popular quarters."[8]

Legitimate businesses patronized by Naco's estimated 1,200-1,500 residents in mid-1902 included J.H. Hughes' saddle and harness shop, O.K. Blacksmith Shop, several custom brokerages, B.J. O'Rielly's insurance agency, a grocery store, several hotels, a photography studio, at least three purveyors of Mexican curios and drawn work, and a Bank of Bisbee branch.[9]

Packard undoubtedly did business at the bank's Naco branch, since he'd expanded his holdings. During January 1900, he and Vickers, as the Packard Cattle Co., exercised their option to buy Ojo de Agua and San Rafael del Valle from the Camou family. This consisted of 112,000 acres in Sonora and about 18,000 acres in Arizona along the San Pedro.[10]

Packard relied upon his foreman, Henry Aston, to oversee his ranches. Packard also regularly saw Robert W. Barr, Turkey Track Cattle Co. foreman, until 1899 when Rufus M. "Babe" Thompson took over the job.[11]

Packard was the Turkey Track's treasurer and manager. Partner Egbert J. Gates, was usually busy in his native California. The same as his older brother Carroll Gates, E.J. worked in real estate and banking. Carroll and Walter Vail leased a large San Diego County ranch, and so Carroll became involved in Vail's Empire Ranch and then Vickers' CCC Ranch. These connections led to links between E.J., Packard and Greene as Turkey Track Cattle Co. incorporators.[12]

Packard was Turkey Track manager because Greene was developing Greene (later Cananea) Consolidated Copper Co., which became the showpiece of his tremendous and diversified fortune. Greene also married again. His bride, Mary Proctor, was 25 years younger than he and became the mother of four children.

In addition to ranching, Packard needed formal banking services as executor of two estates. The first was that of Daniel D. Ross, who died Feb. 25, 1898 in Bisbee. Ross had been, since about 1879, proprietor of a sawmill on the Chiricahuas' west side. The main portion of his estate, however, was a Swisshelm Mountain ranch, which ranchers Peter Johnson and Conlon helped appraise. It took Packard some litigation with an insurance company and over two years to fully settle Ross' estate.[13]

The second estate Packard settled was that of his friend Sweet. In addition to their deep involvement in Democratic politics, the two men were active Masons. Both attended the Episcopalian Church. Packard began doing so because of Dixie, but then became more involved in the church because of Sweet.

A native of Rhode Island Sweet had arrived in 1890 Bisbee to be CQ assistant surgeon. He became chief surgeon the next year, and in 1900 gained the appreciation of all Bisbee residents for his efforts toward reducing typhoid deaths.[14]

During that time, Episcopalians usually met at members' houses, including Sweet's. He set about changing this with a fund-raising campaign. Bisbee's Episcopalians purchased building lots for St. John's Church on Sowle Avenue for $1,500. Sweet, as churchwarden, kept collecting money and the churchwomen, including his wife, Julia, did too. They raised $1,290, while Sweet handed $2,457.47 to Bishop J. Mills Kendrick.[15]

On April 15, 1903 Sweet died of a stroke at age 42. After a widely attended funeral, Copper Queen officials (almost certainly Ben and Lewis Williams) gave $1,898 to the building fund with the understanding that the church would be named St. John's Sweet Memorial Church. Once built, members dedicated a large stained glass window in the church's northeast corner to Sweet's memory, and Phelps Dodge owner Cleveland Dodge gave an 800-pound bell to the church.[16]

To Packard fell the work of settling Sweet's estate for the benefit of his widow and two children. She had been pregnant when Sweet died.

Dr. E.W. Baum (who succeeded Sweet as head CQ physician), Cunningham and Brophy appraised the estate, which included interests in two mines, considerable stock, and a house and lot on Bisbee's Main Street. The latter Packard sold to Maggie Letson, and the rest to other parties so Sweet's widow and children were amply provided for.[17]

Portrait of B.A. Packard, ca. 1905.
Packard family photo

Sweet's death was one of three events that must have discouraged Packard in 1903. A dry spell and importation restrictions caused by tick outbreaks limited Packard's cattle business, and then there was Ives' political venom. For much of January 1904, Packard lay ill in Phoenix in the Adams Hotel and then Casa Loma Hotel. He tried to disengage from his leadership role in Cochise County's Democratic Party,[18] but the *Bisbee Review* refused to let this happen.

In a May 24, 1904 editorial, the *Review* said, "The services of a gentleman like Mr. Packard can not be measured by words. His influence in the county was probably more than that of any other man. He could have a hearing where others could not, and he could obtain that for which he called without a moment's hesitation. His influence in the Territory of Arizona has been and is today felt where it has ever been potent in public affairs."

This steadfastness must have buoyed Packard because he remained a leader in Cochise County's Democratic Party, taking on the chairmanship after Sweet's death. Another thing that raised his spirits was Gertrude's marriage in April 1904 to Max Boardman Cottrell.

He was the first son of Albert Boardman and Isabel (Coon) Cottrell, having been born June 10, 1883. He grew up in Wirt, N.Y., between Portville and Alfred. The Cottrells, the same as the Packards, had New England and Seventh Day Baptist roots. Max's father graduated from Alfred University and was a school teacher and superintendent before involvement in local and state politics.

This similar familial background, plus Max and Trude's education at Alfred University, made for a happy couple. They settled in New York and quickly made Packard a grandfather. First born was Burdette Packard Cottrell in 1905, and then in 1906, Gertrude Louise Cottrell, whom everyone called Louise to avoid confusing her with her mother. Max and Trude's household included Dorothea, who lived with them after the death of the sisters' grandmother a month after Gertrude's marriage.

By then, Ashley was attending Stanford University. He played varsity football, sang in the glee club and was a Delta Kappa Epsilon member.[19]

In Arizona, Packard maintained his connections to those such as Charlie Overlock, who'd established his butcher business in Tombstone during the 1890s drought. His brother, Lemuel, had a meat store in Bisbee at the turn of the century.

One autumn day in 1900, Charlie rode from Bisbee to Slaughter's ranch to buy cattle. He talked with Slaughter's foreman, who mentioned unusual activity he'd seen in the

Sulphur Springs Valley. Riding back to Bisbee, Charlie looked for signs of that activity.

He did this because the railroad everyone thought Phelps Dodge (PD) was going to build to Nacozari had not started from Naco. Charlie found survey stakes pounded into the Sulphur Springs Valley about 25 miles east of Bisbee and realized that's where the A&SE Railroad was headed.

Back in Bisbee, Charlie gathered Lemuel, Bisbee tailor Alfred Paul and two other friends, and they formed a company. Charlie hurried to the federal land office in Tucson to file on an area adjoining the staked land. When he discovered PD hadn't filed on the staked land, he promptly did so in the name of his company. Then he erected a frame building on the claim, which became the office of his first Douglas enterprise – a lumber yard.[20]

This audacity forced PD's directors to file on another parcel and include Overlock and his partners in the International Land & Improvement Co., which platted a town with wide streets and large blocks of business and residential lots. A subsidiary, the Douglas Traction & Light Co., provided electricity, water, an ice plant, telephones and a streetcar system in the town named for PD official Dr. James Douglas.

As Phelps Dodge built its Copper Queen smelter, another Bisbee copper firm erected its own smelter. The smelter of Calumet & Arizona Mining Co. (C&A) was smaller than PD's, but it started operations first, during March 1903. The A&SE Railroad built tracks to Douglas and evolved into the El Paso & Southwestern Railroad (EP&SW) to continue track laying into New Mexico toward Texas.[21]

For Packard, the EP&SW provided an easy way to ship cattle for the Hohstadt brothers, Teachout and other Nacozari-area ranchers. Stock pens and a cattle dip on Douglas' western edge became one of the new town's first features and they quickly assumed economic importance. During just the first two

Cattle at the San Pedro River at the Hereford bridge. Bradshaw Collection. *Courtesy of the Bisbee Mining and Historical Museum.*

weeks of the 1905 cattle shipping season, 150 carloads went from Douglas to points east and 44 carloads to California.[22]

As Charlie Overlock laid the foundation for his future affluence, his brother Lemuel became a Bisbee stockbroker after selling his meat store in 1900 to Edward A. Tovrea. Formerly a northern Arizona butcher, Tovrea began his rise to fortune and fame by selling beef that he and partner, then-Arizona Rangers Capt. Mossman, bought from Packard and sold in Cananea and Cochise County.

Tovrea soon had four meat markets, including one in Douglas. He built feeding pens at Osborn Station, where he was among the first Arizonans to fatten cattle on cottonseed.[23]

Charlie Overlock began selling lumber so Douglas residents could build homes and businesses. Then he sold fire insurance in case the wooden buildings burned down. Along the way, he became Douglas' first postmaster and first mayor.[24]

Another businessman who thrived in Bisbee-Naco and then jumped to Douglas was Benjamin F. Graham. He first appeared on the Bisbee scene in 1898 when he opened a general store. Soon, he had a livery stable, was selling furniture and became a county road overseer. In 1902, he sold his undertaking business and opened a brokerage house.[25]

This led to his involvement with El Tigre Mine, a gold and silver bonanza discovered in 1902 about 45 miles south of Douglas. Graham went to Lemuel Shattuck, head of the then-new Miners and Merchants Bank in Bisbee, and obtained funding to start up the Lucky Tiger-Combination Gold Mining Co. Soon, Graham headquartered the company in Douglas, and built for himself a large house fitted with "most substantial and modern plumbing" at 1047 10th St.[26]

Graham's Lucky Tiger investors included some Arizonans as well as men from Kansas City. In 1905, the Missourians staged a hostile takeover. Graham responded by forming another company and hiring Douglas attorney and Mexican mining law expert David A. Richardson to represent it. Then Graham bought some firearms, hired 10 men and sent them to El Tigre where they took over the mine in the name of his new company.[27]

The success of this expedition was short-lived, and subsequent court action lengthy. The court proceedings exposed Graham's unscrupulous methods, and the Missourians regained control. A judge awarded them $275,000 in damages, and Graham fled to British Columbia to avoid paying. He sold his Douglas house to James G. Cowen, International Land & Improvement Co. executive.[28]

While this was going on, Packard spent considerable time in central Arizona. First, he sold the San Rafael grant, including the Half Moon, to Greene in 1902. The Half Moon house burned down in 1906, but Greene spent $25,000 rebuilding it the next year so it resembled his Cananea house.[29]

Connections: The Life and Times of B. A. Packard

William Greene built this house in 1907 to resemble his Cananea home. This house replaced the one that had been Packard's Half Moon ranch house, which burned down in 1906. Greene acquired the house and the San Rafael land grant from Packard in 1902.

Bisbee Mining & Historical Museum

In 1904, Packard bought the James Sturgeon farm in Kyrene, a water right-of-way and shares in four Tempe-based irrigation companies. In 1905, Packard paid $30,000 ($4.5 million in 2013) for the J.W. Woolf farm and its water rights. Together, the two farms totaled 320 acres.[30]

They were near the Taylor place, which Packard acquired in 1895. The abundance of water produced so much alfalfa that, even after feeding his cattle, Packard yearly filled 500 railroad cars with hay that he sold. He even contemplated living permanently in Kyrene, where his famous trotting stallion Direct View stood at stud.[31]

This didn't happen, however, because business kept drawing Packard back to Cochise County's borderlands. He kept crossing thousands of cattle at Naco and Douglas and brokering them for clients. He attended meetings of the Bank of Bisbee and International Improvement Co. as a board of directors member.[32]

It probably was during one of these trips that Packard became peripherally involved in another of the famous incidents in

Greene's life – the 1906 strike of the Cananea Copper Co. Its 5,300 Mexican workers struck because they wanted the same wages as the 2,200 American workers. Greene and others thought the strikers were after higher wages rather than eliminating a pay scale based upon ethnicity.

On June 1, 1906, some strikers approached the company lumberyard to talk with workers there. The lumberyard manager was William Metcalf, whose brother George had grown strawberries in the Huachucas 20 years before and now was manager of Cananea Copper housing. The brothers confronted the strikers, George armed with a fire hose, which he quickly turned on. Then a shot was fired, from where no one knew, and in the resulting melee, the Metcalfs and three strikers were killed, and the lumberyard burned down.[33]

This so alarmed Walter Douglas, CQ general manager in Bisbee, that he contacted Thomas H. Rynning, then Arizona Rangers captain. Perhaps inspired by Graham's filibustering, Douglas suggested Rynning gather some men, arm them and head for Cananea. This Rynning did but not before he asked Packard to run interference for him.

Gov. Kibbey repeatedly sent Rynning telegrams, which Rynning didn't read because he knew Kibbey was telling him to stay out of Mexico. So Rynning asked Packard to hold the telegrams for him while he went to Cananea, where his force protected Greene's property until Kosterlitzky arrived with his *rurales* to put down the strike.

Rynning said Packard thus became Kibbey's scapegoat in the ensuing controversy,[34] which would account for the animosity Kibbey displayed three years later when he called for Packard's resignation from the territorial fair commission. For his part, Packard maintained his friendship with Greene and two of Greene's connections.

The first was Epes Randolph, the Southern Pacific Railroad's Tucson division manager who was also involved in the CY&P and Southern Pacific affiliates sometimes referred to as "the Randolph lines."

One of those was the Arizona & Colorado Railroad (A&C), whose tracks stretched southward from Cochise (near Willcox) toward Pearce and Gleeson. Another was the Mexico & Colorado Railroad (M&C), which serviced Courtland, a mining community near Gleeson. The A&C and M&C junctioned at Kelton, named for Packard's old San Pedro neighbor, C.B. Kelton.[35]

The second Greene connection was Mitchell. His technical expertise and relationship with Greene shaped the core of Cananea Copper just as Mitchell Economic Hot-blast Furnaces formed the heart of the company smelter. The Cananea Copper triumph made Mitchell a richer man, and in 1902 he established banks in Cananea and Douglas and invested in a copper mine in the Mexican state of Guerrero.[36]

Mitchell received the Douglas City Bank's charter on June 16, 1902. That was just three days before Brophy, Cunningham and James S. Douglas opened the doors of their bank. They hired Charles O. Ellis to be the cashier (manager) of the Bank of Douglas, situated in the town's business center on the northeast corner of 10th Street and G Avenue.[37]

Mitchell's Douglas City Bank opened in 933 G Ave., two weeks after the Bank of Douglas. Douglas City's capital stock was $50,000 ($1.4 million in 2013), and Lewis C. Hanks was the cashier. He'd been assistant cashier in Mitchell's Banco de Cananea.

On Feb. 17, 1903, Douglas City Bank became First National Bank of Douglas upon receiving a charter from the national banking system.[38] This meant First National operated under federal rules, underwent federal inspections and could implement interest rates different from state banks and even issue currency.

This bolstered Douglas residents' confidence in First National and, according to the April 7, 1904 *Douglas International*, they deposited $75,000 in the bank the previous year. This probably played a role in Mitchell's decision to move the bank into a new building.

That building took shape early in 1906 on the southwest corner of 10th Street and G Avenue. Those lots had held Douglas' first two-story building, the Ord Hotel, which Mitchell had bought in 1902. The Ord was torn down to make way for First National.

El Paso architect Trost submitted plans to Mitchell showing a multi-story building made of stone and cement. The bank's interior featured massive pillars that emphasized an impressively lofty interior and mezzanine. The top floor consisted of offices rented to professionals, including attorney Richardson.[39]

Perhaps because Mitchell wanted also a state-regulated institution, he established Arizona Trust & Banking Co., whose office was in the First National building. By March 1907, Arizona Trust was the territory's 22nd-largest financial institution; Shattuck's Miners & Merchants Bank was No. 1 and the Bank of Douglas ranked sixth.[40]

Then came the Panic of 1907, a financial crisis similar to that of 1893. A 10 percent drop in stock prices during March 1907 warned something was amiss with the national economy. This probably was a topic of conversation when Packard, Greene and Randolph traveled together in early April to Guaymas to inspect the railroad Randolph was building to that Sonoran seaport.[41]

Perhaps traveling with Packard was Louis R. Krueger, his private secretary. In 1905, Krueger had been an Arizona Representative, which is probably how he caught Packard's attention, who undoubtedly needed assistance managing his increasingly complex national and international businesses. Krueger concentrated on the Packard Cattle Co. farms in Kyrene.[42]

Packard got additional help beginning in March 1907 when Max, Gertrude and their children moved to Naco. Max managed his father-in-law's interests in Mexico, and quickly received "a B.A. lesson" in how to turn economic hard times into personal advantage.[43]

The 1907 Panic started in October when a scheme to corner the stock of a mid-level Montana copper company failed. This revealed a network of interlocking directorates among New York banks, brokerage houses and trust companies that raised the anxiety of bank customers so much that they descended en masse upon their depositories demanding their money.

In those days, placing money in a savings account involved risk. If a bank closed because of bad investments, depositors who didn't withdraw their money quickly lost it. Closure news spread fast, causing panics with people leaving homes and workplaces to swarm banks and get their money out before the bank shut.

This behavior caused failure of New York's third-largest trust company and triggered runs on banks across the nation. Then financier J.P. Morgan stepped in with timely and selective assistance. The panic subsided but not before related damage occurred, including a copper price drop that temporarily closed the Cananea and Douglas smelters.

In Cananea, this was preceded by a hostile stock take-over of Cananea Copper contrived by Thomas F. Cole, of C&A, and John D. Ryan, of Anaconda Corp., another copper-producing giant. After February 1907, Greene no longer controlled Cananea's mining operations, but he remained a force to be reckoned with because of his diverse borderland holdings.

In Douglas, the smelters reopened in 1908 and Mitchell provided repeated assurances that everything was fine with his banks. Perhaps depositors worried the banks were over-extended, and perhaps they were right for rumors continued that there'd be ownership changes.[44]

On April 11, 1908, the *Douglas International* reported "a story which has not been confirmed" that "Hon. B.A. Packard of Naco, T.A. [sic] Pollack, the prominent banker and sheep man of Flagstaff, Ariz., and Colonel Epes Randolph of Tucson have purchased the stock of the First National Bank formerly owned by George Mitchell and amounting to a controlling interest. It is further stated that Mr. Packard will move to Douglas and make his home in this city."

Although the *International* reporter couldn't confirm the story, he had it exactly right. The four men had met in Douglas to consummate a deal that took effect May 1 in which Packard and Pollack held 75 percent of First National's capital stock, which they increased to $400,000 ($10.5 million in 2013). The deal included ownership of Arizona Trust and Moctezuma Banking Co. in central Sonora. The latter included a mercantile and hotel in a building facing Moctezuma's plaza.[45]

Holding the remaining 25 percent was Randolph, who became a First National director. Much of the excitement surrounding Randolph was speculation he'd build a railroad into Douglas. This didn't happen immediately, but his presence reassured Douglas residents that First National was a solid institution.[46]

Packard reinforced that by taking part in community activities (joining the Chamber of Commerce) and Democratic politics (leading the territory's delegation to the national convention in 1908), while establishing Douglas residency. At

The same as many Douglas residences in the town's early days, the Packard property included a stables. That's where Dixie and Dorothea's horses came from in this circa 1910 photo.

Packard family photo

first, B.A. and Dixie lived in a rental, but early in 1909 they bought the Cowen house on 10th Street.[47]

This connection to Cowen drew Packard's attention to Courtland, a mining camp that sprang up in the southeastern Dragoon Mountains in 1909. After Cowen sold his house to Packard, he managed Courtland's water and ice plant. Packard bought some lots in the boomtown. Richardson and his law partner, Frank W. Doan, represented several Courtland town site companies.[48]

Courtland grew rapidly, aided by the arrival of Randolph's M&C Railroad that eventually reached Douglas, making it the only Arizona town with railroads leaving in the four directions. (The others were El Paso & Southwestern to the east and west, and the Nacozari Railroad to the south.)[49]

Packard knew all about Dragoon mineralization, having invested in the Silver Cloud and other prospects in the 1880s. Courtland, although pushed as a copper claim, proved just as ephemeral as the 1880s silver mines. It was on its way to ghost town status by 1913. Nearby Gleeson, a mining camp owned by another company, hung on a few years longer.

In Douglas, B.A. and Dixie were joined in their house by Dorothea, after she finished at Miramonte School for Girls in Los Angeles. Ashley too in 1909 left California for Douglas upon graduating from Stanford. He started working in First National and had a place of his own. Like his father, Ashley took steps to integrate himself into Douglas life.[50]

One measure was election into the Thirteen Club, a group of 13 prominent bachelors who spoofed superstition while leading Douglas' social life. Club founders Charles and Frederick Nichols invented detailed rites (initiation included kissing a skull), led the town's first baseball team, and put on elaborate dances in which the decorations included skulls and crossbones, miniature coffins and 13 open umbrellas.[51]

Less lighthearted were changes that the purchase of First National brought to Packard's life. On Sept. 7, 1909, he

Cynthia F. Hayostek

How well-watered Packard's farm in the Kyrene area was is apparent by the tall trees alongside the house and the lush alfalfa in the pasture. The large barn stored cut hay and the animals that ate it, while the small building between the barn and house was where Burt Cottrell had his radio lab.
Packard Family photo

incorporated Packard Investment Co. (PIC). Its stated aims included operating banks and trust institutions, handling mortgages and bonds in the United States and Mexico, and operating cattle ranges and related agricultural matters. Capitalization was $1 million and shareholders were B.A., Dixie, Ashley and Max.[52]

Packard used PIC as a holding company to, among other things, arrange his Kyrene properties. He sold 320 acres to the Turkey Track Co., which sold the property to PIC, which sold it to Alfred J. Peters and George Taylor.[53]

In 1910, Max, Trude and children moved to "the Taylor place" and lived there until construction of their home on PIC's other 320 Kyrene acres was complete. This house, with a string of trees on one side and a wide veranda on the other, faced some outbuildings and a large barn.

The barn, where Packard kept mules bought in Missouri and a dozen black Percherons, cost $5,000 to build. Packard maintained race horses, including the fast filly, Betsie Howe, at the fairgrounds, where Allie Fort trained them.[54]

The Taylor place sale was part of the Turkey Track disbandment. Apparently, Gates previously sold out, for the Sept. 7, 1909 *International* didn't mention him. The article does mention that Packard's Turkey Track share amounted to $300,000 ($7.9 million in 2013), and Packard got some Turkey Track land in Kyrene as well as in Mexico.

The legalities accompanying this divesture plus a business trip to Kansas City prevented Packard from attending festivities held in Douglas Sept. 21, 1909, which included a Chautauqua at which Bryan was the featured speaker. Event organizers, knowing of Packard's connections to Bryan, scheduled breakfast for the by-then three-time Democratic Presidential candidate in the Packard house. But only Dixie, Ashley and Dorothea greeted Bryan.[55]

Packard's nonattendance did not garner much attention until a month later when Kibbey stirred up the partisan rumpus over Packard's Territorial Fair leadership. Then a Republican-oriented newspaper in Bisbee printed a snide article about Packard's absence, which was followed by a January 1910 attempt to besmirch Packard.[56]

The man holding "the handle of the muckrake" was W.K. Meade, the former U.S. Marshall who'd organized the rescue of Gov. Zulick 25 years before. Meade, a Republican, told a grand jury that Packard mishandled the Ross estate in 1898. Since Meade was a recognized "grouch" and never "perfectly satisfied with but one official record in Arizona ... and that was his," the grand jury examined the probate records and then totally disregarded Meade's ham-handed effort to stir up trouble.[57]

A portion of this response was attributable to B.A. and Dixie's good reputation stemming from incidents such as a house fire they fought. One day in 1910, the Packards were on their way home when they noticed the house of Harry Rice, who'd moved to Douglas not long before, was on fire. B.A. got a yard hose and started fighting the flames, while Dixie evacuated the Rices.[58]

At the time, Packard focused his business efforts on First National. Because the 1907 Panic was caused partially by customer doubts of bank sustainability, Packard emphasized First National's reliability. Reports of directors' meetings appeared in Douglas newspapers, and ads such as one promoting safety deposit boxes ("your valuable papers are absolutely safe") stressed trustworthiness.[59]

Promoting First National's reliability wasn't an easy task because national unease about undependable banks was intensified in Cochise County by what happened in Bisbee. About the time Packard purchased Mitchell's banks, First National Bank of Bisbee closed its doors, and soon its president was on trial for making false entries in bank books.[60]

The same sort of scandal touched First National of Douglas but caused no harm to Packard. That's because early in 1909, Packard sold Arizona Trust to Fletcher M. Doan, an Arizona Supreme Court judge. His son, Frank, was the attorney partnered with Richardson in First National's second-floor offices.[61]

Judge Doan moved Arizona Trust to 1029 G Ave. and hired James A. Howell as temporary cashier. Howell, brother of Slaughter's second wife, Viola, had served in the 1903 Arizona House and worked in two Cochise County banks before becoming Turkey Track foreman about 1908 when he replaced "Babe" Thompson.[62]

Howell served only six months because Judge Doan brought his son, John, from Yuma to be cashier. Hanks and bookkeeper Earl Davis, who'd arrived with Hanks, were let go. Hanks found a job in Globe and Davis with Douglas' International Laundry, which was owned by the Nichols brothers and Pollack.

Packard and Judge Doan knew they'd made the right decision because late in 1909, federal examiners discovered false entries and misapplied funds in First National's accounting done by Hanks and Davis during the 1907 Panic. Hanks claimed, "that while he may have been irregular in handling certain features of the bank business during the panic, that

Connections: The Life and Times of B. A. Packard

The Douglas City Bank, top left photo, opened in 1902 at 933 G Ave. in Douglas. Sharing the storefront (on the right-hand side) was E.A. Von Arnim, real estate, insurance and investments broker. The bottom photo shows the First National Bank of Douglas in 1910 when a men's clothing store, Scott & Co. (under awning), occupied part of the bank building. Second-story windows carry signs for Dr. L.B. Cary, a dentist, and attorneys D.A. Richardson and F.W. Doan. Entrance to the upstairs offices was the doorway by the horse and buggy. In 1916, a remodeling (upper right photo) of the interior eliminated First National's corner entrance. Attorneys Samuel W. White and Richardson occupied second-floor offices then.

Douglas Historical Society

was made necessary to keep the doors open and protect the patrons of the bank as well as its owners."[63]

Davis didn't try to impress anyone with this rationale. On April 19, 1910, he pled guilty to 36 counts of making false entries in a federal bank's books, and was sentenced to five years in territorial prison. He began his term in Yuma, then was moved to Florence after a few months when the new prison opened there.[64]

Hanks' case wasn't heard until late November 1910. Then it took a jury only 10 minutes to find him guilty of misapplying federal bank funds, and sentence him to five years in Florence. Hanks wept as he entered prison, in part because he knew he'd never see his seriously ill wife again; she died less than a week later.[65]

Packard replaced Hanks with Elbridge W. Graves, an experienced banker even before he arrived in 1889 to work in Consolidated National Bank of Tucson. There he met Petra Etchells, oldest child of prominent Tucson blacksmith Charles T. Etchells and his wife, Soledad, and married her in 1892.[66]

Tragically, Petra died Aug. 11, 1894, just hours after the birth of a daughter named for her. Young Petra's harrowing entry into the world caused her mental retardation. Elbridge's parents helped care for their granddaughter until 1902 when Elbridge married Sarah "Sadie" Etchells, his first wife's sister.[67]

Elbridge W. Graves

Author's collection

Connections: The Life and Times of B. A. Packard

Early in 1910, Sadie and Petra moved to Douglas, where Elbridge had been working since Dec. 1, 1909 as cashier at First National. He quickly developed a deep loyalty to and friendship with Packard as Packard's right-hand man, first as cashier and then as First National's elected vice-president in 1921.[68]

The Graves family lived in 1125 10th St., the block east of Packard's home. Across the street was Wright W. Lawhon and his wife, Cecelia, in 1160 10th St. Packard hired Lawhon, member of a Texas ranching family, as assistant cashier in April 1909. With employees as neighbors, Packard could travel for pleasure (including a 1910 cruise to Japan) and look after his cattle business while leaving day-to-day running of the bank to Graves and his underlings.[69]

Bank business included a full range of services -- savings accounts, safety deposit boxes, checking accounts and loans. The latter sometimes resulted in court cases but most were simple transactions.

An example of a court case was an action First National filed in 1908 against D.R. Archuleta, manager of Hacienda Mababi, a 400,000-acre ranch between Cananea and Fronteras, about 45 miles southwest of Douglas. With Richardson and Doan as its attorneys, the bank obtained a garnishment on Archuleta's loan. Soon after, Mababi changed hands.[70]

B.A. Packard posed casually during a cruise.

Packard family photo

Other First National loans had more successful outcomes. Even a partial list from a seven-month period in 1913 shows how First National helped develop Cochise County's economy by assisting small businessmen and ranchers. The loan list included:

– Will D. Glenn, $4,000 to buy 200 native stock cattle that ranged in Buck Creek Canyon, on the Pedregosa Mountains' east side. The Glenn family still ranches in the Pedregosas.

– Earl McKinney, $3,147.55 to purchase 22 dairy cattle, 75 stock cattle, 15 horses and dairy fixtures. McKinney then established one of the Douglas area's long-running dairies.

– Davis McDonald, $600 to buy 600 stock cattle ranging in Cottonwood Canyon of the Peloncillo Mountains. McDonalds still ranch today in the Peloncillos.

– Juan Rocha, $100 to buy 80 head of cattle and 30 mules and horses for his ranch, five miles north of the EP&SW's Bernardino Station in the San Bernardino Valley.

– H.H. Carlisle and J.S. Booger, $300 to establish a barber shop at 1120 G Ave. in Douglas.[71]

Graves was just one of Packard's shrewd employee choices. Another was Bessie McInernay, who started as First National's stenographer and notary public, then received promotion to collections. In 1918, she was one of eight women on First National's staff, along with six men.[72]

One of those six was C. Ygnacio Soto, a Bavispe, Son., native. He attended school in Moctezuma, where employment in the town's bank seemed a natural career choice for a young man with an aptitude for accounting.[73]

Soto caught Packard's attention during his visits to the Moctezuma Bank. The company apparently lost money because in July 1910, Packard went to Moctezuma and shut down the bank. Soto moved to Douglas then to became paying teller in First National.[74]

Connections: The Life and Times of B. A. Packard

In 1906, Packard had said, "Mexico will suffer from a general uprising."₇₄ Four months after he closed Moctezuma Bank, Packard's prediction came true. The Mexican Revolution began in November 1910. It ravaged Mexico for 10 years, and Packard, Graves and Soto played a vital role in its final outcome.

NOTES

1. Hart, Mary Nicklanovich, "Merchant and Miner, Two Serbs in Early Bisbee." *Arizona Journal of History*, Autumn 1988, pp. 314-5.

2. Wood: "Bisbee Items," *Prospector*, Jan. 28 and Feb. 15, 1895.

The Feb. 22, 1902 *Review* told of Packard, Angius, Sweet, two CQ executives and some wives boarded buggies for a day trip from Tucson to San Xavier Mission. The horses ran away and Angius was injured.

3. Hart, p. 319; *Bisbee Orb*, March 15, 1900.

4. Cochise County Superior Court Civil Case No. 2137. The dispute over Packard's $500 deposit transferred to Pima County courts, and apparently was resolved without ill will since Packard and CQ principals maintained cordial business relations.

5. Schwikart, Larry, *A History of Banking in Arizona*. Tucson, Ariz.: University of Arizona Press, 1982, pp. 30-1. Packard bank director: *Review*, March 4, 1908. Geisenhoffer: "Vizina Lease," *Nugget*, Dec. 13, 1881.

6. "Slowly, but sure, banks began...," *Review*, Aug. 30, 1987.

7. "Removed to Naco," Orb, Nov. 20, 1899.

8. "Naco Enterprises," *Review*, Feb. 18, 1900.

9. "Our Naco Advertisers," Review, Aug. 9, 1902. Population: Review, July 3, 1902.

10. Cochise County Deed Book 2, p. 487; "The San Rafael Grant Purchase," Orb, Jan. 24, 1900.

11. Thompson: 1896-1908 Cochise County voting registration; letterhead stationery in possession of Watkins.

The July 8, 1898 *Prospector* identifies Barr as foreman of the Turkey Track Cattle Co. That Barr held the position six months after Greene's murder trial makes Barr a prime contender for the "inside man" during Greene's trial.

There's long been speculation that Greene received deferential treatment during the murder proceedings or that bribery was part of the trial. Sonnichsen in *Colonel Greene and the Copper Skyrocket* mentions Sheriff White and District Attorney Allen English as part of the easy handling Greene received before the trial but dismisses bribery because, Sonnichsen believed, Greene had no money.

Greene sold his Sonoran gold mine before the trial, but apparently the proceeds were tied up in bank transfers and weren't available to influence the trial. If there was any collusion, it may have involved Barr for he was a member of the jury (*Prospector,* Dec. 16, 1897). When he became Turkey Track foreman is unknown.

Barr was also a Cochise County Supervisor until he moved away for unknown reasons. The Dec. 29, 1899 *Orb* told of Hugh Conlon filling out Barr's supervisor term.

12. Bailey, *Silk Hats,* p. 178; 1880 and 1910 Census.

The Jan. 5, 1910 *International* noted the Vail family and Carroll Gates had divided their property following Walter Vail's death. His estate included the Empire, other ranches and much Los Angeles real estate. In 1928, the Vails sold the Empire to the CCC, whose partners had acquired it from Theo White. Assisting in all those deals was Vickers.

13. Sawmill: Wilson, John P., *Islands in the Desert.* Albuquerque, N.M.: University of New Mexico Press, 1995, p. 211. Cochise County Superior Court Probate No. 232. The litigation is mentioned in Nov. 29, 1899 *Orb.*

14. *Review,* Aug. 14, 1900.

15. Service in Sweet house: *Review,* Jan. 19, 1900. Fund raising: "Historical Sketch, St. John's Church, Bisbee, Arizona," no date or author, church office files.

16. "Dr. Frederick Arnold Sweet," *Arizona Republic,* April 16, 1903; "Eulogy," *Review,* April 16, 1903; notes collected by Virginia F. Hodge for "On the Occasion of the 90th Anniversary Calendar." Notes emailed by Hodge to author Aug. 18 and Sept. 9, 2000.

17. Cochise County Superior Court Probate No. 562.

18. Ticks: *Review,* Jan. 30, 1903. Dry conditions: *Review,* April 3, 5 and May 7, 1904. Ill: *Review,* Jan. 5, 13 and 15, 1904. Disengage: "Democratic Central Committee...," Review, May 22, 1904.

An April 27, 1904 *Review* article headlined, "Assailing Packard," said supporters of William Randolph Hearst had accused Packard "of trying to manipulate the politics of Cochise County and strangle the Hearst sentiment" at a party convention in Tucson. The "Hearst contingent" then blocked Packard's election as Cochise County chairman, said the May 15, 1905 *Dispatch.* A week later, Packard tried to leave the party, saying "recent party events in this county had rendered his service in the future as useless... ."

19. Ashley Packard and Dorothea Watkins; "Naco Had Enthusiastic Meeting," *Review,* May 5, 1904; "A.B. Packard," *Shattuck Spectator,* no date.

20. Tailor: Review, July 10, 1900. "The Beginning of Douglas," *International,* Nov. 20, 1920.

21. Jeffrey, Robert S., The History of Douglas, Arizona. Master's thesis, University of Arizona, 1951.

Connections: The Life and Times of B. A. Packard

22. "Cattle Shipping Season Opens," Review, April 13, 1905.

23. Overlock: *Review*, March 2, 1901. Four: Review, Aug. 7, 1903. Buy from Packard: *Review*, Jan. 26, 1902 and Dec. 10, 1904. Douglas market: *Review*, Feb. 19, 1905. Pens: *Review*, Jan. 28 and Feb. 7, 1904. Cottonseed: *Review*, Dec. 10, 1904.

24. "Charles A. Overlock...," *Dispatch*, Feb. 19, 1926.

25. General store: *Orb*, May 22, 1898. Livery stable: *Orb*, Aug. 12, 1899. Furniture: *Orb*, Oct. 23, 1899. Overseer: Review, Feb. 9, 1900 and March 17, 1902.

26. Fathauer, Isabel Shattuck, *Lemuel C. Shattuck*. Tucson, Ariz.: Westernlore Press, 1991, pp. 74-5. House: March 11, 1905, *Review*.

27. Fathauer, pp. 80-5.

Leader of the 10 men was John Brooks, who'd been the Arizona Rangers' lieutenant until Capt. Tom Rynning learned of the expedition and, fearing legal repercussions, forced Brooks to resign. Shortly after the filibuster, Brooks began working for Greene in Chihuahua. Brooks' father, Ross, who probably was one of the 10 men, is a great grandfather of Sandra Day O'Connor. (*Borderland Chronicles* No. 4.)

28. Court: Fathauer, pp. 87-9. Sold house: "Graham Residence...," *Dispatch*, Dec. 19, 1906.

29. Packard sells: Cochise County Deeds, Book 2, p. 487. Burn, rebuild: "Great Growth...," *Review*, Jan. 13, 1907. Rafael sold: "Boquillas Company...," *International*, April 23, 1912.

Greene retained the San Rafael grant until his death. His estate sold a portion to the Boquillas Land and Cattle Co. in 1912. The family retained another portion until 1999 when it became an Arizona state park.

30. Maricopa County Deed Book 79, pp. 577-9; *Prospector*, Oct. 16, 1905.

31. Another farm: Maricopa County Mortgages Book 48, pp. 414-15, and Book 51, pp. 201-3. Registered: *Review*, March 11, 1906. Living in Tempe: *International*, May 3, 1906; *Review*, May 4, 1906. Stud: "Packard Has Fast Horses," *Dispatch*, March 16, 1908.

32. Directors: *Review*, March 7, 1905 and May 3, 1906.

33. Sonnichsen, pp. 182-3.

34. Rynning, Thomas H., *Gun Notches*. San Diego, Calif.: Frontier Heritage Press, 1971, pp. 296, 311-2.

35. Myrick, p. 349.

36. Sonnichsen, p. 48; "George Mitchell's Mining Property," Review, Aug. 2, 1902; "First National Bank...," *International*, June 11, 1921.

37. Hait, Pam, *The Arizona Bank, Arizona's Story*. Phoenix, Ariz.: Heritage Graphics, 1987, pp. 32-3.

38. Open: "Cochise County Banking Business," *Review*, June 5, 1903. Location: "1st National Bank...," International, Dec. 21, 1916. Hanks assistant: http://papermoneyofsonora.com, accessed June 12, 2012. Federal charter: "First National Bank Chartered....," *Dispatch*, May 28, 1930.

39. "New Douglas Building," *Review*, Sept. 5, 1905. Bought 1902: "Progressive Douglas," *Review*, Sept. 7, 1902.

40. Arizona Trust location: 1907 Douglas City Directory. Rankings: "Condensed State Of The Reports...," Review, April 14, 1907.

41. "Packard Returns...," *Review*, April 6, 1907.

42. "Visitors From Naco," *Review*, Jan. 22, 1907; Goff, John S., *Arizona Territorial Officials, Vol. VI*. Cave Creek, Ariz.: Black Mountain Press, 1996, p. 150.

43. "To Become Arizonians," Review, March 7, 1907.

44. Takeover: Sonnichsen, pp. 214-19. Fine: "Mitchell Tells...," Review, Jan. 11, 1908; "Douglas Growth...," *International*, Jan. 11, 1908; *Review*, March 13, 14, 17 and 20, 1908.

45. "First National Bank Changes," Dispatch, May 2, 1908.

46. "A Bright Future For Border City," Review, April 12, 1908; "Douglas Future...," *Review*, May 9, 1908.

47. Community activities: "4th July Business Active," *Dispatch*, May 13, 1908; "Tucson People Visit Douglas," *Dispatch*, May 19, 1908; "Local Men...," *International*, Aug. 4, 1908. Democratic politics: "Packard May Head...," *International*, June 5, 1908; "Packard To Denver...," *International*, June 9, 1908; "Headquarters...," *International*, June 20, 1908. Rentals: "For Summer," *Dispatch*, July 14, 1908. Buy house: Cochise County Deeds Book 48, pp. 67-9.

48. Cowen job: International, April 1 and 15, 1909. Buy lots: Cochise County Deeds Book 51, pp.217-9. Town site: Bailey, *Dragoons*, p. 195.

49. Myrick, p. 343.

50. Dorothea: *International*, Sept. 22 and 29, 1908; and Watkins. Ashley: *Dispatch*, June 21, 26 and 30, 1908.

51. "Thirteen Club...," *Dispatch*, March 13, 1987.

52. Cochise County Incorporations Book 5, pp. 596-8.

53. Maricopa County Deeds Book 79, pp. 578-9; Book 86, pp. 78-9; Book 87, p. 71.

54. "A Valley Stock Farm," undated clipping from unknown newspaper in Watkins' possession. "Packard's Filly Fast Flyer," *International*, April 6, 1910.

55. Trip: *International*, Sept. 18, 1909. Bryan: "City Welcomes Commoner," *International*, Sept. 21, 1909.

56. "Why Packard Didn't Stay...," Bisbee Evening Miner, Oct. 1, 1909.

Connections: The Life and Times of B. A. Packard

57. "Packard Has...," *International,* Jan. 10, 1910.

58. "Fire Extinguished...," *International,* Feb. 17, 1910. The Rice house occupied 959 10th St., in the block west of the Packard house.

59. Meetings: "First National Holds Meet," *International,* Jan. 11, 1910. Ad: *International,* May 9, 1908.

60. "An Additional Charge...," Dispatch, April 2, 1908; "Bisbee First National Bank," *Dispatch,* April 22, 1908.

61. Sold: "New Directorate...," *International,* Jan. 18, 1909. Frank Doan: Connors, *Who's Who,* pp. 171-2.

62. Move trust: 1912 Douglas City Directory. Howell: "New Superintendent...," and "Back To Ranch...," *International,* June 29 and July 22, 1908. Doan, May Cargill, "I Wouldn't Trade These Yesterdays." *Arizona Journal of History,* 1966.

63. "District Court Monday," *International,* April 19, 1910.

64. "Five Years In Pen...," *International,* April 20, 1910; record of Convict 3206, Territorial Prison, Pinal County Historical Society Museum, Florence, Ariz.

65. *Dispatch,* Nov. 29, Dec. 2, 3, 4 and 6, 1910; *International,* Nov. 30, Dec. 1, 4, 10 and 16, 1910; record of Convict 3440, Pinal County Historical Society Museum.

66. Birth: 1870 U.S. Census; California Death Index, 1940-1997. Early career: "E.W. Graves...," *Dispatch,* Aug. 19, 1937. Meets Etchells: "Looks Back," *Star,* Sept. 26, 1947.

67. Marriage, death: "Obituary," Aug. 11, 1894, and "Death of Mrs. Graves," *Tucson Citizen,* Aug. 12, 1894. Retardation: John H. Davis Jr., Douglas, Ariz., interviews with author, July 1996. Marry: Connors, *Who's Who,* p. 267.

68. Move: "E.W. Graves...," *Dispatch,* Aug. 19, 1937. Family move: *International,* Jan. 14 and Feb. 10, 1910.

69. Live: Douglas City Directories. Lawhon: International, April 20, 1909. Japan: "Douglasites In Tokio, Japan," *International,* Sept. 22, 1910.

70. Cochise County Superior Court Civil Case No. 5153.

71. All loans mentioned are in Chattel Mortgages Book 5, beginning on p. 24.

72. Douglas City Directories; "Murray McInernay...," *Dispatch,* Sept. 8, 1928.

73. Escobosa Gámez, Gilberto, "El Gobernador Caballero," *La Jornada,* Sept. 25, 2008, Hermosillo, Son.

74. *Dispatch,* June 26, 28 and July 12, 1910; *International,* Nov. 9, 1912.

75. "Packard Was Here," *Review,* July 29, 1906.

Cynthia F. Hayostek

Revolution

> "The Revolution was not the work of saints but of men of flesh and bone, men of passions and of many defects."
> – Francisco L. Urquizo, 1891-1969, Mexican general, writer and historian

The Cananea strike against Greene's copper company quickly gained a mythology and today is seen as a precursor to the Mexican Revolution. But a largely forgotten incident, the kidnapping of Manuel Sarabia in Douglas, had a larger influence for it engaged the sympathies of men such as Packard and his connections.

By 1907, Mexican President Porfirio Díaz had been in office about 30 years. During that time, the finely tuned system that preserved his dictatorship had come to include international kidnapping among its techniques.

One Díaz system target was the *magonista* movement, named for brothers Ricardo and Enrique Magón. They published an influential newspaper, which advocated overthrow of Díaz. To continue publishing and to save their lives, the Magóns and their connections, including Sarabia, fled to the United States. In Douglas, Sarabia worked for the *Douglas International*, a daily newspaper published by Progressive Democrat George H. Kelly.

On June 30, 1907, Arizona Ranger Sam Hayhurst arrested Sarabia on a Mexican murder warrant and put him in Douglas' jail. What Hayhurst and his fellow law officers didn't know was that the warrant was false; it simply was the Díaz government's way of getting Sarabia back into Mexico where he could be eliminated.[1]

During Sarabia's transfer from the jail to a car for a trip to the border, he tried to escape. He yelled he was being kidnapped but was choked into submission. Sarabia, however, created enough of a commotion that, although he was turned over to Mexican authorities, his plight became known.₂

Kelly put banner headlines across the *International's* front pages the next three days. A rally the evening of July 2 in front of city hall drew 1,000 people. Charlie Overlock and Richardson spoke. Richardson gave an "impassioned speech" stating Sarabia "was not wanted for murder but was wanted for expressing criticism of the existing government... ."₃

Indignant Douglas residents signed a resolution sent to Presidents Theodore Roosevelt and Díaz. Mary "Mother" Jones, the nationally known labor firebrand who was speaking in Douglas the day before the kidnapping, also generated a loud outcry.

Local law enforcement officials as well as the Mexican consul who participated in the incident were arrested and arraigned. Charges were dropped later because Sarabia was released. On July 12, he returned to Douglas and thanked "the people of Douglas for the kindly interest they have taken in my affairs. It is wonderful how a people could be so kind to me when I was not known to scarcely a soul among the Americans."₄

Sarabia's story helped some borderland Americans comprehend Mexico's status quo. Although Díaz had brought stability and some economic development to Mexico, the predominate form of labor, especially in remote mining towns and on large *haciendas*, remained debt peonage. This meant a small percentage of Mexico's population was incredibly rich and a large percentage perpetually poor with little hope of change because of the regime's repressiveness.

Packard undoubtedly knew this as owner of a large Mexican ranch. It seems unlikely, however, that he went along with the peon system, given the way he'd implemented eight-hour work days in his Tombstone mines while other owners held to 10 and 12-hour shifts. Once owner of First National Bank, Packard became more closely connected to *revoltoso* sympathizers such as Richardson, who spoke publicly about changing Mexico's government.

Violent changes began in November 1910 when Francisco Madero and his followers launched a revolutionary attack on the Díaz regime in Chihuahua. Madero adherents in Sonora joined in.

On April 13, 1911, about 150 rebels under the direction of Arturo "Red" Lopez took over the Nacozari train and used it as a Trojan horse to enter Agua Prieta. In a three-hour battle, the rebels captured Agua Prieta and forced the *federales* to take refuge across the border in Douglas.[5]

Some Americans, including Graves, hastily organized a Red Cross chapter, which gathered and transported the wounded and dead. Red Cross services were required again on April 15 when other *federales* attempted unsuccessfully to retake Agua Prieta. Bullets whistled into Douglas, peppering people and buildings as far north as First National.[6]

On the 18th, the rebels were low on ammunition and abandoned Agua Prieta just hours before reinforcements arrived. Although the *revoltosos* retreated, their four-day occupation of Agua Prieta validated their movement's strength.

Lopez and many other *revoltosos* then went to Juarez, Chih.,[7] which the *maderistas* captured May 9. Shortly afterward, Díaz fled to Spain. Madero was elected Mexico's President and assumed office in November 1911.

Unfortunately, he proved to be a weak leader. One of Madero's mistakes was authorizing local militia formation instead of a national army. Chihuahuan militias, organized by Pascual Orozco and Pancho Villa, soon were in revolt against Madero.

Other militias, using Orozco's red banner, quickly descended into banditry and terrorized northern Mexico. In 1912, "red flaggers" complicated a trip Soto took to Moctezuma.

While still living there, Soto had courted Rosa Durazo. When he moved to Douglas, they wrote every day but then Rosa's letters stopped. Early in September 1912, Soto asked Graves for a week off so he could travel to Moctezuma to check on the Durazo family and present Rosa with an engagement ring.

Soto reached Nacozari by train and went by stagecoach to Moctezuma. He entered the town soon after the red flaggers left and was much relieved to find the Durazos unharmed. Rosa accepted his proposal, and Soto returned to Nacozari. There he learned regular train service had ceased because of red flagger activity.

Soto's leave was almost up and in desperation, he asked Maj. E.C. Muñoz, who was organizing a federal military company headed for Agua Prieta, if he could accompany the soldiers on their 75-mile trip northward. The major agreed but was reluctant because, Soto said, he was dressed in his "Sunday clothes, low shoes, a cap and [held] as the unnecessary impedimenta, a suitcase."

On a Tuesday evening, Soto and the soldiers climbed aboard a flatcar pushed by an engine, which only inched along because of the danger from land mines. Their ride ended after seven kilometers when the lead car ran into a burro and derailed. The jolt flung the men down an embankment.

This happened a short distance from the first of eight burned-out bridges the men walked around. They marched through the night but were still south of Fronteras when they encountered a freight train that took them into town.

They left Fronteras on the train Wednesday night, but their ride was cut short by damaged tracks. So they trudged northward, skirting around four red flagger camps. At 11 a.m. on Thursday, the need for water forced them to look for some. It wasn't until 6 p.m. Friday that Soto crossed the border and telephoned Graves of his arrival.[8]

Conditions soon calmed enough that the tracks were repaired. On Oct. 19, 1912, a little more than a month after his marathon journey, Soto married Rosa in Moctezuma and brought her to Douglas. He kept working at First National, and the couple established a home in 810 Seventh St., where the first of their eight children was born.

The red flaggers who bedeviled Soto's trip brought to the forefront a man named Álvaro Obregón, born in 1880 near Alamos, Son. The same as Packard, Obregón had a well-developed sense of humor, impressive memory and keen interest in human character that made him a poker player extraordinaire. Like Packard, he'd gone into business at a young age and suffered an early set-back, but recovered while working for others.

By the time the Revolution started, the mechanically minded Obregón owned a farm on which he grew garbanzos and harvested them with a machine he'd invented. He'd been elected Mayor of Huatabampo, an agricultural town in the heart of Mayo Indian country in southern Sonora. Obregón spoke Mayo as well as Spanish, which helped him get elected as well as recruit men for a militia supporting Madero.[9]

On Sept. 16, 1912, red flaggers occupied El Tigre and threatened Nacozari until Obregón's unit showed up. The marauders deserted El Tigre, but Obregón found them eight miles north of Fronteras. Late on Sept. 20 at Hacienda San Joaquin, Obregón's 150 infantrymen attacked 550 red flaggers. The battle, cut short by nightfall, resumed the next morning with the Mayos routing the red flaggers, who left behind two machine guns and more than 100 horses.[10]

Phelps Dodge attorney Edward L. Tinker happened to be with Obregón, probably in much the same arrangement as Soto had with Col. Muñoz. Tinker's report resulted in Phelps Dodge and Lucky Tiger officials hosting a banquet for Obregón in the Gadsden Hotel, where Packard first met Obregón. Prominent Mexicans later gave Obregón a second banquet in the Douglas home of Sonoran rancher Hilario Gabilondo; among the speakers was another young up-and-comer named Plutaro Elías Calles, who was then Agua Prieta *comisario*.[11]

Sonoran Gov. José M. Maytorena assigned Obregón to Sonora, and he lived in the Gadsden until February 1913 when Victoriano Huerta seized power and murdered Madero. In the months preceding those Ten Tragic Days, Obregón had opened an account at First National and, given the nature of the two men, almost certainly played poker with Packard.₁₂

By this time, First National was a respected Douglas institution. The bank held City of Douglas bonds and handled the payroll of American troops stationed at Camp Douglas, on the town's east side in case the Revolution spilled into the United States. The bank's total assets neared $1 million, just $100,000 or so behind the Bank of Douglas.₁₃

B.A. Packard portrait taken in 1916.
Author's collection

This was due largely to Packard's adept handling of the bank, which included his choice of directors. They were Pollack, Graves, Randolph, Louis W. Powell, C&A vice-president and general manager; James Wood, C&A smelter superintendent in Douglas; and George Dawe, chief clerk at the C&A smelter. The Moctezuma directors included Pollack, Henry C. Beauchamp, manager of the Transvaal Copper Mining Co. near Cumpas, Son.; and Francisco Gallego, the Moctezuma cashier.₁₄

These choices were designed to produce confidence in First National. Pollack, who owned two banks in northern Arizona, traveled regularly to Douglas and seems to have been the person upon whom Packard most relied for banking advice. But it was Packard's varied and large body of international experience that undoubtedly made him "the go-to guy" for borderland ranchers, miners and political figures.

Packard was a stockman who was a politician and banker in addition to his cattle business. He liked a country lifestyle and its people, and fellow cattlemen on both sides of the border clearly liked and trusted him. He did business cattleman's style – on a handshake or via letters. He did bank business that way too.

His mining knowledge was a plus. When Packard bought First National, one of its assets was the Roy Mine, near El Tigre.[15] The Roy Consolidated Mining Co. was one of numerous, small mining firms located in Sonora that had Douglas offices, thus invigorating the borderlands economy. Another was the Transvaal operation, 100 miles south of Douglas, that consisted of a mine and smelter.

Packard's American enterprises also prospered. Cottrell planted bountiful wheat and barley crops on the Kyrene farm, which also hosted registered Hereford cattle that B.A. bought during his trips each October to the Kansas City Livestock Show. Dorothea lived with the Cottrells while she attended the Phoenix Music Conservatory and trained her alto voice.[16]

In Douglas, Dixie was a popular social hostess. It was through her that B.A. gained a nickname that stayed with him the rest of his life. That nickname was "Daddy" and obviously stemmed from an inside joke between B.A. and Dixie that was a result of people's reaction to their age disparity. About this time, he also received the honorific "Colonel."[17]

While Packard's American businesses ran smoothly, the Mexican ones did not. In April 1911, around the time of the Agua Prieta battle, red flaggers looted the Moctezuma store. On Aug. 2, 1911, Packard went there to inventory and sell the store's merchandise to E.C. Soto, a relative of Ygnacio's. This trip caused Packard to miss Greene's funeral.[18]

Although by 1911 Greene had not controlled Cananea Copper for three years, he retained a string of ranches managed as the Cananea Cattle Co., as well as timber and mineral rights in Sonora and Chihuahua serviced by his own railroad. All this mattered naught on July 31 when the pair of horses pulling Greene's buggy ran away and crashed into a Cananea telephone pole. Greene was thrown onto a wooden fence in front of the church.

Greene downplayed the incident, as he had previous horse accidents in his life. He insisted he was all right, got up without assistance and walked off, but his injuries were life-threatening. Doctors diagnosed a fractured collarbone, broken ribs and a punctured lung. Pneumonia set in and he died Aug. 5. Dixie went alone to the funeral held Aug. 7, 1911 in Greene's Cananea house.[19]

Although Packard sold the Moctezuma store, he was forced to deal with the company another year. That's because he and Pollack filed a suit against Randolph in an attempt to get what they felt was owed them.

"The dispute in the case was whether or not a verbal agreement had been made between Pollack, Packard and Randolph to share the losses equally among themselves in making good the deficit of the bank," explained the Nov. 30, 1912 *Douglas Dispatch*. The "verbal agreement ... was to sell all the property of the company, and with the money derived from the sale ... settle all obligations of the company.

"Should there be a deficit, ... the agreement was that each director, on the account of the trust in which people reposed in him, should stand one-third of this from his personal estate. It was stated that this was thought to be the best plan of action, since the people in that section had placed their money in the bank because of the known integrity of the men back of the concern."

When Packard closed the bank, its deficit was slightly over $39,000. He paid out the money to account holders in Moctezuma after transferring it from First National. Randolph refused to pay his share, forcing Packard and Pollack to sue. After two days' testimony in a Tucson courthouse, a jury decided in favor of Randolph. Shortly thereafter, he resigned from First National's board of directors.

What was left unsaid at the time came out 20 years later. Reading between the lines of an interview Packard gave in 1931 reveals what really was the cause of the Packard and Pollack's disavowal of Randolph – he'd gone back on what he'd agreed to do, which apparently was build a railroad.

"Some years ago," Packard told the *Dispatch*, "with my good friend Tom Pollack and one or two others, I engaged in a banking enterprise at a Mexican point because of the outlook for railroad development. The development did not come and so we withdrew from the field."[20]

In January 1912, red flaggers raided Mababi. Since it was a short distance from Ojo de Agua, Packard was uneasy because of "a large number of fine horses ... exposed to the roving bandits." So he traveled to Ojo to oversee the horses' removal since "loss of the horses would be a great hardship just at this time when it would be hard to replace them in time for the spring round up work."[21]

In March, "regaled in a regulation cowboy suit," Packard returned to "his Turkey Track ranch in Mexico, south of Crook [railroad] tunnel." By then, everyone called the ranch the Turkey Track, although the corporation had ceased to exist. An estimated 5,000 corriente cattle dominated the place.

"Packard is enjoying life to the fullest extent," the *International* reported. "He keeps in close touch with the 'chuck' wagon, and ... is the first man to roll up in his blankets at night and the first man to unroll himself in the morning and stir the boys into action."[22] He was 65-years-old.

In August 1912, with red flagger activity building toward the September outbreak that placed Obregón center stage, Packard again went to Ojo de Agua to "bring fifty head of his ranch horses to this side of the line. The reported presence of a good sized band of rebels in the Ajo Mountains led Col. Packard to the conclusion that his horses would be safer on this side of the line, as he has no desire to mount any of the soldiers in Mexico, no matter what calling they are seeking to uphold.

"Only enough horses will be left on the ranch to serve the few cowboys employed at this season and the ones brought across the line today will be kept in pastures in the vicinity of Naco until there are more peaceful conditions in Mexico, or until they are required for the fall roundup."[23]

Bandits looted Ojo de Agua on Sept. 2, 1912.[24] There were no other raids for two years, but Revolutionary events made life difficult for Packard and other borderlands cattlemen. He expressed his frustration anonymously in a 1913 newspaper interview.

"I have been in the cattle business in Mexico continuously for the last 24 years and the worst conditions that have ever existed ... exist there now...," Packard told the *International*. "The Mexicans who work for me used to try and do their best.... At the present time it is exactly the opposite. ... Nearly all my old employees have left me in the last two years and joined the various sides of the revolution... ."[25]

After Huerta became Mexico's President in 1913, several state governors refused to recognize him. Foremost was Venustiano Carranza, Coahuila governor. Gathering like-minded leaders into a coalition, Carranza established a provisional government in Sonora and named himself First Chief of the Constitutionalist Army. Leading that army was Obregón.

The Constitutionalists were just one faction in northern Mexico; Villa led another. It was important for these factions to control a border town because the town facilitated flow of the three Ms – money, munitions and men. One way a faction could raise money was imposition of taxes on border commerce. Early in March 1914, Carranza applied an export duty of $20 per head on all cattle crossing the border at Agua Prieta.

"The decision ... will probably bankrupt many Sonora cattlemen who have agreed to deliver to buyers on the American side of the border cattle at a stipulated price made before they were aware of the prohibitive duty imposed by the official decree," the *International* reported. "Several large shipments which were en route to the border have been stopped, and in spite of the efforts of their owners, have been refused exportation without payment of the duty."[26]

Later, Carranza reduced the tax to $5 per head, but only if the exporter deposited $50,000 in gold coin into the Constitutionalist coffers as surety. Charlie E. Wiswall, the Cananea Cattle Co. manager; Marion Williams, a neighboring rancher; M.M. Sherman, who ranched near Nacozari but lived in Kansas, and the Hohstadt brothers banded together and paid the $50,000. This was widely seen as submission to graft.[27]

The *International* delineated another problem cattlemen faced when it said, "Col. B.A. Packard gathered more than 1000 head of cows and calves from his Turkey Track range in Mexico, below Naco, ten days ago, but had to hold them for a week waiting for a permit from the state government... . He had [railroad] cars for these cattle, but because of the delay in getting his permits the cars were given to other shippers and there being also a shortage of cars on the Southern Pacific, he was not able to ship yesterday... ."[28]

Then there was an old difficulty. "Deputy United States Veterinarian Dr. Harry Hart issued an order yesterday preventing the cattle taken by the constitutionalists from the Arturo Morales ranch from entering the United States through the Douglas port on the grounds they came from a district exposed to the fever tick," said the *International*. "If this ruling is sustained, ... the seizures of cattle at other places will not be likely to do the state troops as much good as they anticipated... ."[29]

To Sonoran ranchers, it must have seemed as if everything was conspiring against them. For Packard, the situation came to a head during October 1914 when Maytorena troops besieged Naco, which was held by Constitutionalist Gen. Benjamin Hill. This took place shortly after the Aguascalientes Conference, which was supposed to decide which faction would rule Mexico after Huerta's resignation.[30]

Packard didn't care about that. He was upset because both the Naco besieged and besiegers helped themselves to 2,000 head of his cattle without paying for the provisioning. Hill bluntly told Packard not to move the cattle because his troops needed them. Packard appealed to then-U.S. Secretary of State Bryan, for permission to move his Mexican cattle across the line, but he was ignored.

When political means proved inadequate to solve his difficulties, Packard's innate self-reliance led him to do what he thought was right, even if it was at odds with government policy. Early in November, Packard instructed his foreman, James H. Pyeatt (who'd assumed the job in 1911 following the retirement of his uncle, Henry Aston) to gather a dozen or so cowboys, arm them and lead them onto Ojo de Agua. There they rounded up 6,000 head and herded them across the line.[31]

Packard's action caused a sensation. Newspapers ranging from the *Los Angeles Times* to the *Olean Times Herald* printed stories about the roundup, which included criticism of Bryan. The *Herald* began its story with, "They raise some good men in Cattaraugus County even if all of them do not stay here."[32]

On Nov. 12, Tom Lea, a Texas resident shortly to become El Paso Mayor, sent Packard a telegram. It read, "You don't know me nor I you but if you sent the word to Bryan which the papers say you did my hat is off to you and I would like to meet you when you come to El Paso I join with you in saying that we have no Secretary of State."[33]

Shortly before these events, Packard became involved in rescuing Valley Bank of Phoenix. Founded in 1883 by William Christy, an innovative rancher, farmer and banker, Valley was in trouble after loaning out 85 percent of its deposits. Because it was the leading bank of the state's leading town, other Arizona bankers joined in trying to prevent Valley's closure and a possible panic.

Packard, representing First National; Pollack, Arizona Central of Flagstaff; Ellis of the Bank of Douglas; and several others met regularly for two months attempting to save Valley Bank. But it wasn't until R.E. Moore, C.E. Mills and L.D. Ricketts of Gila Valley Bank & Trust in Solomonville (east of today's Safford, Ariz.) joined the group that a viable rescue plan took shape.

It was a struggle, but "by an amazing exhibition of all-around cooperation ... the situation was saved without receivership, without litigation [and] almost without loss. Just as Westerners had always clubbed together on a voluntary yet individual basis to pool their combined vigor ... so they had met this disaster in finance, aided by bankers who had learned their trade in Arizona's copper mining camps, and who had the well-being of their state deeply at heart."[34]

Shortly after this rescue, changes occurred in First National of Douglas. One change involved formation of the Federal Reserve System, which created a nationwide check-clearing system that attempted to solve problems contributing to the 1907 Panic. In 1914, First National participated in the new insurance system by placing $20,000 of its reserve in a district bank in Dallas. That year for the first time, First National topped $1 million (today about $12 million) in assets.[35]

Other changes, involving personnel, began in 1915 after Edward C. Bradford resigned as First National's receiving teller. Bradford's varied work experience led him to form East, Lawhon & Bradford, a real estate and insurance agency.[36]

James East was a New Mexican lawman who'd once helped capture Billy the Kid. In Douglas, he interspersed stints as city marshal with managing saloons and a beer distributorship. He did well enough that his money funded Lawhon and Bradford's start-up.

Lawhon trained Soto as First National's paying teller, and then resigned to devote himself to his own firm. It succeeded admirably. Lawhon and Bradford quickly bought out East, then opened branches in Bisbee, Tucson and, in a few years, Phoenix.[37]

The employees of First National Bank of Douglas posed for this photo on March 31, 1918. They were, right to left, Eugene C. Hempel, receiving teller; Ashley B. Packard, assistant cashier; Ygnacio Soto, International Commission Co.; Mrs. Bertha Paddock, stenographer; Ruby Brummer, bookkeeper; Merle L. Hartley, liberty bonds and general books; Edgar A. Poe, receiving teller; William Alberts, teller; Mae Stillman, exchange; Frances Sexton, bookkeeper; Harriet Browder, statements; Jean Thomas, bookkeeper; Bessie McInernay, collections; Florence Seebaum, clearing house.

Cochise County Historical Society

About the time of his promotion, Soto moved his family into 1017 11th St. There he had an encounter that put him in the *International*. During the early hours of Feb. 11, 1915, a drunken soldier from Camp Douglas wandered into Soto's house.

"There was not a gun in the house and Soto was at a loss to know what to attack the burglar with," said the *International*.

"But when his eyes fell on a heavy golf stick called a mashie lying nearby, the problem was solved."

Grabbing the mashie, Soto rushed the soldier. Brandishing the golf club in the air, Soto shouted, "Fore!"

"Don't hit me," cried the astonished soldier, who promptly sat down after Soto told him to do so. The police took the soldier away.

"Mr. Soto figures that this experience with a golf stick should bring him luck ... the next time he goes to the country club," added the *International*, and he'll "play the greatest game of his life. Incidentally, he warns all opposing players that when he hollers 'fore' he means business."[38]

A few months after his golf adventure, Soto resigned from First National. With borderlands small mine owner Sutter A. Gardanier, Soto founded a customs brokerage, the International Commission Co., in 927 H Ave. Helidoro Rivera owned the two-story building. He had a wholesale grocery operation and customs brokerage in one part of the building and rented another part to the U.S. Postal Service.

It may seem odd that Rivera and Soto had the same sort of business in the same building. What wasn't readily apparent were Rivera and Soto's connections to the Constitutionalist cause. By September 1915, Soto was opening International Commission branch offices in Nacozari and Cumpas.[39]

Ashley took over Soto's bank job shortly before marrying, on May 24, 1915 in Tucson, Rachel Williams. Born in New York, she was the daughter of Elliott S. and Rachel (Wood) Williams. Rachel had taught in the Douglas school system since 1911.

That created a problem, the *International* said, since Miss Williams had signed her teaching contract for the next school year before she became Mrs. Packard. The school board overlooked this breach. But then another teacher did the same thing, and then rumors "whispered of more desertions from the ranks of the pedagogues... ." So the school board met and, with tongue firmly in cheek, issued an ultimatum titled "Notice to Men:

"We have had our attention called to the fact that quite a number of our teachers have entered into matrimonial contracts ... subsequent to signing of contracts with us to teach, and you are hereby warned that all contracts of marriage made with teachers who are already contracted to teach school in Douglas during the coming year are hereby declared null and void, and all men, parties to such contracts, will be held to strict accountability and will suffer the penalties prescribed for such offense."[40]

Having escaped the wrath of the school board, Ashley and Rachel settled into 1150 10th St., next door to the Lawhons. On Aug. 21, 1916, their only child, Ashley Burdette Packard, Jr., was born in the house. By then, Ashley Sr. was assistant cashier at First National, and had the same close relationship with Graves that B.A. had.[41]

Becoming a grandfather again was just one facet of Packard's abundant life during this time. At the 1916 state fair, 22 of his show Herefords won 24 blue ribbons and two grand championships. He sold these animals to upgrade borderland herds, including those of Sonoran rancher Francisco Elías, a relative of Plutarco Elías Calles.

Packard's Hereford bulls appeared on First National checks and savings book covers. The bank's agricultural underpinnings also showed when Sulphur Springs Valley farmer James Brogan began commercially canning "Honest Pack" brand tomatoes.

"The brand is said to have taken its name from the Hon. B.A. Packard of this city, but instead of his well-known smiling countenance, it[s label] bears a portly red tomato as a trade mark," said the *Dispatch*.[42]

First National apparently was Brogan's financial institution – not Arizona Bank & Trust. That's because the institution closed late in 1913, a victim of "overloaning and slow

~ 188 ~

collections." A state auditor inspected the books and declared cashier John Doan had a clean record but the bank was overextended. John moved back to Yuma, while his brother and father maintained an active law practice in their First National building office.[43]

About this time, Packard transitioned from a horse and buggy to an automobile. The process was not easy, as the Oct. 6, 1913 *International* reveals.

"As a result of a collision between an automobile and horse and buggy last Saturday evening near the [railroad] roundhouse on the Bisbee-Douglas road, Ross Taylor, a smelter employee, will be the recipient of a good horse and new buggy to take the place of a smashed vehicle and dead horse, the same to be presented by Mr. B.A. Packard, president of the First National bank.

"The accident happened just after dark at a point in the road where neither party could see the other until within a few feet of meeting. Mr. Packard was driving his big Cadillac car at a pretty fair speed ... when all at once Mr. Taylor, driving a horse and buggy, turned into the road directly in front of him, and there was a head-on crash which smashed the buggy to pieces, broke one of the legs of the horse and threw Mr. Taylor violently to the ground, but fortunately not injuring him. As soon as he got a glimpse of the vehicle, Mr. Packard swerved his machine to the right, but it was too late. Constable Sam Hayhurst was called to the scene and found it necessary to shoot the wounded animal.

"It was one of those peculiar accidents for which neither party was really to blame, and it is only because of the fact that Mr. Packard has a kind heart and does not wish to see Mr. Ross the loser by an accident for which neither could be held responsible that he will make him a present of another horse and new vehicle."

Packard was in a "fender bender" two years later. Apparently, he was too closely following a vehicle driven by Louis A. May, a contractor, who swore out a warrant claiming Packard had left the scene of the accident. Witness testimony, presented by Packard's attorney Richardson, showed this wasn't true, and the case was dismissed.[44]

These incidents so affected Packard that from then on, he always kept his automobile in first gear when driving in town. Despite this, Packard felt his car was a useful tool, as a Nov. 21, 1914 *International* article conveys.

"Hon. B.A. Packard drove in yesterday afternoon from his pastures north of the city, stopping his big Cadillac machine in front of the Gadsden Hotel. 'Bah! Bah! Bah!' came from the bottom of the machine behind the front seat. Several present were startled by this unusual sound... . Examination ... revealed a young bull calf which its owner declared was less than ten hours old. ... Mr. Packard ... said he found the calf in a herd of cattle which he was sending to his pastures near Tempe...; it was unable to travel and was too valuable to leave,

In the yard of the Packard home on 10th Street, Gertrude Packard holds the Jersey heifer whose picture would soon adorn delivery trucks of the Douglas Dairy Co. The heifer looks as if she wants to grab some of the alfalfa at Gertrude's feet in this 1913 photo.

Packard family photo

so he loaded it into his machine and brought it home where it will receive every care."

Packard put the calf on his dairy cow, an animal of some fame for a portrait of her adorned the door of the Douglas Dairy delivery truck. The Jersey grazed in the almost half-block yard surrounding the Packard house on alfalfa Packard had planted there.[45]

Winifred Paul, Alfred's daughter, used to walk two blocks east from her home to the Packard house and pick alfalfa to feed her pet rabbit. B.A. would sternly say, "You're not supposed to take anything without asking," said Winifred, but she knew he was teasing because of the twinkle in his eyes.[46]

Winifred's father, after joining the company that upset PD's plans for early-day Douglas, established a quarry northeast of Douglas. In 1905, the quarry produced tufa stone, used to erect many Douglas buildings, and 18 railroad carloads of limestone each day. All area copper companies bought ground-up limestone to use in their concentration process.

In 1911, Paul began managing a C&A silica quarry 15 miles west of Douglas. This prompted him to develop some claims he had nearby, and they turned out to have higher-grade limestone than the quarry northeast of Douglas. Paul moved his plant in time for the boom in copper production that took place during World War I, and a village known as Paul Spur took shape near the new quarry.[47]

In 1916, Packard put together a ranch a mile south of Paul Spur. He bought most of it from Charles P. Hunt and three of his 10 children, James, John and Caroline "Carrie" Nolan. Packard paid a total of $7,280.[48]

The Hunts were Texans, who'd mostly arrived in Cochise County around 1900. They homesteaded and received patents on their land, but by 1916 they wanted to leave the Sulphur Springs Valley, which they felt was beginning to fill with farmers. The Hunts moved their cattle to the Animas Valley in New Mexico's boot heel but maintained numerous ties to Cochise County, as did their cousin, Stewart Hunt, who ranched on both sides of the international borderline.[49]

Packard always called his ranch near Paul Spur "the Hunt place." It was adjacent to where Texan George M. Slaughter briefly ran some cattle. George was the son of Christopher C. Slaughter, prominent Texas rancher and banker, and cousin of John Slaughter. George's brother, Robert L., managed the Slaughter Land & Cattle Co., near Moctezuma. Robert's close friend was attorney Richardson.[50]

Packard, with Richardson's assistance, handled the considerable estate of another Texan, "Babe" Thompson, who died in 1914. Packard and Thompson became friends when Thompson was Turkey Track foreman. Thompson also ran his own San Pedro ranch, whose assets Packard sold to the Boquillas Co. to benefit Thompson's heirs.[51]

At the time of Thompson's demise, he was leasing the Rancho Gallardo, two miles east of Agua Prieta, with partner William Neel. He'd arrived in Cochise County about 1895 to manage the Ryan Brothers Ranch, which acquired the Erie Cattle Co. holdings after the Shattucks moved to Kansas.

About 1901, when the Ryans succumbed to changing conditions, Neel and Omaha cattle buyer C.J. Hysham formed the Four Bar Ranch. It included Mud Springs (just north of Paul's first quarry), ran across the Sulphur Springs Valley's width and into the Dragoons, where it incorporated what had been the Packard and Tweed Ranch. Neel died early in 1915; his widow, Ellen, and their son, Walter, then ran Four Bar.[52]

The deaths of Thompson and Neel meant that neither of them suffered from the anxiety involved in Gallardo serving as an assembly point for Pancho Villa's attack on Agua Prieta late in 1915.

By then, the Mexican Revolution had deteriorated into civil war on state and national levels. In Sonora, Constitutionalist Gen. Calles battled Villa ally Maytorena. Nationally, Obregón led the Constitutionalist Army, which administered several defeats of Villa, who retreated to Chihuahua to resupply during autumn 1915.

Villa, however, no longer controlled any Chihuahuan border town. Agua Prieta, lightly held by Calles, seemed vulnerable and relatively close. Villa's army marched toward it from the east and southeast during October 1915. Calles' men encircled Agua Prieta with breastworks and barbed wire entanglements.

Calles also received cannons, other equipment and reinforcements via El Paso, Texas. The Constitutionalist soldiers crossed the Rio Grande, traveled on American trains, then disembarked in Douglas and marched to Agua Prieta. This enraged Villa because it was accompanied by American recognition of Carranza's government.[53]

At Gallardo on Oct. 31, Villa learned of the recognition and reinforcements but attacked anyway, losing thousands of men during three days of battle around Agua Prieta. On Nov. 3, 1915, what was left of Villa's army began staggering around northern Sonora, generating mayhem in its quest for food, supplies and revenge on Americans and Constitutionalists. The *villistas* looted El Tigre, and forced Robert Slaughter Jr. and ranch foreman J.P. Hall to hide in a cave near Moctezuma for six days before making their way across the border.[54]

Obregón and Calles concentrated on controlling the borderline and repelled *villista* attacks at Naco and Nogales during November. On Dec. 3, 1915, Obregón met with Maj. Gen. Frederick Funston, U.S. Army departmental commander, in the Gadsden Hotel. (They'd previously met in Nogales.)[55]

After Funston left, Obregón remained in Douglas for some time while tracking *villista* movements and socializing. He appeared in full dress uniform at a dance in Douglas' Acacia Hall on Dec. 6, 1915. This seeming frivolity can be seen as Constitutionalist public relations for it emphasized the contrast between a civilized Obregón and a raging Villa, perhaps changing passive supporters of the Constitutionalist cause into active ones.[56]

Packard was certainly among the active supporters. For one thing, Constitutionalist money flowed, more or less openly, through First National. Soto, as a former employee, had his International Commission Co. account there.

Another example of Packard's support of the Constitutionalist cause was, during the summer of 1915, he allowed Calles, by then Constitutionalist military governor of Sonora, to store $162,000 worth of silver pesos in First National. The currency's presence didn't become publicly known until eight months *after* Villa's attack when Calles shipped it to the Valley Bank office in Phoenix.[57]

By that time, First National had $1.5 million in assets ($149 million today), and the directors decided to remodel. The process took five months while operations moved to an adjacent building. In addition to revamping the layout and installing black-veined marble from Colorado and an oak and mahogany interior, the remodel beefed up bank security with a massive new vault.[58]

The bank's growth was part of Douglas' overall prosperity brought about by World War I, which created high copper demand. Both smelters operated at capacity, and the town's population exceeded 17,000.

That figure didn't include men stationed at the Army camp east of Douglas. Renamed Camp Harry J. Jones, to honor a corporal killed by a stray bullet during the 1915 Battle of Agua Prieta, the camp became a training facility upon American entry into WWI. Camp Jones was a divisional headquarters with 10,000 men and officers stationed there. One of those officers became Dorothea's husband.

Dorothy was a popular figure in Douglas society. She helped Dixie entertain Nan Hayden, wife of Arizona's lone Congressman Carl Hayden, during a Douglas visit; "merrily tormented the curious [as] a cunning little Dutch boy" during a masquerade ball; and was such a good tennis player that people ignored a dance band to watch a mixed doubles match she played at the Douglas Country Club.[59]

Dorothy's groom was Capt. John A. Parker. Born in 1878, Parker was the son of a North Carolina farmer. He was a University of North Carolina graduate who became an attorney and practiced law for 12 years before joining the Army. He became an officer of the 308th Cavalry, known as "Arizona's Own," since it was organized in Douglas at Camp Jones on May 1, 1918.

Married June 27, 1918 in St. Stephen's Episcopal Church by the rector, Rev. Ernest W. Simonson, Dorothy and John moved to Ft. Sill, Okla., before the end of WWI because the 308th converted into an artillery regiment. Promoted to major, Parker stayed in the Army with the adjutant general's office after the war, receiving postings overseas and stateside.[60]

Although WWI ended, military action continued in Mexico as the Constitutionalists and Carranza consolidated their hold on power. Firearms and other supplies were still needed and, despite a U.S. embargo, Soto's International Commission Co. provided them. The International Commission did so well that Soto erected a building on the northwest corner of G Avenue and 12th Street in 1919. It featured three brick veneer storefronts, an expansive basement and direct access to a railroad spur behind the building.[61]

That Soto's business included arms smuggling is clear from a case the U.S. government brought against him in 1920. The U.S. Bureau of Investigation (predecessor to the FBI) reported "27,500 rounds of ammunition and a Colt machine gun, purchased in Los Angeles during the week of May 4, [1920] by Ygnacio Soto, were seized by agents of the Department of Justice at Nogales, Arizona, to which place they had been shipped in caskets."[62]

Soto, with Frank Doan as his attorney, faced charges in federal court in Tucson for false billing of merchandise and exporting firearms and ammunition into Mexico in violation of the American arms embargo. The government claimed to have 127 witnesses, but on June 2, 1920 Soto entered a guilty plea of conspiring to smuggle arms, paid a $10,000 fine, and left the courthouse.₆₃ The episode didn't negatively affect International Commission business, which remained solid through the last writhings of the Mexican Revolution.

In them, Obregón ran for the Presidency, harassed at every turn by Carranza, who'd assumed the office under a Mexican Constitution written in 1917. In the culmination of a long series of events, Carranza tried to imprison Obregón in southern Mexico while pressuring Sonora. This led Calles to issue *El Plan de Agua Prieta*, a rationale for revolt against Carranza. In ensuing events, Carranza was killed and Obregón elected President of Mexico.

There can be no doubt that Packard backed Obregón monetarily and in other ways through much of the Revolution. A bit of proof is that before Obregón's inauguration, he sent a special railroad car to Juarez to pick up B.A. and Dixie. Among those boarding with the Packards were five other couples: Mr. and Mrs. Paul, Ygnacio Soto, James P. Harvey, and James

Álvaro Obregón and his son are in the center of this photo taken at Chapultepec Castle, Obregón's official residence in Mexico City. To the boy's right are Mabel Paul and Dixie Packard (large hat). Elbridge Graves is behind Dixie and Plutarco Elías Calles is third on her right.

Author's collection

S. Williams; as well as Francisco Elías, Rafael Gabilondo, Eduardo Gabilondo Sr. and Jr., and George Stephens. Harvey owned the Canario Copper Co. near Nacozari; Williams ran the Nacozari Railroad; and the five unaccompanied men were all border ranchers with political connections.

Another train, formed as an excursion from Nogales, took over a dozen other Douglas residents to Mexico City as well as people from as far away as Illinois.[64] Obregón met the Douglasites from the special train at Chapultepec Palace, had his photo taken with them the afternoon of Dec. 1, 1920, and was inaugurated that night.

After the festivities, the Packards and other Douglas residents returned home and resumed their lives. For B.A. that included traveling to Kyrene to see acreage Cottrell had planted in long-staple cotton, promoting First National, visiting his Herefords at the Hunt place, and dealing cattle with Elías, the Gabilondos and others.[65] It was a pattern he followed the rest of his life.

NOTES

1. Raat, Dirk W., *Revoltosos*. College Station, Texas: Texas A&M University, 1981, pp. 17-21.

2. "Mexican Political Prisoner Kidnapped," *International*, July 1, 1907.

3. "Douglas Is Stirred...," *Review*, July 3, 1907.

4. Arrested: "Maza, Shropshire, ...," *International*, July 3, 1907. Arraigned: "Maza And Local...," *International*, May 11, 1907. Release: "Sarabia Here...," *International*, July 13, 1907.
Transporting Sarabia back to the United States from his Sonoran prison was Arizona Rangers Capt. Harry Wheeler. Given that 10 years later Wheeler led the Bisbee Deportation, one wonders what Wheeler and Sarabia talked about on their train ride to Douglas.

5. "Agua Prieta In Hands...," *International*, April 14, 1911.

6. Graves: "Perfect Arrangements...," *International*, April 18, 1911. Pepper First National: "Stray Bullets...," *International*, April 18, 1911.

7. "Scouts Appear...," *International*, April 18, 1911; Christiansen, Larry D., "Bullets Across the Border, Part I," *The Cochise Quarterly*, Dec. 1974.

8. "Has Strenuous Trip...," *Dispatch*, Sept. 14, 1912; "Soto Recalls...," *Dispatch*,

Connections: The Life and Times of B. A. Packard

Sept. 20, 1939.

9. Hall, Linda B., *Álvaro Obregón*. College Station, Texas: Texas A&M University, 1981, pp.19-31.

10. El Tigre: "El Tigre Captured...," *Dispatch*, Sept 17, 1912. San Joaquin: Hall, pp. 31-4; "Federals and Rebels...," *Dispatch*, Sept. 21, 1912; "Thirty Men Killed...," *International*, Sept. 21, 1912.

11. Banquet: Hall, p. 35; and "3,000 Troops Start ...," *International*, Sept. 23, 1912. Second banquet: "Banquet Given ...," *International*, Nov. 13, 1912. That the Lucky Tiger Co. participated in the Gadsden banquet is apparent by the presence of James W. Malcolmson, consulting engineer for El Tigre. Although Packard isn't specifically mentioned in newspaper coverage, he certainly was in attendance, given his social predominance and connection to Walter Douglas, banquet host. That Packard was in Douglas the night of banquet is clear from "B.A. Packard Denies Interview," published in the Sept. 25, 1912 *Dispatch*.

12. Hotel: "Obregon Lived...," *Dispatch*, July 18, 1928. Obregón residency and bank account: Hall, p. 35.

13. Bonds: "Douglas City Funds...," *International*, Sept. 14, 1911. Payroll: "City News," *International*, May 11, 1911. Assets: "Report on...," *International*, Feb. 26, 1912*International*.

14. Douglas directors: ads in *Dispatch*, Nov. 22, 1910 and International, Dec. 21, 1912. Moctezuma directors: "Moctezuma Bankers Meet...," *International*, Jan. 18, 1910.

15. Cochise County Superior Court Civil Case No. 5081.

16. Grain: "Raise Fine Barley...," International, June 13, 1910; "From the Harvest Field," *International,* June 12, 1911. The barley returned almost 3,000 pounds per acre; the wheat 40 bushels per acre. Cottrell also sold alfalfa at $8 per ton.

Show: "Packard Planning...," Nov. 17, 1912 and "Packard Purchases...," Nov. 24, 1912, both *Dispatch*. A few head went to Rancho Mababi, which had been purchased by a British syndicate that undertook an ambitious development program terminated by the revolution. (*Borderland Chronicles* No. 15).

Dorothea: "Studying in Phoenix," *International*, Jan. 21, 1912.

17. Hostess: "Notes Of Society," *International*, Jan. 15, 1910 and April 30, 1910. First media use: "Daddy Packard...," *International*, July 22, 1911.

18. "Sold Stock...," *International*, Aug. 9, 1911.

19. Sonnichsen, pp. 255-6; "Returns From Tucson," International, Aug. 9, 1911. Previous horse-specific accidents were: lameness from colt in corral, *Epitaph*, Feb. 14, 1886; thrown by horse, *Tombstone*, July 14, 1886; broken ribs after thrown from buggy, *Prospector*, Sept. 17, 1897. Other Greene incidents drawing newspaper attention were: serious injury, *Tombstone*, Sept. 4, 1886; broken shoulder blade, *Prospector*, Feb. 9, 1892; stopping runaway,

Epitaph, Feb. 20, 1898.

20. "Packard Loses His Suit," *International*, Nov. 30, 1912. "Purchase of Western Sonora...," *Dispatch*, Feb. 23, 1931.

21. "Packard Uneasy," *International*, Jan. 21, 1912.

22. "Packard to Ranch," *International*, March 29, 1912; "Packard Following...," *International*, April 14, 1912.

23. "Col. Packard Brings...," *International*, Aug. 6, 1912.

24. "Rebels Left...," *Dispatch*, Sept. 4, 1912.

25. "Cattleman Says...," *International*, Feb. 25, 1913.

26. "Mexico Export Tax...," *International*, April 8, 1914; "Fifty Thousand Paid...," *International*, March 13, 1914.

27. "Carranza Refused...," *International*, March 4, 1914.

28. "Cattle Shippers Are Inconvenienced," International, Oct. 16, 1913.

29. "Cattle Cannot...," *International*, April 24, 1913.

30. Mumme, Stephen P., "Battle of Naco: Factionalism and Conflict in 1914-15." *Arizona and the West*, Summer 1979, pp. 157-86.

31. "Packard Central Figure...," *International*, Nov. 10, 1914.

32. "Cattle Baron...," Los Angeles Times, Nov. 8, 1914; "Took Bull By The Horns," *Olean Times Herald*, Nov. 10, 1914.

33. Telegram in possession of Watkins.

34. Hopkins, Ernest J., *Financing The Frontier.* Phoenix, Ariz.: The Arizona Printers, 1950, pp. 127-139.

35. "First National...," and "Report of the Condition...," *International*, both Nov. 6, 1914.

36. "J.B. Speed Sells...," *International*, Aug. 11, 1915. Bradford's experience included being an Illinois bank teller and working with Douglas real estate developer Elmo Pirtle. Bradford started his business by buying the real estate office of James B. Speed, a fellow Thirteen Club member.

37. "Succeeds Lawhon," *International*, Nov. 15, 1915. "Packard Named...," *Dispatch*, Nov. 14, 1915; "Branch Office...," *International*, Feb. 7, 1917.

38. "Soto Captures Burglar...," *International*, Feb. 11, 1915.

39. "Local News," *International*, July 26, 1915; and "Y. Soto Forms...," *International*, Sept. 16, 1915.

40. "The School Board Warns...," *International*, May 30, 1914.

41. "Succeeds Lawhon" and "Packard Named...," *Dispatch*, Nov. 14, 1915.

42. State fair: "Win Prizes," *Review*, Nov. 22, 1916. Sell cattle: "Hereford Cattle ...," *International*, May 26, 1916. Brogan: "Cans Tomatoes From His Farm," *Dispatch*, Oct. 25, 1912.

Connections: The Life and Times of B. A. Packard

43. "Arizona Bank & Trust...," *International*, Nov. 4, 1913.

44. "Packard Found Blameless...," International, Sept. 16, 1915.

45. "A Water Color," *International*, Aug. 29, 1913.

46. Interview with Winifred Ames, Nov. 20, 1996, Douglas, Ariz.

47. "Our Mining Heritage," *Pay Dirt Magazine*, December 1997.

48. Cochise County Deeds Book 66, pp. 73-77.

49. Hunt, Norman K., *The Killing of Chester Bartell*. Phoenix, Ariz.: Cowboy Miner Productions, 2006, pp. 13-16.

50. George: "Horse Thieves Are Active Now," *Dispatch*, April 5, 1908; "Border Cattlemen Lose Many Horses," International, April 6, 1908; 1904 Cochise County voting registration. Robert: "Texas Cattleman And Millionaire...," International, Jan. 25, 1919; Joan Jenkins Perez, "Slaughter, Christopher Columbus," *Handbook of Texas Online* (http://www.tshaonline.org/handbook/online/articles/fsl01), accessed April 07, 2013.

51. "'Babe' Thompson...," *International*, July 30, 1914. Cochise County Superior Court Probate Case No. 862.

52. "W.H. Neel...," *International*, Jan. 11, 1915; and "Thursday Will Be...," Jan. 12, 1915. Cochise County Superior Court Probate Case No. 1177. Cochise County Deeds, Book 16, pp. 518-30.

53. East and southeast: "Troops Pour...," Dispatch, Oct. 24, 1915. Cannons: "Big Guns...," *Dispatch*, Oct. 27, 1915. Reinforcements: "Rebel Leader...," *Dispatch*, Oct. 31, 1915. Recognition: "Learns For First Time...," *Dispatch*, Oct. 31, 1915.

54. "El Tigre Camp...," *International*, Dec. 6, 1915; "Slaughter Safe...," *International*, Dec. 27, 1915.

55. "Gen. Funston...," *International*, Dec. 4, 1915.

56. "Obregon Attends...," *International*, Dec. 6, 1915.

57. "Sonora Mexicans...," *International*, June 28, 1916; "Graves Recalls...," *Dispatch*, July 1, 1936.

Twenty years after the incident, Graves insisted the amount was $60,000. But perhaps his reticence overrode reality. The 1916 *International* says $162,000; a 1916 *Arizona Republic* article about the money's arrival mentions $160,000.

58. "First National...," Aug. 3, 1916; "New Quarters...," Oct. 11, 1916; "First National Bank...," Dec. 21, 1916; all *International*.

59. Hayden: "Society," Oct. 30, 1915; ball: "Society," March 17, 1917; tennis: "Dancing Stops...," Dec. 20, 1915; all *International*.

60. "Engagement Announced," June 11, 1918; "Society," June 28, 1918; "Visiting In Douglas," Jan. 9, 1919; "Maj. and Mrs. Parker...," Oct. 29, 1921; all *International*.

61. "International Commission...," *International*, June 11, 1919.

62. Situation survey for week of May 26, 1920, U.S. Bureau of Investigation case file, accessed Aug. 5, 2011 via www.footnote.com.

63. U.S. District Court for State of Arizona, Case nos. 12-25 and 12-19. "Soto Pleads Guilty...," and May 28, 1920; "Soto Pays $10,000 Fine...," June 3, 1920, all *International*; "Fine Soto...," *Dispatch*, June 3, 1920. Also *International*, May 19 and 27, 1920.

64. Special car: "Party Leaves...," *Dispatch*, Nov. 23, 1920. Another train: "Nearly Dozen ...," *Dispatch*, Nov. 4, 1920; "Five States ...," *Star*, Nov. 22, 1920.

65. Cotton: "Will Stay With Cotton," *International*, Dec. 10, 1920. Promote: "Christmas Club" ad, Dispatch, Dec. 5, 1920. Visit: "Looking Over Cattle," *International*, Nov. 4, 1920. Deal: "Shipping Beef Cattle," *International*, Feb. 1, 1921.

Final Years

"That's the way nearly all those old-timers was. Plumb sound and sweet inside no matter how they'd been scarred up by bad luck along the trail."
– *Thomas H. Rynning, 1866-1941, first captain of the Arizona Rangers*

The end of hostilities in the Mexican Revolution and World War I meant national copper demand dropped sharply. In 1918, Phelps Dodge smelted almost 187 million pounds of copper. In 1921, PD's production dropped to less than 22 million pounds.[1]

This dramatically affected Douglas' economy. PD reduced smelter workers' wages, then temporarily closed Nacozari and its Douglas smelter. C&A did much the same. The effects showed up in First National status reports. In late 1919, the bank's assets topped $2 million ($130 million today); in 1921, the amount fell to $1.5 million ($107 million).[2]

During autumn 1921, as a national recession gripped the country, Douglas merchants and businessmen cast about for something to boost the local economy. What they came up with was a county fair, and their "go to" person was the man who'd started the state fair 10 years before and still was a state fair commissioner – Col. Packard.

Early in September 1921, a Douglas fair committee elected Packard its president and announced its headquarters would be in First National. Various subcommittees organized displays, events, concessions and prizes. For exhibits, the Army loaned its quartermaster's buildings, which were around the YMCA at the western terminus of 10th Street – a block from First National.[3]

On Nov. 17-19, 1921, thousands of fair-goers listened to the Sonoran State Band (sent by recently named Gov. Francisco Elías), watched horse and automobile races, and toured booths displaying the best agricultural and merchandise efforts of Cochise County. The fair's continued success the next two years led to formal incorporation in 1924 and a move to grounds a mile north of Douglas.

One feature of the 1921 fair was a meeting of the Cochise County Pioneers Society, of which Packard was president.[4] By then, he had been a Cochise County resident for more than 40 years and was 74 years old.

B.A. Packard in the early 1920s
Author's collection

His health was good, although he'd begun to suffer from rheumatism. In 1919, he and Dixie went to Battle Creek, Mich., and its famous Kellogg Sanitarium where imposition of dietary rules and other practices promised sufferers relief from their ailments.

"The colonel heard all the talk of scientific food units, had the proper number of calories in each meal, rested, thought he starved part of the time, and now is in the best sort of health," reported the *Dispatch* after the Packards returned to Douglas. "As usual with Colonel Packard, he took advantage of his trip to buy a carload of prize-winning cattle for stock for his Phoenix ranch. He stopped off in Chicago and Kansas City to attend the Hereford sales."[5]

Connections: The Life and Times of B. A. Packard

The Herefords Packard bought that year stayed in Kansas on a place near Garden City, an area Packard had frequented since the 1890s drought. In addition to the Garden City land, Packard held shares in Kansas City's Royal Stock Show Association and a Kansas City bank. Packard connections also occupying Garden City area land included Slaughter and the Krentz family.

About 1906, the Krentzes began ranching in the San Bernardino Valley and took on management of Tovrea's meat market in Douglas as a way to sell their beef. A few years later, Tovrea resumed control of the establishment, which

Late in 1921, poker buddies John Slaughter, Hugh Conlon and B.A. Packard had their photo taken at the San Bernardino station cattle pens, northeast of Douglas on the El Paso & Southwestern Railroad. Slaughter had sold his herd and was shipping for the last time in his long life. Slaughter died the next year and Conlon three years later, but Packard lived another 14 years.

Cochise County Historical Society photo

became part of what eventually was one of the largest meat-processing businesses in America.[6]

Other Packard Herefords spent time in Kyrene before moving to the Paul Spur ranch, which Packard expanded eastward with judicious purchases. The same as his poker-playing buddy Slaughter, Packard had a personal gate in the border fence to facilitate moving cattle. The well-watered Kyrene farm, under Cottrell's supervision, continued to produce bounteous crops of long-staple cotton, grain and hay. Packard even cut hay on his Douglas house lot.[7]

Some of Packard's cattle brokering was for Mexican ranchers sending animals to Mexico City, where post-Revolutionary demand, and thus prices, had become high enough to make worthwhile the effort needed to send cattle south. In 1922, Elias shipped cattle under bond on the EP&SW from Douglas to El Paso, where they crossed for a trip south. Rafael Gabilondo drove small herds monthly from Sonora to Ojo Caliente, Chih., where the cattle boarded Mexican Central Railroad cars headed for Mexico City.[8]

While coping with the post-WWI recession, First National Bank underwent changes. Some were due to Pollack's disengagement. In 1921, business reversals in northern Arizona led him to reduce his role in First National. Bank directors elected Graves vice-president in place of Pollack. The next year, Pollack sold out to Packard, who remained bank president.[9]

Graves oversaw a rapid expansion that by 1922 had First National offices on Fort Huachuca and in Agua Prieta, Cananea and Nacozari. Ashley Sr. joined the board of directors and replaced Graves as cashier in what was the sixth largest national bank in Arizona. Ashley also took on management of the Roy Mine, overseeing installation of a new mill and concentration process.[10]

Ashley expanded his community role also. Douglas Country Club members elected him president in 1920, and he served on the Douglas school board. Appointed in 1919 to fill out the term of a member who moved away, Ashley was overwhelmingly re-elected in 1921.[11]

In 1924, Ashley ran for re-election without opposition – or so he thought. On voting day, someone noticed more people showing up at the polls than an uncontested election would warrant. Packard supporters suspected a write-in opponent and rushed about telling voters to go to the polls. Despite this, he lost by 57 votes to Katherine S. Harsell, whose husband, Thomas, was a CQ smelter foreman.[12]

Ashley's adherents questioned the legality of Mrs. Harsell's election without nomination and filed suit on his behalf. She responded with an interview in the *Dispatch* in which she said people asked her to run to provide a feminine influence on the school board.[13]

The implication that Ashley didn't understand a woman's point of view was belied by his management of First National. In the 1920s, the bank continued to have a large number of female employees and actively solicited female business. A First National ad in 1923 stated, "Women of Today are prominent in business and many carry savings accounts with this bank ... and will be rewarded with a happy and independent future."[14]

The suit, which challenged the Arizona Constitution's write-in voting procedure, was dismissed after transference to Graham County. The whole incident, as did his father's troubles with Ives 20 years before, convinced Ashley to stay out of politics. Another reason for this decision likely was his health.

Early in 1921, Ashley spent six weeks at a health resort in Paso Robles, Calif. Six months later, he went to another health resort and, upon his return to Douglas, underwent a stomach operation.[15] After recovering, he resumed managing First National, allowing B.A. to become involved in various endeavors.

One was a multi-year term on the Arizona Banking Association's executive committee. In 1920, Douglas hosted the association's convention, with Packard handling the preparations.

Packard also handled the arrangements for a state cattlemen's convention in 1915 Douglas and a Shriner's convention in 1917. He'd become a Mason in Portville and advanced through the degrees while in Arizona.[16]

Lawhon, before he left First National, served on the Douglas YMCA board of directors. Packard followed him onto that board, and this focused his charitable instincts on local causes. For instance, he was a generous donor to Douglas' Mexican Methodist Church building committee in 1920.[17]

Both father and son supported the Douglas Chamber of Commerce and Mines. In the early 1920s, that group promoted development of Cochise County highways to places such as the "Wonderland of Rocks." In the northern portion of the Chiricahua Mountains, the Wonderland features eroded rock spires and formations bearing fanciful names.

Packard's next-door neighbor, Dr. J.J.P. Armstrong, took photos of the formations, which First National displayed in its 1923 county fair booth. Packard must have prevailed upon his old political ally, Gov. George W.P. Hunt, because in 1924 that worthy visited the area. The following year, President Calvin Coolidge created the Chiricahua National Monument, which soon was drawing large numbers of tourists to the Wonderland.[18]

In 1922, Packard campaigned for a road to connect Agua Prieta and Cananea. He contacted Elías, who pledged government funds for construction. Douglas' Chamber of Commerce sponsored a motorcade of vehicles from Douglas and Agua Prieta to Cananea. Packard led the 50 cars because, for much of the way, the proposed road's route was on Ojo de Agua.[19]

Little resulted from this first effort (since Elías completed his term as governor), but in 1924 road-building interest revived. That's because excitement over the California oil boom seeped into the borderlands.

Packard went to Mexico City to see Obregón, who issued drilling permits to his old friend. Whittier Southern Oil Co., prominent in the Bakersfield area, sent an exploratory drilling crew to Ojo de Agua. No oil was found, but the venture accelerated northern Sonora road building.[20]

This activity kept B.A. and Dixie in Arizona when they probably wanted to travel and see Dorothea in Washington, D.C. She was there because John had been named Consul to the Assistant Secretary of War, and was director of surplus property sales as the country demobilized from WWI.[21]

On April 15, 1924, Dorothea participated in a ceremony dedicating placement of Arizona's stone (a block of petrified wood) in the Washington Monument. She unveiled the stone and sang "Arizona," the state's official anthem, written by Douglas residents Margaret Clifford and Maurice Blumenthal.[22]

"I am awfully thrilled over my experience of unveiling our beautiful Arizona stone,"

In 1924, Dorothea and John Parker stiffly posed for this photo in front of the Washington Monument after Dorothea sang the state song "Arizona" during a ceremony dedicating placement of her native state's stone in the monument.

Packard family photo

Dorothea wrote in a long letter to Dixie, "and I only wish you and Dad could have been here to witness it.

"The stone was veiled with flags and Arizona greens... . It was a lovely little ceremony and went off without a hitch. It was most thrilling and exciting for me to stand up and sing in the presence of the President of the United States and so many other notables.

"I got through it all right and wasn't as nervous as I was afraid I'd be. The Marine band orchestra played my accompaniment – and though I was inwardly quaking, no one knew it. It was one of the proudest moments of my life when I pulled up the flags and unveiled our beautiful Arizona stone."[23]

Another proud moment for B.A. undoubtedly was when he took grandson Ashley Jr. to "Onion" Miller's annual picnic. The picnic was the end of a long sequence of Packard connections.

The string started in 1921 when B.A. bought some land from Bruce Stephenson, an attorney who briefly partnered with Judge Doan after his son, Frank Sr., died from injuries suffered in a 1920 automobile accident. Frank Sr. was killed on the Bisbee-Douglas Highway less than two weeks after the judge helped dedicate the highway as Arizona's longest hard-surfaced road.[24]

The Stephenson property was in the Double Adobe area, where the Erie Cattle Co. headquarters had been 35 years before. B.A. added other parcels until he had a good-sized holding that hosted his Herefords, including the calf that received a ride to the Gadsden Hotel in Packard's Cadillac.[25] In 1924, the land gained value during the Valencia onion boom.

A leading enthusiast of Valencia onion cultivation was James T. "Tom" Hood. He was cashier of Lem Shattuck's bank before becoming a Douglas car dealer. Hood's wife, Mary, was a daughter of Peter Moore, the farmer who sold B.A. his place on the San Pedro in 1889. Tom and Ashley Sr. became better acquainted serving together on the Douglas school board.[26]

They also became officers of a group promoting Valencia onions. Tom's brother, Joe, a former Cochise County Sheriff, planted Valencias on land he owned near the C&A smelter, and Tom planted some on his own property. Others joined them, their truck farms dotting the Sulphur Springs Valley in a patchwork spread the Hunts had dreaded and avoided by moving to New Mexico.[27]

During September 1924, about 150 people attended a dinner put on by William G. Miller. His farm 1½ miles north of the Double Adobe School grew so many onions that neighbors nicknamed him "Onion." Miller's dinner became a yearly event, drawing politicians on the stump and voters wanting to hear them. In 1932, more than 1,200 people swarmed Miller's farm for the annual picnic.[28]

B.A. always attended Miller's picnic, and it was an event at which the elder statesman was welcome. His age, vast experience, long Cochise County residency and well-known humor made B.A. a welcome guest at any gathering and a prime choice to represent Douglas.

When Eddie Rickenbacker, famous race car driver and WWI ace, talked with Alfred Paul Sr. about investing in a mine, the Packards joined them at dinner. When famed humorist Will Rogers landed at Douglas Municipal Airport, B.A. was there to trade quips and talk business with him. When U.S. Vice-President Charles O. Curtis visited Douglas, B.A. greeted him, even though Curtis was a Republican.

An example of a Packard quip was when Frank M. King, associate editor of the *Western Livestock Journal*, kidded Packard about the paradox of being a banker and a poker player. Packard replied, "Well, Frank, there ain't much difference, only banking is legalized."[29]

Packard judged a parade of automobiles filled with bathing beauties as part of festivities marking the opening of the Douglas American Legion swimming pool near Joe Hood's place. Packard judged equine pulchritude in a Fort Huachuca horse show celebrating the 60th anniversary of the 10th U.S. Cavalry.[30]

Packard represented Douglas at meetings of the Bankhead National Highway and Broadway of America Associations. Both promoted hard-surfaced highways to link the nation, and the 20-plus miles of cement road between Bisbee and Douglas was a focal stretch for both associations. In 1925, the Bisbee-Douglas road became part of U.S. Highway 80.[31]

Packard didn't travel by highway in 1924 for a trip to New York; he went on the train as he always had. But his time in his native state was not the same as when he attended his long-lived grandmother's annual birthday celebrations. Rebecca (Rose) Packard, born in 1795, became one of those remarkable individuals who lived in three centuries. She did not die until 1903, when she was nine days short of her 109th birthday.[32]

Her death, plus his children living in Arizona, had eliminated Packard's regular trips to Cattaraugus County. So when he did return there in 1924, Packard got "a peculiar feeling of sadness ... in visiting the scenes of his childhood. He said that the boys and girls with whom he had grown up were all old men and women now and all seemed to have the blues, telling him of deaths among his old friends and making him exceedingly uncomfortable.

"He said that on two occasions ... he started out to visit the old homestead where he had been raised. It is sold now and occupied by strangers. He said that on both trips ... he experienced such a queer sensation upon nearing the house that he told the driver to go on down the road and did not enter the house.

"[Packard] said that everything seemed much the same as when he had lived there 40 or 45 years ago. He said that the hills and valleys had not changed ... but that an avenue of maple trees which he had planted in 1882 were great trees now where they had been but switches then."[33]

Although Packard's nostalgia was apparent, he was not afraid of change. In the late 1920s, he advocated removal of the county courthouse from greatly diminished Tombstone.

Additionally, he relinquished ownership of his Second Street property, where he'd lived with Ella, by allowing it to be sold for taxes.

"No one better than I could hark back to the 'good old days' and color a vote with sentiment," said Packard. "I got my Arizona start in Tombstone. I admit there is a considerable liking on my part for the old town. ... Things of this world do not stand still. Either we progress or we go backward."[34]

The same year as his New York trip, some of Packard's many friends gave him a party to celebrate his 77th birthday. An indication of the regard Douglasites had for Packard was this birthday party received newspaper coverage then, and for the next 10 years.[35]

Other Packard activities receiving newspaper coverage were B.A. and Dixie's trips. In 1927, they traveled to Georgia, staying with Dorothea and John at Fort Benning before going to Florida and Havana. The next year, the Packards cruised to Panama, again to visit Dorothea and John. As was his custom, Packard stopped off on his way home at the Democratic National Convention or Midwestern livestock shows. A couple of bulls he purchased spent time in the 10th Street house yard.[36]

Making the Packards' travel possible was the smooth way in which First National ran. Ashley, clearly being groomed to succeed his father, continued with management of First National's Douglas branch. Graves became so well-regarded within the banking industry that in 1929 he was elected a member of the Federal Reserve Board's 11th District advisory committee.[37]

Another connection string made B.A. a director of Valley National Bank.[38] That institution was created from The Valley Bank of Phoenix, which escaped closure in 1914 through the combined efforts of Packard and other Arizona bankers. In 1928, the "new" Valley Bank's president was Charles E. Mills. He was a taciturn Midwesterner nicknamed "El Indio" (the Indian) by Mexican miners at Phelps Dodge's Morenci, Ariz., operation, where Mills was superintendent.

Mills had one great friendship. It was with a man as brilliant and strongly silent as Mills. Louis D. Ricketts, Ivy League-educated but with years of hands-on experience, was America's premier mining engineer. In 1898, Ricketts built the world's first all-steel-and-concrete concentrator for PD in Nacozari. It was the Morenci prototype.

Nicknamed "El Palo Seco" (the dry stick) by Mexican workers for his lanky build,[39] Ricketts knew Packard at Nacozari and later when Ricketts lived in Warren. Ricketts appreciated their similarities – business expertise, independent thinking and unpretentiousness – enough to suggest Packard as a Valley director 20 years after its rescue.

This took some of Packard's time, but he remained involved in the day-to-day management of First National. That's plainly shown by bank advertising. An ad in the March 28, 1925 *Dispatch* displayed Packard's humor and philosophy.

"Said Uncle Silas," the ad began, "When I was young and full of pep, I made plenty of money and never had a care. I was as happy as a jay bird in a tree full of doodle bugs. Things changed as I grew older.

"No doubt there was a change. There always is. If you spend all as you go along, you are sure to find the going much rougher at the very time when you are least able to stand it. 'Come easy, go easy' is all right so long as things continue to come. After that, needy and dependent old age stares you in the face. Save a little as you go along and keep it in our bank. That is the sure remedy."

Other ads revealed Packard's personal philosophy while promoting his bank. "The happiest man is the busiest man," declared a Sept. 18, 1925 *Dispatch* ad. "He is ambitious to achieve; disposes to do; desires to serve; cheerfully meets difficulties; expects disappointments. The pleasure he enjoys from the results of his accomplishments pays back many times the disappointments. This man is known at the bank."

A Feb. 2, 1926 *Dispatch* ad declared, "To reach worthwhile places, it seems necessary to pass some stretches that test one's sticking power. Those who save money and keep on toward a fixed point usually reach it."

Packard emphasized saving during 1926, partially as good banking business but also in response to the Valencia onion bubble. Many who tried to grow Valencias in Cochise County were lured there by real estate promoters, who encouraged the newcomers to buy land on which to try dry farming. As Packard concluded years before, access to water was key to Arizona agriculture. Only growers such as Miller, who had windmills and pump jacks, successfully grew Valencias for more than a season or two.[40]

During the latter part of July 1927, Packard suffered a slight stroke. He survived, but the event scared both him and Dixie. They went to a Paso Robles health resort, where B.A. wrote Ashley Jr. and sent a check for his grandson's 11th birthday.

"My Dear Boy,

"Please find enclosed my check for eleven ($11.00) dollars, amount due tomorrow as per agreement made with you some years ago. Your birthday is to me a very important event for numberless reasons, one of which is my anxiety to see you a young man of importance, and as you know, my time is short. You must grow fast in every respect."[41]

Upon returning from California, Packard consolidated his Herefords at Paul Spur under foreman Felix Christiansen, a neighbor who'd replaced John D. Rust. Packard had previously directed Frank Hillman, Ojo de Agua foreman since 1917, to sell the ranch's corriente stock. Selling 5,000 head was a large undertaking and took more than a year to implement, but just as he had during the 1893 financial troubles, Packard sold at a time when prices were high.[42]

During 1928, Dixie and B.A. moved into 805 Ninth St. This house had a first floor bedroom – an important accommodation following Packard's stroke. He sold the 10th Street house to the

Cynthia F. Hayostek

During autumn of 1927, Dixie and Daddy hosted a family gathering upon his return to Douglas from a California health resort where he'd recuperated from a stroke. It afflicted Packard's left side, which Dixie is supporting; in his right hand Daddy holds his customary cigar. Ashley Sr. and Rachel with son Ashley Jr. are in top right photo. Burt Cottrell and his parents, Gertrude and Max Cottrell, are in bottom photo.

Packard family photographs

Company Of Mary, an order of Mexican nuns led by Mother Serrano, who'd been chased out of Mexico when Calles tried to reduce the Roman Catholic Church's influence.[43]

After Obregón finished his presidential term in 1924, Calles succeeded him. In 1928, Obregón was re-elected President. But before he assumed office, he was assassinated by a religious fanatic in the Cristero movement, which had sprung up following Calles' restrictions upon the church.

In 1929, the short-lived Escobar Rebellion arose and once again Ojo de Agua hosted insurgents besieging Naco. During an agricultural show at that time, Packard encountered Kelvin K. Henness, the Pinal County extension agent. Henness was accompanied by an acquaintance from Illinois who, to make conversation, asked Packard a naïve question: "Do you feed cattle?"

"No," replied Packard with a wry smile. "I feed Mexicans."[44]

Events in Mexico were not the only things that concerned Packard in the late 1920s. The national economy heating up to near-frenzy level obviously worried him. Packard told the *Dispatch* on July 3, 1927:

"During the past few years, the tide of money has flowed freely ... it has been a source of real concern among men who think and look ahead. The average citizen has been saving almost nothing for a rainy day.

"The banker [obviously Packard] has seen many people grow old without having laid away any money. He has seen them come into the bank and ask for a loan... [and] the banker knows this is a heartbreaking thing to witness. He doesn't want to see the people who live all around him in that fix... ."

Packard held onto this cautionary attitude even as First National assets grew in the late 1920s. In June 1929, First National's resources, for the first time since WWI, exceeded $2 million ($360 million today). The economic crash that shocked America during autumn 1929 took a while to reach Douglas.

Then it hit hard; the smelters shut down and First National's assets fell to $1.4 million. So 1930 for Packard was much the same as 1893 had been. He struggled with financial difficulties and personal loss.

That loss was Ashley Sr., who early in 1930 suffered a reoccurrence of his stomach affliction. B.A. took him for treatment in El Paso and then Los Angeles, but Ashley died from stomach cancer on May 7, 1930 at age 46. Rev. Simonson conducted his service in St. Stephen's, and the cortege to Calvary Cemetery included three cars carrying just floral tributes.[45]

B.A. "never fully recovered from the shock of the death of his only son," wrote King in the *Western Livestock Journal*. "He had trained the boy to take over his banking, cattle and other extensive businesses. At the time, he told me he didn't expect to live another year, but he kept carrying on... ."[46]

So did Ashley Jr. In September, he entered Shattuck School, which his father had attended 30 years before. Following his grandfather's example, Ashley persevered at Shattuck. In 1931, his best friend, Jack Davis, joined him at Shattuck.

They and Jack's younger brother, Herb, and Frank Doan's son, Frank Jr., were close friends. They saw each other in school and church and on special occasions such as Halloween when they went to the Graves' house to show Petra their costumes.

"I liked Ashley's dad," recalled Davis, "as he was interested in us boys. He liked to hike and tell stories. He taught us to make and fly kites.

"As we got older, Ashley and I were recruited as acolytes at St. Stephen's Church. This was not a chore as Rev. Simonson was a delightful man, very good with boys. In fact, we liked him so much we agreed to his tutoring us in Latin one whole summer.

"At about age 11, our fathers got us interested in Boy Scouts. They took us on our first camping trip in the Chiricahuas. The two dads hiked seven miles up the mountain while Ash and I rode burros.

"Ash's grandfather treated us pretty good too. He was an ample man with a large girth and well into his 70s then. Despite this, he was quite active and very sharp. He'd take us to his Paul Spur ranch in an old Dodge four-cylinder sedan that he used to herd cattle. When he did that, he'd let us ride anywhere on the car we wanted.

"Ashley's mother would have died. My mother would have forbidden me such outings if she had known, but our secret was safe with 'Daddy.'"[47]

B.A. kept going after Ashley Sr.'s death with activities he'd always enjoyed. He judged horse races at the state fair, celebrated the birth of twin Hereford calves, joined a Broadway of America motorcade, and encouraged Sonoran rancher Jose Ruiz in his road construction project between Agua Prieta and Bavispe.[48]

Another pleasure for Packard was the wedding of his granddaughter Louise on July 9, 1932. She'd obtained a degree from Alfred University before marrying Russell W. Henness, whose brother had received a sample of Packard's humor in 1929 when he said he "fed" Mexicans.[49]

After Ashley Sr.'s death, B.A. searched for a replacement on First National's staff and board of directors. Assistant cashier E.E. Friday received promotion, and Floyd C. Kimble joined the board. A cattleman whose registered Herefords challenged the dominance of Packard's animals in southwestern shows, Kimble was the third of three directors joining the board as the Great Depression got underway. The other two were Harry A. Clark, Douglas smelter superintendent following the merger of PD and C&A, and Ben Levy, Douglas department store owner.[50]

As a veteran of panics and recessions in 1873, 1893, 1907 and 1921, Packard advised borderlands residents to "think more and talk less" about America's economic difficulties. "If you must talk about conditions, know what you are talking about and try to say something encouraging.... . Quit wearing the old shoes to save money. Buy a new pair. Buy the usual amount of clothing and other goods for your money keeps circulating that way and keep business normal [which] is the best thing you can do."[51]

First National's new directors plus stalwarts Dawe and E.W. Adamson worked with Packard and Graves to get First National through the worst of the Great Depression. Thousands of banks failed in the early 1930s, including Arizona Southwest Bank, a Tucson-based firm that became Douglas' third financial institution in 1926.

On June 22, 1931, Arizona's Superintendent of Banks closed Arizona Southwest to protect "depositors from loss because of depleted reserves." First National, with almost $2 million in

Packard's enthusiasm for registered Hereford cattle is apparent in this photo as he displays a polled animal. Packard helped found the Kansas City Livestock Show and was elected to the American Hereford Breeder's Hall of Fame.

Packard family photo

assets, and Bank of Douglas, with almost $3.4 million, did not face that problem, but were temporarily closed in 1933.[52]

Just days after taking office in 1933, President Franklin D. Roosevelt declared a bank holiday so provisions of the quickly passed Emergency Banking Act (EBA) could take effect without a panic developing. The EBA permitted the U.S. Treasury Department to reopen previously closed banks, and authorized formation of the Federal Deposit Insurance Corporation, eliminating the risk that had always been part of savings accounts by insuring deposits.

Roosevelt's holiday created a division between Douglas' two remaining banks. On Friday, March 3, Packard said First National, as a federal bank, would follow Roosevelt's directive as issued through Arizona Gov. Benjamin B. Moeur and not open on Monday, March 6. James S. Douglas, president of Bank of Douglas, directed cashier John Crowell to keep its doors open.[53]

Douglas declared a bank holiday was unneccessary in the town that bore his father's name, especially since "misfortune has come to Arizona through the action of the adjoining states." Douglas insisted Moeur had no legal basis for issuing the decree.

Packard agreed a holiday wasn't needed, but said Moeur had the power to publish the decree. Packard added, "Fairness could be had only when all banks observed" the closure.[54]

There was much talk about scrip as the holiday lengthened.

"I anticipate that when those in authority ... get the plans for issuance of scrip worked out," said Graves, "we will be much better satisfied around business generally than we are now. We are keeping our doors open during the usual banking hours and allowing our customers or anyone who so desires to come in and get change or visit."[55]

On March 15, banking business resumed in Douglas and across the nation.

"We will carry on along the usual lines and will be glad to see and to accommodate our customers and the public as usual," said Graves. "We have been cognizant all of the time that our bank needed no holiday because at all times we have been a solvent concern and have neither asked for nor needed any protection."[56]

After the holiday, many Douglas residents, the same as other Americans, redeposited into their local banks cash they'd previously stripped out, and the country began a slow recovery. Just four days later, Packard suffered another personal blow.

On March 19, John was killed near Petersburg, Va., along with two other officers. All were on Army business and en route to Washington, D.C. when their Army plane caught fire and crashed.[57]

Dorothea returned to Douglas and moved in with B.A. and Dixie. She started working in First National and registered to vote as she reintegrated herself into the Douglas community.

"Dr. F.T. Wright lured her to the city hall," wrote Nichols, "and induced [Dorothea] to register to vote as a Republican, although she was not a qualified voter in Arizona at the time. When her father heard about it, he immediately took his daughter to task and gave her a long lecture about disgracing the family traditions. Daddy declared

The ravages of BA's stroke show in this 1930s portrait.

Packard family photo

that he would challenge her vote if she attempted to go to the polls, as a last resort to save the family honor."

Nicholas said, "I heard Dorothy and Dr. Wright discussing the incident ... years after it happened. Dr. Wright, with his characteristic frankness, said he was always ashamed of his rash act."[58]

At First National, Dorothea provided Daddy with eyes and ears when he couldn't get to the bank. His visits to health resorts became more frequent, but his concern for Douglas and its residents remained strong. In the early 1930s, he became involved in cattlemen's drought aid, and donated whole beefs to Douglas relief agencies.[59]

During this time, Packard deepened his friendship with Simonson. He too was at the end of his career, which included almost 30 years as rector of St. Stephen's and services in Nacozari and along the borderlands. The two friends held lengthy, philosophical conversations as they discussed current events and their long lives, which were reflected in Daddy's public pronouncements.

He talked about his admiration for President Woodrow Wilson and his Progressive ideals because he'd promoted "the welfare of humanity." Packard felt humanity was best served by application of the Golden Rule and "if it were always applied, little more would be required to make this a world of peace and happiness."[60]

He also believed in counting his blessings, large and small. On his 87th birthday, a reporter visited Daddy in First National.

"[U]pon Colonel Packard's desk stood a bouquet provided by the employees of the bank with an appropriate note and upon the floor was a bouquet of exceptional beauty... . There were several messages, letters and telegrams from friends at distant points.

"As he pointed to the flowers and the messages, Colonel Packard smiled and remarked, 'Hasn't a fellow who has been blessed with 87 interesting years and still has friends that send him those things, have something to be happy about on a birthday?'"[61]

Not long before Daddy spoke those words, Ashley Jr.'s many and varied activities, including leadership of Shattuck's silent drill team, caught the attention of Capt. (later General) Lewis C. Beebe, the school's military instructor. He recommended Ashley as Shattuck's honor appointee to the U.S. Military Academy, and Ashley went there. Davis also continued his schooling in upstate New York at Cornell University, and the two friends stayed in touch.[62]

On Jan. 5, 1935, Ashley wrote:

> Dear Granddad,
>
> It does not seems possible to me that I have been at the Academy for six months or that it has been exactly a year since I was last in Douglas.
>
> The "plebes" have just finished the Christmas holidays and we have started in the regular routine again. At times the routine is a trifling tiring, but there are many interesting events to break the monotony. Our Christmas holiday started on Dec. 22 and lasted until Jan. 2. During that time, all the upper classmen were gone and we had the Academy entirely to ourselves. We had no duties to perform, so we managed to catch up on sleep and get better acquainted among our classmates. There were dances every night, which made the evenings enjoyable for the young ladies present were good dancers and good lookers to boot.
>
> On Christmas, I was invited to the quarters of a major who was born in Phoenix. ... He is married and has a young daughter whom I escorted to one of the dances. The family are very nice, and the dinner which Mrs. Felch, the major's wife, cooked was delicious. It reminded me a good deal of home. ...
>
> I guess everyone is very happy that Louise had a baby girl. It must be quite a thrill to be a great grandfather. Congratulations! I just received a letter from mother telling

of her visit up to Tempe. She says the baby is very good looking, so it must be taking after its mother. Aunt Trude and Uncle Max wrote me before Christmas and she seemed quite worried about Uncle Max. I am sorry to hear that he is worse. ...

I see by the Dispatch that a good heavy rain fell last week. Glad that rain has finally come and I'm sure next year's hay crop will be better than it has been the first part of last year. Did the rain harm any of Uncle Max's lettuce crop? ...

Please give my love to Aunt Dixie and Aunt Dottee. Whenever you can spare a moment, please write. I promise my correspondence shall be more regular hereafter.

Much love,

Ashley[63]

The correspondence did not become regular because Packard experienced an attack of pleurisy in February. He spent 10 days in the hospital before going home in time to listen to the radio broadcast of the inaugural Santa Anita Derby since, he declared, "a hoss race" still had the power to thrill him. A few days later, pneumonia set in and Daddy died March 12, 1935.[64]

His bank, all Douglas stores and city hall closed the afternoon of his funeral, which filled St. Stephen's to overflowing. Simonson preached from Ecclesiastics: "A good life hath but a few days, but a good name endureth forever." An additional 250 people who stood outside the church during the service joined the cortege to Calvary Cemetery, where Packard was buried in the family plot next to his son.[65]

Tributes poured in from all of Packard's connections. "I am profoundly touched by the passing of my good friend for whom my affection never wavered through all the long years," cabled Mossman.

"Just learned of your misfortune. You have our deepest sympathy but we will all soon be with Daddy," telegraphed Frank Moson, Greene's stepson.

"To express to you our real feeling in your loss of our dear old 'Daddy' Packard, it would indeed be difficult for the words are inadequate," wrote Honor G. Moeur, the governor's wife, to Dixie. "He was so good, kind and such a true friend, a friendship we greatly valued and seldom find. He left you so many monuments to his memory, which I know will be a great comfort... ."

Among the monuments Packard left were his many connections. Pollack mentioned these in a Nov. 29, 1913 letter to his colleague following the death of Packard's former secretary, Lewis Krueger.

"I have you in mind this morning and know that the loss of an old time friend means as much to you as any man that I ever knew," Pollack wrote. I "believe that it is such a great gift given us which we do not, in this age of rush, appreciate as much as we should. I know that you appreciate your friendships and know that the loss of a dear friend is something that comes to you, especially at the present time of life, with a good deal of shock.

"This world is full of people that the word friendship is foreign to ... and all they have in this world is simply acquaintance but never friends. You are very fortunate indeed in friendships that you are able to form because it is more or less a test of a man's character and you are especially fortunate."[66]

NOTES

1. Cleland, Robert Glass, *A History of Phelps Dodge*. New York: Alfred A. Knopf, 1952, pp. 199 and 302.

2. Reduction: "Smelter Wages...," International, Dec. 11, 1920. Ceased: "Phelps Dodge Will Stop...," *International,* March 29, 1921 Assets: "Report of

the Condition...," *International*, Nov. 17, 1919 and Dec. 31, 1921

3. "Col. Packard Heads...," Sept. 8, 1921; "Cochise Fair Assc. Appoints...," Sept. 9, 1921; "Buildings Loaned...," Sept. 27, 1921; all *International*.

4. "Cochise County Pioneers...," *International*, Oct. 3, 1921.

5. "Col. B.A. Packard...," *International*, Aug. 25, 1919; and "Col. Packard Is Back...," Oct. 8, 1919.

6. Packard in Garden City: *International*, Aug. 1, Oct. 26, 1921, and March 23, 1922. Slaughter and Krentz: *International*, April 25 and Sept. 25, 1916; May 23 and Oct. 21, 1921. Tovrea: *International* ad Oct. 28, 1916.

7. Kyrene: "Shipping Cattle," *International*, Nov. 28, 1922. Expansion: Cochise County Deeds Book 67, p. 49; Book 107, pp. 51-2; Book 109, p.322; and Book 112, p. 316. Gate: Oct. 8, 2008 letter from James E. Christiansen, College Station, Texas. Bounteous crop: *International*, April 30, 1920 and March 15, 1922. House lot hay: "First Alfalfa Cutting," International, May 8, 1922.

8. International, Jan. 17, 1921, Aug. 14 and Oct. 4, 1922.

9. "Pollack Company Creates...," *Dispatch*, Nov. 29, 1920; "First National Bank Holds...," *International*, Jan. 11, 1921; George Kelly column, *International*, Dec. 7, 1922.

10. Expansion: "First National After...," *International*, Aug. 26, 1921 and "First National Has...," Jan. 3, 1922. Rank: *International*, Nov. 13, 1920. Roy: "Returns From Mexico," *International*, Jan. 13, 1920, and "Cinco De Mayo...," May 25, 1920.

11. Country Club: "Country Club Directors," *International*, March 10, 1920. Fill out: "Packard Is New School Trustee," *International*, April 14, 1919. Re-elected: "Packard Wins...," *International*, Oct. 31, 1921.

12. "Mrs. Harsell Voted...," Dispatch, Oct. 26, 1924.

13. "Harsell Case Set...," *Dispatch*, Jan. 24, 1925; "Woman School Trustee...," *Dispatch*, March 15, 1925.

14. Employees: Nov. 6, 1922 and Sept. 12, 1923; ad: June 23, 1923; all *International*.

15. Health: March 10, April 18, Sept. 8, 23 and 28, 1921, all *International*.

16. Bank: Sept. 14, Nov. 11 and Nov. 13, 1920, all *International*. Cattlemen's: Jan. 3, 5, 6, 1915, all *International*. Shrine: April 13, 14, 1917, all *International*.

17. "An Historical Sketch," Young Men's Christian Association Railroad Branch, May 1917, no printer listed. Photocopy in author's possession. Cash book of Mexican Methodist Episcopalian Church, ca.1920. Photocopy in author's possession.

18. Both support: "Nominations...," *International*, April 22, 1914. Photo display: "Commercial Exhibits ...," *International*, Oct. 12, 1923. Highway, tourism: "Arizona's Longest Hard-Surfaced Highway and the Doan Family Tragedy," *Borderland Chronicles* No. 14, pp.17-18.

19. *International*, March 11, April 18, April 29 and May 1, 1922.

20. "Contract Closed...," *International*, Jan. 15, 1924; "B.A. Packard's Trip...," *Dispatch*, March 11, 1924; "Road To Oil Well ...," *Dispatch*, May 24, 1924.

21. "Major and Mrs. Parker...," *International*, Oct. 29, 1921.

22. Clark, Ethel Maddock, *Arizona State History of the Daughters of the American Revolution*. Greenfield, Ohio: Greenfield Printing & Publishing Co., 1929, pp. 32-35.

23. Letter dated April 22, 1924 in possession of Watkins.

24. *Borderland Chronicles* No. 14, pp. 10-11; 1925 Douglas City Directory.

25. Cochise County Deeds Book, p. 401; Book 92, p.351; Book 98, p. 491.

26. Bailey, Lynn, "Lemuel Shattuck," pp. 66-7; 1922 Douglas City Directory; Cochise County Marriages Book 3, p. 261; Wiggins, Genevieve, "A History of Douglas the Douglas Public Schools 1901-1965," unknown publishing information, p. 63.

27. "Syndicate To Promote...," *Dispatch*, Sept. 26, 1924. "Ten Acres...," *Dispatch*, April 12, 1925.

28. *"Onion Miller Gives...," Dispatch, Sept. 23, 1924.* "Colonel Packard Was Representative...," *Dispatch*, Aug. 24, 1932.

29. Rickenbacker: *Dispatch*, March 3, 1920. Rogers: "Rogers Arranges...," *Dispatch*, Nov. 8, 1931. Curtis: "Douglas People Greet...," Dispatch, Nov. 17, 1931. King quip: *Epitaph*, April 4, 1935.

30. "Name Judges...," *Dispatch*, May 13, 1924. "10th Cavalry's Horse Show...," *Dispatch*, July 28, 1926.

31. Bankhead: March 27 and April 2, 1918; "Goes To Phoenix Tuesday," April 22, 1922, all *International*. Broadway: "Packard, Home...," *Dispatch*, April 24, 1928; *Borderland Chronicles* No. 14, pp. 13-4, 19.

32. Ashley B. Packard, Lion's Bay, B.C., Canada.

33. "Col. Packard Returns...," *Dispatch*, July 15, 1924.

34. "B.A. Packard, Pioneer...," *Dispatch*, Nov. 3, 1929.

35. "B.A. Packard Celebrates...," *Dispatch*, Nov. 1, 1924.

36. *Dispatch*, Feb. 26, 1926; March 4, 1927; June 8, 1928; and Dec. 27, 1929; all *Dispatch*.

37. "Douglas Banker...," *Dispatch*, June 21, 1929.

38. "B.A. Packard Is Elected...," *Dispatch*, Jan., 19, 1928.

39. Hopkins, *Financing The Frontier*, pp.56-60.

40. "Valencia Onion...," Dec. 4, 1924; April 21 and June 17, 1925 ads; all *Dispatch*.

41. Letter dated Aug. 20, 1927 in possession of Watkins.

42. "Packard Sells...," Dispatch, May 21, 1927.

43. *Dispatch*, "Packard Home...," Jan. 20, 1928; and "Packards Move...," March 15, 1928.

44. Watkins interview.

45. "Ashley Packard, Son...," *Bisbee Ore*, May 8, 1930; "Ashley Packard, Douglas...," Dispatch, May 8, 1930. "Casket Is Hidden...," *Dispatch*, May 19, 1930.

46. King, Frank M., "Colonel Packard Will Be Missed," *Western Livestock Journal*, March 28, 1935.

47. John H. Davis, Jr. reminiscence written Sept. 5, 1991. Copy in author's possession.

48. Judges races: Dispatch, Nov. 11, 1928, Nov. 11, 1931, and Oct. 23, 1932. Twins: "Packard's Purebred Cow...," Dispatch, *Dispatch*, May 27, 1932. Bavispe road: "Excursion Trip...," *Dispatch*, Aug. 26, 1933.

49. "Gertrude L. Cottrell ...," *Dispatch*, July 31, 1932.

50. "First National Bank Fills Vacancy," July 1, 1930; "Clark Is Made...," Jan. 10, 1929; "Report of Condition...," Jan. 8, 1930; all *Dispatch*.

51. "Colonel Packard Says...," Dispatch, Sept. 7, 1930.

52. "Arizona Southwest...," *Dispatch*, June 23, 1931. "Report of the Conditions of The Bank of Douglas and First National Bank," *Dispatch*, Jan. 7, 1931.

53. "Banking Holiday...," *Dispatch*, March 3, 1933.

54. "Scrip May Be Used ...," *Dispatch*, March 4, 1933.

55. "Douglas Bankers Awaiting...," Dispatch, March 8, 1933.

56. "Local Bankers...," *Dispatch*, March 15, 1933.

57. "Officers Killed," *Dispatch*, no date 1933; "Three Officers Killed In Fall," unknown date and publisher, newspaper clippings in possession of Watkins.

58. Nichols, *Dear Old Cochise*.

59. Health resorts: Dispatch, March 6, 1931; April 10, Oct. 23 and Dec. 23, 1932. Drought relief: "Drought Relief ...," *Dispatch*, June 13, 1934. Give beef: *Dispatch*, Feb. 6, 1932 and Aug. 26, 1933.

60. "...Tells Kiwanis Club...," *Dispatch*, March 4, 1932.

61. "Colonel Packard Says...," *Dispatch*, Nov. 2, 1934.

62. Davis interview.

63. Letter in possession of Watkins.

64. "Packard's Old Friend ...," *Dispatch*, Feb. 23, 1935. "Packard Is Near Death," *Dispatch*, March 12, 1935. "B.A. Packard's Long Career...," Dispatch, March 13, 1935.

65. "Douglas Honors...," March 14, 1935, and "Packard Funeral...," March 15, 1935, both *Dispatch*.

66. Telegrams and letters in possession of Watkins.

Epilogue

Packard set up his estate to benefit Dixie. It was first administered by Graves and then Pollack,[1] who sold three major pieces of Packard's realm within two years of his death. The first to go was the Paul Spur ranch to Walter E. Holland in 1935.

Holland had worked closely with Thomas Edison to develop alkaline storage batteries, which led to an executive position with Philco Radio Co. Holland's daughter, Virginia, married Alfred Paul Jr. Holland called his place Rancho Sacatal and stocked it with Herefords whose showability would have gained B.A.'s approval.[2]

In the early 1960s, Alec Clarkson, inventor of an autopilot still used today, bought the ranch. Some acreage had been sold, including a portion to Arthur Bergman that his brother donated in 1962 to become the main Cochise College campus. Rancho Sacatal remained in the Clarkson family until the early 1990s.

The second piece of Packard's holdings sold was Ojo de Agua in 1936. The buyers were brothers Daniel and Kemper Marley of Phoenix. Daniel's first wife, Esther, was a sister of Frank Hillman, Packard's last Mexico foreman.[3]

Daniel kept Ojo de Agua until his 1958 death, after which it was sold to Armando Varela Sr. His son, Armando Jr., ran the ranch and married Janet Glenn, a great niece of Will Glenn, recipient of a First National loan in 1913.

The third major component of Daddy's empire sold was the bank. In 1937, First National Bank of Douglas became the 19th institution in the Valley National Bank chain. Graves retired when Valley took over. Petra had died in 1934, so Elbridge and Sadie moved to California.[4]

When Valley bought First National, it bought only bank operations. The estate retained the building, and transformed the upstairs offices into apartments. Pollack helped oversee this conversion shortly before his 1938 death.$_5$

In 1946, Valley National bought the building, remodeling it in early 1960s, and then demolishing it in 1971. A new modernistic structure replaced Daddy's bank that year.

Following Pollack's death, Dorothea became executor of her father's estate. She and Dixie lived in the Ninth Street house until Dorothea died in 1944. Then Dixie moved into a Gadsden Hotel apartment. She held forth in the lobby, displaying her own brand of Packard humor.

One day, austere Sam Applewhite, James Douglas' former secretary who'd gone into real estate, walked into the Gadsden wearing a cowboy hat. Someone asked Dixie if he was a rancher. "No," deadpanned Dixie. "He's a Presbyterian."

Dixie died in 1947, and was buried in the Packard family plot, alongside Gertrude and Max, who'd died in 1936 and 1940. That left Rachel as the sole Packard family representative in Douglas. She'd resumed teaching and become best friends with the Davis brothers' mother, Ethel.

Ashley Jr. graduated from West Point in 1938, entered the Army Air Corps and married Francesca "Frenchie" Hagood, daughter of then-retired Maj. Gen. Johnson Hagood. Ashley advanced through the ranks, becoming a lieutenant colonel in 1944 while chief of pilot training in the Army's western flying training command.

Ashley B. Packard Jr., 1944 portrait
Packard family photo

Late that year, he went to Guam to command the 475th Fighter Group and earn a Bronze Star. In 1945, despite hospital care and Rachel's ministrations, Frenchie died of Crohn's disease and was buried in South Carolina.

After the war, Ashley assumed command of the 27th Fighter Escort Wing, SAC. He met Eve Medwid, an Army nurse with Canadian roots, and married her. The couple had two sons, Ashley named for his father, and John, named for his father's best friend.

Late in 1950, the 27th went to Korea and that Cold War conflict. There, the unit racked up over 10,000 hours of combat flying time in less than six months. Ashley Jr. was in Japan arranging his command's transfer back to the United States when the plane in which he was riding crashed. He was buried in the family plot.

It may thus seem that B.A. Packard has no lasting legacy, but that's not true. His other grandson, Burt Cottrell, graduated from MIT and became a noted electrical engineer who participated in the development of radar, the tests at Bikini Atoll and creation of the Technicolor process.

Daddy's benevolence is part of the heritage behind the work of his great granddaughter, Dorothea Watkins. She established Wings of Angels Foundation to alleviate the suffering of Mexico's extreme poor in the Arizona-Sonora borderlands.

The foundation's initial project in 1997 was Mexico's first class teaching Mexican sign language to deaf children and their families; classes are now taught throughout Mexico. Wings of Angels partnered with Douglas and Utah Rotarians to offer Mexico's first-ever EMT training; these classes are also spreading across Mexico.

Wings of Angels provides wheelchairs and prosthetics to those who have none. The foundation also focuses on families of the medically needy, providing solar hot water heaters and sometimes even houses, through Rotary partnerships.

Another part of Packard's legacy were his protégées. One of the first notable ones was H. Merle Cochran, who came to Arizona for his health in 1910 and punched cows on Packard's ranch. In 1913, Cochran graduated from the University of Arizona and joined the State Department. By 1930, he was the American Consul in Paris.[6]

Other Daddy protégées got their start in the financial world at First National.[7] The most prominent was Soto. After founding the International Commission Co. and an Agua Prieta bank, he became a member of the Calles administration in Mexico City. In 1929, Soto returned to the borderlands, where he founded another bank, promoted international tourism and participated in building the Agua Prieta-Cananea road.

He also founded Agua Prieta's public utilities company and Sonora's first Portland cement franchise. In the 1930s, that firm's cement built Angostura Dam, which became the foundation of Sonora's vigorous produce-growing industry today.

In 1949, Sonoran voters elected Soto their governor,[8] and it all started because Packard spotted a capable young man in a Sonoran hamlet almost 40 years before. That Soto recognized this is clear from his condolence letter written to Dixie upon Packard's death.

Because B.A. "lived so many years and [was] always doing so much good for so many of us," Soto wrote, "he is entitled to a long rest. As for myself, I know his memory will live with me until my time is up. He was awfully good to me – Good old Daddy."

NOTES

1. Cochise County Probate 4276, Clerk's office.
2. "Packard Ranch becomes...," *Dispatch*, June 2, 1935.
3. "Packard Sonora 100,000-Acre Ranch...," Dispatch, July 8, 1936.
4. "Graves Quits Banking ...," *Dispatch*, Aug. 19, 1938. "Miss Petra Graves...," *Dispatch*, April 29, 1934.

5. "Packard Estate...," *Dispatch*, June 5, 1937. "Pollack Funeral...," *Dispatch*, March 3, 1938.

6. "Former Resident...," *Dispatch*, June 15, 1930.

7. Packard's banking protégées included: Bradford, teller 1915, Arizona State Bank Examiner 1920; Friday, assistant cashier 1928, Federal Land Bank executive 1933; M.L. Hartley, teller 1915, Phoenix Title & Trust executive 1929; Eugene C. Hempel, receiving teller, 1918, Bank of Douglas department manager, 1953; Lawhon, assistant cashier 1909, Phoenix Chamber of Commerce president 1921; Michael McCue, teller 1929, Douglas business owner 1946; E.C. Piper, assistant cashier 1912, Douglas business owner 1940; Fred P. Ramirez, bookkeeper 1916, cashier Cananea Merchants Bank 1924; W.C. Winegar, assistant cashier 1907, vice-president Sonora Bank & Trust 1927.

8. Hayostek, Cindy, "Two Exceptional Men of the Borderlands and Electrical Power, *Borderland Chronicles* No. 11.

Cynthia F. Hayostek

Connections

"We don't accomplish anything in this world alone ... and whatever happens is the result of the whole tapestry of one's life and all the weavings of individual threads from one to another that creates something."
— Sandra Day O'Connor, former Supreme Court Justice

During his lifetime, Packard and his connections helped develop a distinctive culture in the Arizona-Sonora borderlands. They conducted their business and lived their lives in a region that just happened to include an international border.

Today, many recognize that the borderlands hosts its own culture – neither Mexican nor American, but Border. Packard and his associates helped create a place where languages and lifestyles meld, where residents share a strong entrepreneurial and self-reliant outlook, and where interaction counts more than exclusion.

Even a brief review of the biographies that follow makes it clear how Packard and his connections wove together a community that still links Arizona and Sonora with a borderlands ethos that emphasizes inclusion rather than marginalization.

The dates below in parenthesis are followed by a letter. The letter refers to newspaper from which the citation came. Letters are: "C," *Tucson Citizen*; "D," *Douglas Dispatch*; "E," *Tombstone Epitaph*; "I," *Douglas International*; "N," *Tombstone Nugget*; "O," *Bisbee Ore*; "P," *Tombstone Prospector*; "R," *Bisbee Review*; "R-E," *Tombstone Record-Epitaph*; "S," *Arizona Daily Star*; "T," *The Tombstone*; "WN," *Weekly Tombstone Nugget*; "WO," *Bisbee Weekly Ore*. Example: (29JY1891P) would be July 29, 1891 *Tombstone Prospector* issue.

Birth and death certificates accessed on www.genealogy.az.gov. Cochise County voting registration books held in Recorder's office, Bisbee, Ariz.

Adams, John C. born 15SP1863 to John Quincy and Margaret Adams in Kingston, Ont. Reared in Illinois; Chicago attorney 1890-96. After wife, Anna C. Dimick, needed better climate, moved to Phoenix where built Adams Hotel 1896. After it burned 1910, he rebuilt to include popular bar dubbed "third legislative branch." Phoenix Mayor 1899-1901, Phoenix Postmaster 1898-1902; founder Phoenix Chamber of Commerce and Arizona State Fair; director of both. Died 09MY1926 Phoenix. Only child, Margaret (Mrs. Foster Rockwell), managed hotel until she became Republican National Committeewoman. Her son, John, was third-generation manager. Hotel demolished 1973 but new owner rebuilt 1975; now part of Marriott chain.

Sources: McClintock, Arizona Vol. III. Peplow, Edward H., "Memories Of The Old Adams," Phoenix Magazine, May 1975. Sloan, Richard E., edit., History of Arizona, Vol. 3. Phoenix, Ariz.: Record Publishing Co., 1930.

Adamson, Edward William born 23SP1879 Cass City, Mich. Graduate University of Michigan; arrived in Douglas 1906 as C&A physician. Superintendent 40 years of Cochise County Hospital; First National director. He and wife, Anna, had no children. Died 14JY1968. A scholarship bearing his name is given every year to Douglas High School graduate hoping to become physician.

Sources: Hayostek, Cindy, Borderland Chronicles No. 13, 2011.

Angius, John Basilic (Ivo Vasov) born 28AP1858 in Adriatic coastal village on Balkan Peninsula. Emigrated to U.S. 1874; became citizen 1880 Storey County, Nev. Tombstone merchant 1881-89; to Bisbee ca.1889. Operated several businesses, most notably Angius Hotel, which also held mercantile and first Bank of Bisbee office. Director: Bank of Bisbee, Bisbee Improvement Co., Bisbee Lumber Co., Bisbee Publishing Co. On first Bisbee City Council 1902; active in Serbian Orthodox Church. Died 24AG1904 Bisbee (26AG1904R). Married Stana Medigovich; five children. Eldest, Dan, served on Bisbee City Council and eight terms as Arizona State Senator.

Sources: McClintock, Arizona. Hart, Mary N., "Merchant and Miner," Arizona Journal of History, Autumn 1980. 1902 Cochise County voting registration.

Aston, George W. (misspelled Askin or Astin) born June 1866 Texas to John Monroe Aston and second wife, Jane (Riley). Largely reared by half-brother John, after father died ca.1868 and Jane remarried. In 1886, George accompanied John to Cochise County, where they incorporated Reloj Cattle Co., headquartered near today's Nicksville. In 1890, married Elmiretta "Mittie" Ann Kelly, daughter of Tombstone lawman Jim Kelly. Four children. George shot 29DC1901 during prolonged scuffle in saloon tent in Brown's Canyon, on Huachuca Mountains' east side. George was one of six men playing poker for drinks in unlit tent. He was only one killed in fight occurring after Albert Benningfield uttered racial slur and firearms came into play. Ramon Moreno and Cruz Figueroa tried for George's death; acquitted 1902 and 1904. Mittie managed family cattle until killed in 1902 horse accident (18SP1902R). Children raised by Pyeatt relatives after probate court found estate "has greatly deteriorated in value by reason of the mismanagement of John. M. Kelly..." and he resigned as guardian.

Sources: 1850, 1860, 1870, 1880, 1900 U.S. Census. Cochise County Marriage Book 2, page 296. First Judicial District coroner's inquest No. 39. Cochise County Territorial criminal cases Nos. 883 and 953. Oral history tapes of Roland Pyeatt, recorded by Gene B. Pyeatt, Bakersfield, Calif.; provided to author in 1998. Cochise County Probate Case No. 446.

Aston, Henry J. (misspelled Askin or Astin) born 27FB1861 Texas to John Monroe Aston and second wife,

Jane (Riley). Largely reared by half-brother, John. In 1886, Henry accompanied John to Cochise County, where they incorporated Reloj Cattle Co., whose cattle ranged borderlands (09MR1887E). Henry was Packard foreman 1888-1911. Henry opened Douglas' first grocery store early 1901, but after George's death sold it. Never married; died Douglas 01MY1914 (02MY1914P and 01MY1914I).

Sources: 1850, 1860, 18870, 1880, 1900 U.S. Census. Arizona Bureau of Vital Statistics death certificate. Pyeatt oral history. 1902 Cochise County voting registration.

Aston, John Monroe (misspelled Askin or Astin) born 1848 Texas to John Monroe Aston and first wife, Rebecca, both Alabama natives. Following mother's death ca.1858 and father's in 1868, John became head of family. It included stepmother, Jane, and six siblings. About 1873, John married neighbor, Anna Elizabeth Pyeatt; three children. In 1886, John gathered 1,000 head of cattle, some family and friends and moved to Arizona. Spent a winter in San Bernardino Valley, where spring is named for family, before moving to San Pedro Valley, where brothers incorporated Reloj Cattle Co. John accidentally killed near Ochoaville 21DC1887 by friend, H.W. Hartson, as they shot at birds. Hartson cleared of any wrongdoing.

Sources: 1850, 1860, 1870, 1880, 1900 U.S. Census. First Judicial District coroner's inquest No. 1. Pyeatt oral history.

Axford, Joseph "Mack" born 1880 in Michigan. To Arizona 1894; hired by Packard to work on Half Moon Ranch. By 1908 was Greene Cattle Co. (GCC) foreman (24JA1908R) when he appeared before Cochise County's Board of Equalization. GCC disputed county assessor's tax valuation. Axford testified GCC had driven many head onto its Mexican land and so Cochise County assessment was incorrect. He requested reduction from 2,000 to 1,000 head; board allowed 1,750. Axford died 26JU1970 in Mesa, Ariz.

Sources: Axford, Joseph, Around Western Campfires. Tucson, Ariz.: University of Arizona Press, 1969. Cochise County Board of Equalization July 21, 1908 minutes, held in Arizona State Archives, Phoenix.

Barron, Augustus (aka "Gus" Baron) born ca.1846 Germany, where became mining engineer. Worked central Arizona mining camps mid-1870s, Tombstone 1878, Mexico 1879. Returned to Tombstone 1879; spent rest of life there. Worked for Packard on Stonewall; supervised Lucky Cuss, Contention, other mines. Became U.S. citizen in Cochise County 27DC1889. His job, plus six claims he located in Huachucas, enabled him to become Tombstone landlord and First National Bank of Tombstone stockholder. Died 08DC1913 Bisbee. He and wife, Christine, had no children.

Sources: Cochise County Superior Court Minute Book 4, p. 463. Cochise County Probate No. 805. Bailey and Chaput, Stalwarts Vol. 1. Cochise County Probate No. 805. 1902. Cochise County voting registration.

Bayless, Alexander H. born ca.1839 to William H. and Anne (Green) Bayless, New Yorkers who founded Highland, Kan., in 1850s. There, Alexander became country merchant; married Julia Irvin. In 1860 with brother William, Alex participated in Colorado gold rush, but didn't make fortune. In 1879, Tombstone lured Alex and William. Alex traveled there with goods to sell, and profits enabled him to lease Mountain Maid Mine (10DC1881N). In 1884 was "efficient clerk and collector of J.V. Vickers" (29SP1886T), and deputy agent for Louis Hohstadt (21FB1886T). By 1889, flush enough to be Packard Cattle Co. capitalizing partner (11SP1885R-E). William and son Charles remained in Arizona ranching and public service. Alex moved to Alameda, Calif., became realtor, served in 1920 state assembly.

Sources: 1865 and 1875 Kansas Census. 1870, 1880, 1900, 1920 U.S. Census. Santiago, Dawn Moore, "Charles H. Bayless," Arizona Journal of History, Autumn 1994. 1886 Great Register of Cochise County.

Beauchamp, Henry Clay born 23NV1871 Baltimore, Md. Mine engineering graduate of East Coast school. Arrived 1907 in Douglas to oversee mines and smelter for Transvaal Copper Mining Co., headquartered in Cincinnati (10FB1910I). Split residence between Gadsden Hotel and Cumpas, Son. Director Moctezuma Bank (18JA1910D). Also did freelance geology work utilizing connections with S.A. Gardanier. Married Luella Hill 28MR1916; divorced by time he died 02JY1938 in Douglas (03JY1938D).

Source: 1912-1937 Douglas City Directories. Arizona Bureau of Vital Statistics death certificate. Cochise County Marriage Book 11, p. 611. Herner, Charles H., "Gringo Miners Along the Rio Moctezuma," Arizona Journal of History, Spring 1988.

Christiansen, Hans Lorenz born 07FB1861 Denmark. As young man, pressed into German Navy; jumped ship in Texas. Worked as miner; eventually got to Bisbee. Established ranch west of Paul Spur; gradually expanded it. Naturalized 21MY1894 in Cochise County. Married Rose (Bittiner) 07JU1897; two sons. Oldest, **Felix Christiansen**, born 24MR1900, became Packard ranch foreman. Felix married Douglas school teacher Ada Naomi Squire (26MY1929D). Two sons: James, Texas A&M University professor emeritus; Richard, retired Phelps Dodge chemist. Hans died 10FB1944 (11FB1944D), Felix 09JY1973, Richard 20JA2012.

Sources: Jorgensen, Avis E.K., Early Danish Pioneers. Tucson, Ariz.: privately printed, 2012. 1894, 1902 Cochise County voting registration. Christiansen, James E. and Jean M., The Felix and Ada Christiansen Home and Ranch, A Bit of Arizona-Mexico Border History. Privately printed, 2006, College Station, Texas.

Christiansen, Hans M. (no relation to H.L. Christiansen) born ca.1851 Denmark. In October 1877 began digging, by himself, irrigation ditch off San Pedro River, south of Fairbank. Completed it 1879; developed prosperous farm. Sent for childhood sweetheart Christina Beck; married 1884; three sons. Died 05AP1891 in Tombstone of pneumonia (07AP1891P), and Christina 15MY1893 of poisoning (21MY1893E); her murderer never discovered. Her sister Johanna and husband, Charles Gaetjens, raised boys; lost lengthy court battle for "Danish Ranch" since it was on Spanish land grant recognized by U.S. government (31MR1894P). Danish Ranch, acquired by Kern County Land Co., became Boquillas Ranch headquarters. Christiansen/Gaetjens family moved to Gleeson area, where H.M. and Christina's oldest, Henry M., developed well-known ranch that remained whole into 1960s.

Source: Jorgensen, Early Danish Pioneers. Cochise County Marriages Book 10, p. 71.

Clark, Harry Allen born 05NV1871 Minneapolis to Frederick P. and Martha (Daley) Clark. Educated, worked in Minnesota. Moved to Arizona and position with C&A 1910. Installed Douglas smelter roasters 1912; smelter manager 1926; plant superintendent 1928. Married Emma Schroeder 1897; six surviving children. Served on First National Bank board of directors, Douglas school board, Arizona Game & Fish Commission, Arizona Welfare Commission. Owned today's Southwest Research Station in Portal, Ariz. Died 01AP1930 in home on smelter grounds.

Sources: "Harry A. Clark Dies Suddenly Friday Morning," April 2, 1930 Dispatch. Arizona Bureau of Vital Statistics death certificate. Sloan, History of Arizona V.3.

Conlon, Hugh E. born 24SP1862 St. Louis, Mo., to Peter and Julia (Ward) Conlon, Ireland natives. Conlon was: Tombstone merchant 1888; San Pedro Valley rancher 1890-5; Sulphur Springs Valley rancher associated with Erie Cattle Co. 1892-6 (20AP1892P); Bisbee drug store owner (18AG1896P); Bisbee livery stable owner (08NV1897P); Cochise County Supervisor 1899-1900 (29DC1899O); Arizona cattle inspector and Cochise County undersheriff 1900-04 (27DC1900R); Sonoran mining operations supervisor 1905-14 (07FB1904R and 17NV1905R). From 1914 until death 29SP1925, machinist in C&A's Douglas smelter (30SP1925D). Widow, Mary E. (Signaigo), helped Anna Gardanier run Douglas boarding house until 1930 when she moved to St. Louis (06JU1938D). Died there 21DC1938 (06JA1938D).

<small>Sources: Arizona Bureau of Vital Statistics death certificate. 1902-14 Cochise County voting registration. 1915-30 Douglas City directories.</small>

Curry, Avery Griffin and **Joseph Enoch** born to Enoch J. and Narcissa (Rowland) Curry in Visalia, Calif.; Avery 23FB1859 and Joe 14AP1870. Avery in 1879 Charleston, cowboyed with cousin John Hohstadt and other young borderlanders. By 1882, when parents and Joe moved to Cochise County, Avery well-established stockman (31MY1897P). Married Hughella Pyeatt 04SP1888; four children. Joe was a CQ miner 1888, then advanced into accounting ranks. In 1901, during Joe's stint as Naco, Ariz. postmaster, he and Avery established The Emporium, men's clothing store. In 1894, Joe married Barbara Brown, sister of Bisbee dentist Louis R. Brown, whose wife, Ada K., was close friend of Viola Slaughter (28DC1906R). After Naco declined, Avery moved The Emporium to Douglas, and Joe returned to bookkeeping ranks; eventually Apache Powder Co. general manager in St. David. Avery served in first state legislature before farming in Wellton, Ariz. (30SP1914I). He died 05NV1932 in Casa Grande, Ariz. (06NV1938D) and Joe 20SP1947 in Tucson (23SP1947D).

<small>Sources: Sloan, Richard E., edit., History of Arizona, Vol. 4. Phoenix, Ariz.: Record Publishing Co., 1930. McClintock,, Arizona. Connors, Who's Who. Arizona Bureau of Vital Statistics death certificate. Theobald, John and Lillian, Arizona Territory Post Offices & Postmasters. Phoenix, Ariz.: Arizona Historical Foundation, 1961.</small>

Dawe, George born 16OC1875 Santa Barbara, Calif., to Thomas R. and Mary Dawe, England natives. After graduation from business college, worked for Joseph Sexton, Santa Barbara business owner with Cochise County family members. In 1902, Dawe became CQ bookkeeper in Bisbee. Switched to C&A 1904. By 1926 was C&A smelter superintendent. Married 1907 Martha Griffith, daughter of C&A executive Preston A. and Mary Griffith (25NV1930D). Two children: son, George, became physician; daughter, Marjorie, New York City executive secretary. First National Bank of Douglas director over 30 years; also on Douglas school board. Following PD-C&A merger, retired to California. Died 18AG1936 El Monte, Calif. (19AG1936D).

Sources: Sloan, History of Arizona.

Doan, Fletcher Morris born 21JY1841 to John and Maria Doan in Circleville, Ohio. Graduate Ohio Wesleyan University and Albany (N.Y.) Law School. First practiced in Missouri, where married Anna Murray 1873; four sons. In 1888, family moved to Yuma where Fletcher promoted unsuccessful irrigation company. Pinal County Attorney; Associate Justice of Arizona Supreme Court 1897. Retained position until 1912 when resumed private practice, first in Tombstone then in Douglas with son, Frank. Known for logical arguments and clear presentations built upon hands-on knowledge. Among important decisions were complex Gila River water rights case and Elías vs. Territory of Arizona, delineating fair trial rules. Arizona Trust & Banking Co. ownership and law practice kept him active until 28OC1924 death in Tucson. Son John multi-term state representative, son Fletcher Jr. multi-term Mayor of Nogales, Ariz., grandson L.L., four-star Army general.

Sources: Connors, Who's Who. Hayostek, Cindy, "Arizona Longest Hard-Surfaced Highway and the Doan Family Tragedy," Borderland Chronicles No. 14, 2011. Goff, Arizona Territorial Officials, Vol. I.

Doan, Franklin Wilson born 28FB1877 to Fletcher M. and Anna (Murray) Doan in Bowling Green, Mo. Law degree from Stanford University 1901. Practiced in California and Tucson before settling in Douglas and busy partnership with David A. Richardson. On 20OC1912, Frank married Florence House, mother of youngest of his three children. Frank killed in 19SP1920 auto accident on Bisbee-Douglas Highway which, at time, was Arizona's longest hard-surfaced road. His father spoke at dedication ceremony less than two weeks before.

Sources: Connors, Who's Who. Hayostek, "Longest Hard-Surfaced Highway."

Dunbar, John Oscar born 19MY1853 in Maine into Scot-Irish family. Moved 1880 to Cochise County at behest of brother **Thomas Dunbar**. Born ca.1830, Thomas in Arizona ca.1872, farming at Tres Alamos on San Pedro River. His place was nucleus of settlement of which he was postmaster 1875-86. Served 1881 and 1891 Arizona Territorial House. In 1881, introduced successful bill separating Cochise from Pima County. John ran Cienega stage station, west of Tres Alamos (08AP1880WN) before establishing Tombstone's Dexter Livery Stable with John Behan (17OC1880N and 17DC1881N). Proprietor/editor Tombstone *Republic* (09DC1882E); Cochise County Treasurer 1880-82 (09DC1882E); publisher Tombstone *Record-Epitaph* (28NV1885T), then just *Epitaph* until 1888. Moved to Phoenix 1889 (16JU1889E); part owner/editor *Arizona Gazette*; later with *Phoenix Democrat*. Established *Dunbar's Weekly* 1914 Phoenix. Died 01FB1923 in Phoenix leaving wife, Emma (11FB1923I). Thomas died 25JA1891 in Tucson. He'd married twice, first to Agnes Bergus, five children; then to Catherine Hanley.

Sources: Goff, Arizona Territorial Officials, Vol. VI. 1870, 1880, 1900, 1920, 1920 U.S. Census. Lyon, William H., Those Old Yellow Dog Days. Tucson, Ariz.: Arizona Historical Society, 1994. Arizona Bureau of Vital Statistics death certificates. Bailey and Chaput, Stalwarts Vol. 1. Theobald, Arizona Postmasters.

Elías, Francisco Suárez born 30JA1880 to Manuel Elías Pérez and Eloise Suárez Duarte in Tecoripa, Son. Owner of several haciendas, Elías took up Revolutionary cause in 1913 as Constitutionalist fiscal agent. On 23AP1920 among signees of *El Plan de Agua Prieta*, document that propelled Obregón and

Calles into Mexican Presidency. Appointed Sonoran Governor 17JU1921, a term remembered as when most Chinese were expelled from Sonora. Provisional Governor 1929-31; then his nation's Secretary of Agriculture. Married Bertha Gabilondo 06DC1906; four children. Was in second marriage when died 16AP1963 in Nogales, Son.

Source: Elías, Armando C., The Elías Family. Tucson, Ariz.: U.S. Press & Graphics, 2008.

Emanuel, Alfred H. born ca.1832 in Philadelphia. In 1850s San Francisco and 1860s Nevada. In 1880 Tombstone, freighted before becoming Vizina Mine superintendent (21AG1880E). Resigned to pursue own interests (04DC1880N), which included mining claims and Ash Canyon mill. Survived financial difficulties; became Clerk of Superior Court 1889; established carriage/blacksmith business. Tombstone Mayor 1896-1902; also on school board. Moved to Los Angeles ca.1910; died there 09MR1915.

Sources: Bailey and Chaput, Stalwarts Vol. 1. 1894 Great Register of Cochise County.

Etchells, Charles Tanner born 08JU1837 Ypsilanti, Mich.; probably learned blacksmithing there. Trade led him to 1864 Tucson, where he found work and wife, Soledad Borquez, born 1836 in Tucson. Children: **Petra**, born 1870; **John Charles**, 20OC1873; Sarah **"Sadie"** 1875; Peter, 1877. Their father dabbled in Tombstone mines (13JA1882N and 10OC1885T), ranch south of Tucson. He taught his sons blacksmithing in thriving shop, but John became Consolidated National Bank of Tucson employee 1897. John advanced steadily until 1928; briefly state deputy bank examiner. Then joined Southern Arizona Bank & Trust (SAB&T). After 50-year banking career, retired 1948 as SAB&T vice-president (26SP1948S and 01JA1948S). Married Lenore Baker; two sons. Died 05DC1963 in Tucson (06DC1963S). Proceeded by parents,

Charles 23AG1900, and Soledad 16JY1910.

Sources: Thames, John L., Blacksmiths of Tucson. Prepared for 2000 Conference of Artist-Blacksmith Association of North America in Flagstaff, Ariz. Connors, Who's Who. One undated Arizona Daily Star article; others from 28MY1952, 25MY1964, 10MR1991, 04MR1999.

The **Gabilondo** brothers – **Rafael**, born 1869; **Edgardo**, 1871; **Hilario**, 1872; and **Antonio**, 1876 – children of Hilario and Josefa Gabilondo. Brothers and five sisters reached adulthood. Among sisters were Bertha, wife of Sonora Gov. Francisco Elías; Josefa, wife of borderland rancher Robert Hiller; and Trinidad, wife of PD Nacozari manager Ricardo Quiroga. Brothers founded Bancaria Mercantile y Agricola de Sonora with Elías, Soto and Rivera (17DV1917I). Besides ranching, Antonio worked as accountant; Hilario, Cananea mining concessions (12NV1894P); Rafael grew cotton (17JA1920I). Antonio headed Agua Prieta's immigration office most of 1920s; died 1930 Douglas. Hilario died 1922 in Mexico City on cattle selling trip; Edgardo succumbed from 1943 horse accident; Rafael died 1945 on his Chihuahua ranch.

Sources: "Death of Well-Known Resident In Mexico City," April 13, 1922, International; Body of H.B. Gabilondo Is Laid To Rest," April 17, 1922, International; Leading Mexican Former Official Called by Death," Nov. 28, 1930, Dispatch; "Large Numbers Attend Funeral Of Sr. Gabilondo," Nov. 25, 1930, Dispatch; "E. Gabilondo, Long Time, Resident, Dies," Feb. 17, 1943, Dispatch; "Well-Known Rancher Dies In Juarez, May 25, 1945, Dispatch; "Mass Today For Rafael Gabilondo, May 26, 1945, Dispatch.

Gardanier, Henry Albert born 23SP1850 Marshall, Mich.; followed older brother into Civil War. Afterward began career with Standard Oil that took him west. By 1906 managing Silvinite, Son. Health problems sent him to 1907 Douglas where wife Anna Sutter ran boarding house. Their son, **Sutter Albert Gardanier**, born ca.1876, managed Douglas Assay. In 1915, Sutter and Ygnacio Soto founded International Commission Co. Sutter managed it until his retirement in early 1950s. H.A. died 06JY1932; Anna in 1919; daughter

Irma, Douglas school teacher, 15AP1951.

Sources: "Henry Gardanier, Pioneer Resident, Is Dead, Aged 82," July 7, 1932, Dispatch. 1912-50 Douglas City Directories. Arizona Bureau of Vital Statistics death certificates. Hayostek, Cindy, Borderland Chronicles Nos. 9 and 11, 2010.

Gates, Egbert James born 24JY1869 to Freeman and Adelina (Rhodes) Gates in San Jose, Calif. Older brother, **Carroll W.**, born 1860 in New York. E.J. attended UC Berkeley; both brothers went into real estate. Carroll associated with Walter Vail and Empire Ranch, and J.V. Vickers and CCC. E.J. partnered with Packard and Greene's Turkey Track. Married Dorothy Vernon Stiles 18JU1902 Missouri; four children. Youngest daughter, Tizrah, married Nicolas Roosevelt, *New York Times* publisher and Theodore Roosevelt cousin. Oldest daughter, Dorothy, was first wife of astronomer Fritz Zwicky, whose Cal Tech career included discovery of neutron stars and dark matter. E.J. served multiple terms in California Senate before 01JY1923 death in Grand Island, N.Y.

Sources: 1880, 1910 U.S. Census. California Biographical Index. California State Roster. Missouri Marriage Record. "Former Envoy Wed on Coast," June 7, 1906, Washington Post. "Mrs. Nicolas Roosevelt Dies At 53," May 25, 1961, Pasadena Star News.

Graham, Benjamin Franklin, born ca.1868 New York. Turned up in Cochise County ca.1898. His Bisbee mercantile (22MY1898WO) featured furniture (05FB1898P and 13FB1898E). Diversified with livery stable (12AG1899O) and Dragoons mine (03FB1902R). Bisbee's first street superintendent (09FB1900R); resigned to concentrate on business, which included undertaking parlor (17MR1902R). Opened brokerage house (11NV1902R), leading to Lucky Tiger Mine development (10FB1903R). His unsuccessful 1905 filibuster at Lucky Tiger prompted him to flee to British Columbia to avoid prosecution. Founded timber company there and another transporting lumber. Retired to southern

California as millionaire (06JY1911I).
Sources: Fathauer, Lemuel C. Shattuck. 1898, 1900, 1902 Cochise County voting registration.

Graves, Elbridge William born 14AP1869 Dubuque, Iowa to Rufus E. and Mary C. (Tilden) Graves. Rufus, a banker, born 15AG1835 Keen, N.H., died 19MR1918 Tucson. Mary died ca.AG1912 in Los Angeles streetcar accident (03AG1912I). Elbridge followed in father's footsteps, working in Dubuque and Colorado Springs banks before Consolidated National Bank of Tucson in 1889. Married Petra B. Etchells 1892 El Paso. She died 11AG1894 after giving birth to Petra E. (12AG1894C). Married Sarah "Sadie" Etchells 1901. Elbridge was cashier First National Bank of Douglas (14JA1910I); vice-president 15 years. Retired 1937 to La Jolla, Calif. (19AG1937D), died there 28MR1950 (29MR1950D). Daughter Petra died 28AP1934 in Douglas; Sadie 15NV1963 in Tucson (16NV1963S).
Sources: Connors, Who's Who. 1870, 1900, 1920 U.S. Census. California Death Index, 1940-1997. Arizona Bureau of Vital Statistics death certificates.

Greene, William Cornell born 11AP1852 Duck Creek, Wis. to Townsend and Eleanor (Cornell) Greene. Grew up in New York. By 1880, miner near Prescott, Ariz.; moved to Tombstone that year. Married Ella (Roberts) Moson 09JU1884; two children. Their combined property along San Pedro River led to hay, beef contracts with Fort Huachuca (04OC1886T and 19AP1891E). Successful barley crop (30JU1894P) let Greene invest in Sonoran gold mine (18MR1895P and 24JU1896P). Its profits capitalized Cananea copper operation that made him a millionaire. After Ella's 24DC1899 death, married Mary Proctor 15FB1901; four children. After lost control of Cananea 1907, concentrated on borderlands ranching, timber and railroads. Died from horse accident 05AG1911.
Source: Sonnichsen, C.L., Colonel Greene and the Copper Skyrocket. Tucson, Ariz.: University of Arizona Press, 1974.

Hanks, Lewis C. born ca.1859 Covina, N.Y.; educated in Illinois. First borderlands position probably Banco de Cananea assistant cashier. In 1902, cashier Douglas City Bank that became First National Bank of Douglas. After 1910 imprisonment for 1907 misapplication of federal bank funds, friends signed petition to free him (23NV1911I and 14JA1912I). President Taft paroled Hanks (05SP1912I), who went to San Diego and became successful real estate agent (08MR1913I).
Sources: http://papermoneyofsonora.com; Arizona State Prison records, Florence Historical Museum. 1904 and 1906 Cochise County voting registration.

Harsell, Katherine Mae (Searles) born ca.1881 in Nebraska. Arrived in 1916 Douglas as bride of Thomas Lightburne Harsell, Copper Queen smelter foreman. Douglas school board member 1925-1934; Arizona president of United Spanish-American War Veterans Auxiliary. Died 19SP1943 in Los Angeles.
Sources: "Mrs. Harsell's Body Back To Douglas Today," Sept. 21, 1943, Dispatch. 1916-38 Douglas City Directories. Arizona Bureau of Vital Statistics birth certificate.

Hart, Harry M. born ca.1884 Columbus, Ohio; became U.S. Department of Agriculture border crossing veterinarian in Cochise County ca. 1912 (10MY1912I). His Boston Terrier, "Turkey," well-known, especially after she had "five little turkeys" (30MR1915I). Hart's relationship with John B. George also well-known, especially after they attended christening of USS Arizona together (19JU1915I). Late in 1915, Hart transferred to El Paso district, so he was in Columbus, N.M. 09MR1916 during Pancho Villa's raid. Hart's body, found in burned-out Central Hotel, was identified only by jewelry recognized by delegation of his fellow Douglas Elks (09MR1916D and 11MR1916D).
Source: "Dr. H.H. Hart Is Cremated In Hotel," March 10, 1916, International.

Hohstadt, John Francis and **Lewis Almon** lived longest in Arizona-Sonora borderlands of their family. Sons of John W. and Melissa Jane (Morgan) Hohstadt Jr.; John F. born 25DC1861 Missouri, Lewis 10NV1864 California. In 1875, family left northern California with 275 cattle, arriving in 1876 Sonora with 45 head. Settled near Bacoachi; survived Apache raids (19AG1885T). Ran herd in and around Ajo Mountains so it expanded to 2,000 head (25AH1929 and 19JA1920). Some family members returned to California, but John F. and wife Julia stayed on Turicachi Ranch (north of Nacozari), while Lewis lived in Douglas. Mexican Revolution did not treat their herd kindly, so brothers emphasized their mines between El Tigre and Pilares. Lewis had at least seven children with at least three women. John and Lewis died in Douglas; John 19AG1929 (20AG1920D) and Lewis 15FB1944 (17FB1944D).

Sources: Baker-Reynolds, Muriel, Some Came Sailing. Seattle, Wash.: privately printed, 2004. 1910 U.S. Census. Arizona Bureau of Vital Statistics birth and death certificates. 1904-1942 Douglas City Directories.

Hood, Joseph "Joe" Elmer son of Henderson "Henry" and Mary A. (Thompson) Hood, both Southerners. Born 14FB1879 Arizona as family trekked to California. Grew up there but returned to Arizona to ranch in Chiricahua Mountains. Married Olive Christina Robertson 13NV1906 in Tombstone; three sons. In 1915, opened Douglas harness/saddle shop; also small farm west of town. Sold shop (16JA19I) to become cattle inspector (05JA20I) and Cochise County Sheriff, 1920-21. Moved to Kingman, Ariz., ca.1942 and sold real estate. Died there 25AG1960.

Sources: 1880 and 1910 U.S. Census. Eppinga, Jane, Arizona Sheriffs. Tucson, Ariz.: Rio Nuevo Press, 2006. Cochise County Marriage Book 4, p. 372. Arizona Bureau of Vital Statistics birth and death certificates. 1912-1920 Douglas City Directories.

Hood, James Townsend "Tom" born Arkansas 03JU1876 to Henderson "Henry" and Mary A. (Thompson) Hood. Received education, including time at business college founded by a brother, in California. Worked in Prescott, Ariz., before 1900 Bank of Bisbee job. When Lemuel Shattuck founded Miners & Merchants Bank in 1902, Tom joined him (20SP1913I). Married 25JU1903 Mary Rosalie Moore, daughter of Peter Moore; three sons. In 1905, moved onto Sulphur Springs Valley ranch where managed 10,000 head. Sold ranch 1913 to buy Douglas' Ford dealership. Maintained small farm west of Douglas (20SP1913I). In 1930, opened insurance agency where Tom's humor and encyclopedic knowledge of local conditions made him an institution. Douglas Chamber of Commerce president 1915; school board 1918-26. Sold agency 1953 to Charles O. Bloomquist, Peter Johnson's grandson. Died 24JU1956 (25JU1956D); Mary 09JU1962 (10JU1962D), both in Douglas.

Sources: 1880 and 1910 U.S. Census. Arizona Bureau of Vital Statistics birth and death certificates. 1912-1961 Douglas City Directories.

Howell, James Alonzo born 28JU1872 Hamilton, Nev. to Amazon C. and Mary A. (Tyler) Howell, native Missourians. James' sister, Viola, was John Slaughter's second wife. James served 1903 Arizona House (04DC1902R); assistant cashier Bank of Tombstone and Benson's Citizens Bank 1904-7; Turkey Track Cattle Co. manager (29JU1908I and 22JY91908I); cashier Arizona Bank & Trust 1908; manager San Bernardino Market 1908-12; Douglas City Clerk and Treasurer 1912-14; borderlands rancher 1914-27; Cochise County deputy assessor 1927-35. Married Frankie J. (Todd) when she was assistant cashier of Arizona Bank & Trust – possibly first Arizona female to hold such position (13DC1946D). She later First National Bank bookkeeper. No children. After James died 24JA1936 in Douglas; Frankie married Douglas fireman John Stillman, son of Horace C. Stillman, Bisbee pioneer, later manager Ord Hotel in Douglas.

Sources: Connors, Who's Who. 1912-42 Douglas City Directories. Arizona Bureau of Vital Statistics death certificate. Goff, Territorial Officials, Vol. 6. "James A. Howell Dead...," Jan. 25, 1936, Dispatch.

Charles Phillip and **Susan Mary Hunt** had 10 children; most ranched in Cochise County (05AP1908D and 06AP1908I). In 1916, Packard purchased Hunt properties west of Douglas, and family moved to Animas Valley, N.M. There, brothers Sam and Joe shot and killed Chester Bartell, a neighbor Hunts claimed was harassing them. After seven years of legal action, brothers were discharged, but defense costs forced them to sell Animas ranch. Joe managed Slaughter's Ranch after that worthy's death; then elected state senator. Cousin Stewart Hunt established IV Bar Ranch in San Bernardino Valley (later purchased by Shattuck family), and had several ranches in Mexico. Chester Bartell's widow, Cora, married Lynn A. Mobley, owner of Lee Station Ranch, north of Douglas (30DC1945D). Bartell's grandson, Norm, long-time proprietor of Red Barn, Douglas roadhouse.

Sources: Hunt, Norman K., The Killing of Chester Bartell. Phoenix, Ariz.: Cowboy Miner Productions, 2006.

Ives, Eugene Semmes born 11NV1859 Washington, D.C. to Joseph C. and Matilda C. (Semmes) Ives. Joseph, a West Point graduate, led 1853-54 expedition exploring Colorado River and northern Arizona; later engineered Washington Monument. Eugene graduated from Georgetown University, studied in Europe and earned 1880 law degree from Columbia University. Married Anna M. Waggaman 15JU1889; eight children. New York law practice; state assembly 1885-87; state senate 1888-91. Unsuccessful run for Congress 1894; moved to Yuma, Ariz.; Southern Pacific Railroad attorney. Arizona state senate 1901-03; unsuccessful run for Senate 1912; moved to Los Angeles. Died 24AG1917 in California (27AG1917I).

Sources: Goff, Territorial Officials, Vol. VI. Wagoner, Jay. J., Arizona Territory 1863-1912, A Political History. Tucson, Ariz.: University of Arizona Press, 1970.

Johnson, Peter J. born ca.1863 Norway; naturalized 01NV1888 in Tombstone. Cut Bisbee mine timbers; acquired Naco ranch and ranch near Salton Sea (23AP1895P). Bought Bisbee butcher business, leased land between Cabullona and Agua Prieta (23AP1907R and 13AG1908I). Eventually controlled entire Perilla Mountain range, east of Douglas. Married Malena (Peterson) 1887 Tombstone; four children. Malena died 23MR1920 and Peter 18SP1932, both on their Hog Canyon Ranch in Perillas. Daughter Hannah married John Oscar Bloomquist 25AP1912. Eldest son, Charles Oscar, born 21MR1913 Bisbee, grew up on and became manager of Hog Canyon. In 1949, Charles founded Douglas Realty & Trust Co., which bought Tom Hood's insurance agency. In 1951, Charles elected to Arizona House; Majority Leader 1958. Co-sponsored bill establishing Arizona's junior college system; served on Arizona State Junior College Board and Cochise College Governing Board. Died 17NV1979 in Douglas.

Sources: 1900, 1902 and 1904 Cochise County voting registration. Arizona Bureau of Vital Statistics death certificates. Hayostek, Cindy, Borderland Chronicles No. 8, 2009. Cochise County Marriage Book 8, p. 132.

Kelton, Carlton Brown born 08JY1839 in Baltimore to Frederick P. Kelton. Father and son worked as carpenters until son enlisted First Maryland Cavalry in 1861. Fought Bull Run to Gettysburg; injured (facial saber cut whose scar he hid with a walrus mustache) during capture 1864. Escaped from Point Lookout Prison 1865. In 1879 Tombstone (14OC1922I). Arizona jobs included Deputy U.S. Marshall 1884-89, U.S. Department of Justice special agent in Mexico, U.S. Customs roving inspector, U.S. Customs collector Lochiel, Ariz. San Pedro rancher before 1891-92 term as Cochise County Sheriff (28JU1893E). In 1909, homesteaded northwest of Elfrida where railroad junction named for him (02AP1909OI and 07FB1910I). House member 1912 (20JA1913I); proprietor Tucson's Windsor Hotel (10OC1925S). Never married. Died

08OC1925 Alabama; buried Maryland.

Sources: Connors, Who's Who. Myrick, Railroads of Arizona Vol. I. "Story Of The Life Of C.B. Kelton...," Sept. 17, 1935, Dispatch. 1908 Cochise County voting registration. Eppinga, Arizona Sheriffs.Unknown author, Carlton B. Kelton, Arizona Historical Society file in Tucson.

Kimble, Floyd C. born 1899 Burnett County, Texas to Charles Chester and Sally (Hutchison) Kimble. C.C. held Oklahoma oil well leases, but mostly interested in cattle, as was Floyd. He was WWI vet; married Retha V. Stiltz 1920; moved to Douglas same year. Owner San Bernardino Valley ranch and El Centro, Calif., feeder operation. Floyd's registered Herefords regularly won at national shows (19MR1932 and 21FB1943D). First National director 1930 (01JY1930D). C.C. died 21MR1931, Sally 02SP1940, Floyd 08FB1994. Their descendants still ranch in San Bernardino Valley.

Sources: "Charles C. Kimble, Douglas Cattleman, Victim of Pneumonia ...," March 24, 1931; "Mrs. Sallie Kimble Dead...," Sept. 3, 1940; "Obituaries," Feb. 9, 1994; all Dispatch.

Krueger, Lewis R. born 24MR1876 to Fredrick E. and Augusta Krueger in Michigan City, Ind., where educated. Worked as Chicago newspaper reporter before 1900 Phoenix job as accountant. Arizona House 1905; Packard's secretary after that (22JA1907R). Sen. Mark Smith's secretary when died 12NV1913 in Michigan City (24NV1913I).

Sources: Goff, Territorial Officials, Vol. VI. 1880, 1900, 1910 U.S. Census. "Krueger Dies In Hospital," Nov. 13, 1913, Indianapolis Star.

Land, William Calhun born 1845 Texas to John and Matilda Land. Moved to California; in 1865 married Maggie Dennis. Two daughters and son, **Edward W. Land**, born 1872 Nevada. W.C. ranched in three states, including Cochise County with Tevis, Perrin, Land & Co. It acquired portion Babocomari land grant in 1880s. W.C. divorced Maggie; married Harriett Catchim in 1890; daughter born 1890. W.C.

got through 1890s drought (17FB1895P and 16&20NV1895P) as Kern County Land Co. agent/buyer (17FB1895P). Lived in Stone House (31NV1895P) near today's Huachuca City, until ca.1900. Died 1917 in Nogales (24JA1917I). Edward read for law with Tombstone attorney Allen English; admitted to bar 14MY1894. Tombstone city clerk (02MY1896P, Bisbee law office (12OC1896P), Cochise County Attorney 1902. Married Alice Crable; at least two children. Died 30AG1938 in Douglas.

Sources: 1850, 1880, 1900, 1910, 1920 U.S. Census. 1892-6, 1900, 1902 Cochise County voting registration. Roll of Attorneys in Clerk of Court office. Arizona Bureau of Vital Statistics birth and death certificates.

Lawhon, Wright Way born 13FB1883 to Wright Way and Della Lawhon, Georgia natives who ranched in Texas. W.W. Jr. ranching in 1900 Deming, N.M. There married Cecelia; five children. First National Bank assistant cashier 1909. Founded stock brokerage, real estate and insurance agency 1915. Within few years, branches in Bisbee, Tucson and Phoenix; moved to Phoenix. The 1929 Crash killed business; moved to Los Angeles, where Cecelia died 12FB1933 (14FB1933D). He eventually found work as laundry troubleshooter. Died 12AP1954 in Los Angeles.

Sources: 1900-40 U.S. Census. WWI draft registration. California Death Index.

Leatherwood, Robert Nelson born JU1844 North Carolina to William and Elizabeth (Nelson) Leatherwood. Confederate veteran. First in Tucson 1869; ran stable until 1875. Owned Knoxville Mine 1878 Tombstone. Tucson Council 1874; Tucson Mayor 1880; Arizona Council 1885; Arizona House 1887 and 1893; Pima County Sheriff 1894-98; Committee for Arizona's exhibit 1904 World's Fair. Married; one son. Died 05AP1920 in Tucson.

Sources: Goff, Arizona Territorial Officials, Vol. VI. Eppinga, Arizona Sheriffs. Deposition given by Leatherwood in Boston & Arizona Smelting & Refining Co. vs. Robert A. Lewis et al. in Arizona State Archives, Phoenix. Arizoniana Winter 1960, Arizona Pioneer Historical Society.

Lenormand, Emile born ca.1840 France. Ran 1886 Tombstone bar with fellow Frenchman, Anton Mariluis, born ca.1846. Both claimed naturalization; Emile 1867 San Francisco, Anton 1884 Contention City. Emile died 19JA1896 on Fort Huachuca (21JA1896P). His probate reveals bar stock: barrel of whiskey, 13 gallons gin, five gallons each rum, white and red wine; bottles of chartreuse, curacao, "poussi" café, Florida orange wine, peppermint and bitters; 31 bottles imported ale. Liquor came from Lenormand Bros., "Dealers in Foreign and Native Wines and Liquors" in San Francisco, where lived Emile's two brothers, sister and niece. Emile's estate included Tombstone real estate, two adobe houses near Fairbank, horses, haying and pumping equipment. Estate appraisers declared ranch "unprofitable property" since it was on Spanish land grant with "no title thereto save by occupation and possession... ."

Sources: Cochise County Probate Book 2, p. 112. 1886 Cochise County voting registration.

Levy, Ben born 20MY1882 Hartford, Conn. Older brother Jacob founded small dry goods store in 1903 Douglas. After Ben joined him 1905, store evolved into Levy's Department Store. By 1927, it was Douglas' largest clothing store with branches in Bisbee and Tucson (11AG1929D). Ben's community involvement included serving on First National's board of directors. Married Dora (Dauman) 1908; two sons, Alfred and Samuel. They opened Douglas' first drive-in (05JU1929D), and popular nightspot Top Hat Club (10FB1939D). Alfred became agent for Frank Sinatra, other stars (25FB and 27FB1945D); producer of early television shows (22OC1959D). Ben died 05OC1945 in Douglas (06OC1945D). Levy's Department Store is now part of Macy's.

Source: Hayostek, Cindy, Borderland Chronicles No. 10, 2010.

Cynthia F. Hayostek

Lutley, William "Bill" born 14NV1856 Escott Manor Farm, Somerset, England to William and Elizabeth (Withycombe) Lutley. Of their 13 offspring; eight emigrated to U.S. Fred killed by Apaches 09MY1886; Harry escaped Indians but later killed in gun accident; Arthur became Bisbee blacksmith (23MR1896P). Bill freighted timber from Ross sawmill (05AP1889P), then in Phoenix (20MY1890P), Yavapai County (06JA and 09MR1895P) and Sonora (26SP and 07OC1895P). He mined in Sonora; then purchased cattle (17MY1897P). Drove them to Bar Boot Ranch (05NV1895P) with partners Joe Hood and Meadows (23JA1940D). With Meadows and Lem Shattuck owned OK Ranch, also in southern Chiricahuas. Partnered with McNair in Swisshelm Cattle Co. Married 14FB1890 in Tombstone Alice Fenno Woods, born 08OC1867 to Morgan and Lucy (Fenno) Woods, Baldwinsville, Mass. Alice related via marriage to Viola Slaughter. No children. Bill died 21JA1940 (23JA1940D) and Alice 13AP1960 (15AP1960S), both in Tombstone.

Sources: Sloan, History of Arizona. Vol. 3. "William Lutley: The Laird of the Bar Boot Ranch," Aug. 19, 1934.

Marley, Daniel V. born ca.1888 Mountain Home, Idaho. Ranched near Globe before buying Ojo de Agua 1936. Also acquired Rancho La Morita. Married Esther Hillman, sister of Frank Hillman, Packard foreman. After divorce, married Amy, who became his widow upon his 23AP1958 death in Agua Prieta. Survivors were: brothers Kemper, Phoenix; John, Guatemala; Denn, Young, Ariz.; sisters Gladys Goodnight, Phoenix; Mary Marley, San Francisco.

Sources: 1940 U.S. Census. Watt, Eva Tulene, Don't Let the Sun Step Over You. Tucson, Ariz.: University of Arizona Press, 2004. "Prominent Agua Prieta Rancher Dies," April 24, 1958, Dispatch.

McNair, James C. born 31MR1861 Mill Creek, Penn. to William Elliott and Margaret (Burford) McNair. Because of familial connections to Shattucks, in 1883 living on

Mud Springs Ranch (north of first Paul quarry) as Erie Co. stockholder (05MR1892P). Erie president (28JA1897P). Partner with Lutley in Swisshelm Cattle Co. (20AP1892P). Active in it until 1895 (05JU1895P) when moved to Kansas; married and died there.

Sources: Bailey and Chaput, Stalwarts Vol. II. Bailey, Lynn R., We'll All Wear Silk Hats. Tucson, Ariz.: Westernlore Press, 1994.

Meadows, John born 18FB1869 near San Antonio, Texas to John R. and Rebecca H. (Stacy) Meadows, both Provencal, La. natives. Participated in Texas-Kansas cattle drives before moving to Bisbee 1898 to work for Erie Cattle Co. Switched 1900 to Bar Boot Co.; became company partner with Lutley and Len Shattuck in 1914. Company later bought OK Ranch, which Meadows managed until shortly before his 09NV1947 death in Douglas (11NV1947D). One son, Jack.

Sources: Arizona Bureau of Vital Statistics death certificates. "Meadows, Partner Of Lutley Calls Him True Friend," Dispatch, Jan. 24, 1940.

Metcalf, George Augustus born 28MR1858 Anson, Maine to O.D. and Sarah Metcalf. Reared in Santa Barbara, Calif., where ran store, taught, ranched. 1880 miner Pima, Ariz.; 1886 ranch/farm Ramsey Canyon (06JU1886E). Tombstone school principal (03AG1886T); married Bessie E. Tolman (06NV1886T); not together in 1900. Friend of Jim Kirk (later Cananea mine superintendent) while living in Oso Negro, Son. (06SP1891E). Tombstone school principal (02DC1892P), Bisbee schools superintendent (19JY1894P), Bisbee school principal (25NV1896P). Santa Barbara butcher business (21JA1897P) with brother, William, born ca.1880. Another brother, Winfield, was Santa Barbara County Treasurer. George, while manager Greene Copper Co. lumberyard, killed with William 01JU1906 during miners' strike. Both buried Santa Barbara.

Source: Sonnichsen, Colonel Greene and the Copper Skyrocket. 1886, 1888, 1898 Cochise County voting registration. 1860-80 and 1900 U.S. Census. 1866-98 California Voter Registers. FindAGrave.com.

Miller, William Grant "Onion" born 08AG1868 Ursina, Penn. to Abraham and Anna (McIntyre) Miller, both Pennsylvania Dutch. Pittsburgh laborer before moving to Arizona 1907 with wife Della Boyce (Cressinger) born 12JA1869, Alexandria, Ohio to John and Elizabeth (Anderson) Cressinger. Married 24JU1894. Arrived Double Adobe 1908; developed farm with initial bankroll of $7.35. Grew onions, other vegetables watered from windmill and pump jack; after WWI with power pump. Instrumental in development of Central Highway, rural mail delivery, Double Adobe School District and R.E.A. district (20OC1942D). Son Harry G., born ca.1902 in Ohio, married Arizona native Milicia; two children. William died 16OC1942 (20OC1942D); Della 02AG1952 (06AG1952D).

Sources: 1880, 1900-40 U.S. Census. Cochise County Probate No. 3478. Arizona death certificates.

Mitchell, George E. born 18SP1864 Swansea, Wales. Swansea metal works lab 1880; superintendent South Wales Smelting Co. reverbatories 1883; Baltimore Copper Works 1887. Constructed Boston, Montana Copper & Silver Mining Co. plant 1890 Montana; later assistant superintendent. Managed Verde Copper Co. works 1894 Jerome, Ariz. Invented several processes, most notably Mitchell Economic Hot-Blast Furnace. Built Greene Consolidated Mining Co. reduction works 1898; its general manager (23JU1903R). Left 1902 to pursue own interests, including Mitchell Mining Co. in central Arizona (19AP1907R); La Dicha Mine, Durango, Mexico (26SP1905I); Los Angeles home; presidency First National Bank of Douglas (11JA1907I), interest in Black Diamond Mine in southern Dragoons (10OC1915I).

Sources: "Geo. Mitchell's Biography," May 17, 1910, International. Sonnichsen, Greene Skyrocket.

Moore, Peter born ca.1830 Montreal, Canada. Married Martha E. Herrick; born ca.1838 Clayton, N.Y. Six children. Family lived in Idaho before 1875 arrival near Fort Thomas,

Ariz. To San Pedro Valley where Peter raised hay for Fort Huachuca (26MY1888E); cut firewood for Copper Queen. After selling farm to Packard, bought Rucker Canyon ranch (06DC1890P). Installed cattle, irrigation ditch and grape vines. Moved to Willcox area to dabble with Dos Cabezas mine (27JA1894P and 24MY1895P). Son **Franklin Peter** took on Rucker ranch in addition to his own. Born 12FB1869 Boise, Idaho. Married 24AP1897 Augusta Heyne, daughter Frederick W. Heyne, superintendent Bisbee's Copper Prince Mine (24MY1895P) and member Arizona House 1887, 1891. Director, president Arizona Cattlegrowers Association; director, vice-president National Cattlegrowers Association; twice chairman Arizona Livestock Commission. No children so when he died 17OC1934, brother **Frederick Charles** began managing ranch. Born 12MY1876 near Fort Thomas. Married Lucy A. Ellis 29SP1907; three children. Managed Four Bar Ranch (04JA1910I), homesteaded Bar M Ranch in San Bernardino Valley, started Rafter X Ranch in Rucker. Fred's son, Frank, coached football at Oklahoma, Dartmouth and West Point before becoming member Arizona State Highway Commission (18JY1941D and 05MR1942D). After Fred died 10DC1953 in Douglas, his other son, Lawrence, ran ranch; his descendants do so today.

<small>Sources: Goff, Arizona Territorial Officials, Vol. VI. Arizona Bureau of Vital Statistics birth and death certificates. "Mrs. Moore Passes Away;..." Jan. 13, 1917, International. "Frank P. Moore... Dead...," Oct. 18, 1934, Dispatch. "Pioneer Fred Moore Dies At Home Here," Dec. 11, 1953 Dispatch. 1896, 1898 Cochise County voting registration. Sloan, History of Arizona, Vol. 3. Cochise County Marriage Book 5, p. 163.</small>

Mossman, Burton C. born 30AP1867 Aurora, Ill. Foreman Hashknife Ranch 1884; Navajo County Sheriff 1898; first Arizona Rangers captain 1901-02. Crossed border cattle with Packard and Tovrea (26JA1902R). Married Grace Coburn 12DC1905; two children. Associated with Greene and E.J. Gates in cattle business; purchased Diamond A Ranch near

Roswell, N.M. Died there 05SP1956.

Sources: O'Neal, Bill, The Arizona Rangers. Austin, Texas: Eakin Press, 1987. Hunt, Cap Mossman.

Neel, William Hutton born 05OC1861 Lancaster, Penn. to Walter H. and Mary (Hutton) Neel. To Arizona ca.1895 in employ of Ryan Brothers on Four Bar Ranch in Sulphur Springs Valley. Stayed with ranch when Hysham Brothers bought it; later obtained ownership position. Involved with Thompson Cattle Co. in Sonora (11JA1915I). Married Ellen Joyce Conroy NV1898 Denver; one child, Walter, born 10SP1900. After William died 11JA1915I on ranch, Ellen bought out Hysham. She managed Four Bar until her death 20JU1927 in car accident. Walter ran ranch while Cochise County Assessor; died 09JU1958.

Sources: Arizona Bureau of Vital Statistics birth and death certificates. Cochise County Probate No. 1177. "Thursday Will Be Funeral Of Neel," Jan. 12, 1915, International.

Nichols, Charles Arthur born 01JU1878 Whitesboro, N.Y. to Charles W. and Elizabeth (Stephens) Nicholas. Moved to Douglas 1903; organized Thirteen Club. Proprietor International Laundry with Pollack as partner. Manager Coronado Courts apartments 1940; Douglas historian in retirement. Married 24AG1909 Clare Mabel Kelsey; three children. Youngest, Betty, married Herbert Davis. Clare died 20OC1956; Charles 24AG1970.

Source: Hayostek, Cindy, 100 Years of History: St. Stephen's Episcopal Church in Douglas, Arizona. Privately printed by St. Stephen's, 2007.

Obregón, Álvaro Salido born 17FB1880 near Alamos, Son. to Fernando and Cenobia (Salido) Obregón. Worked as mechanic before obtaining farm and inventing garbanzo harvester. Married Refugio Urrea ca.1904; two sons. Elected Mayor Huatabampo, Son. 1911; organized militia 1912. April

1912 Battle of San Joaquin launched military career. Although lost arm 1915 Battle of Celaya, his tactical prowess propelled Constitutionalists into national prominence; Minister of War 1916. Married Maria Tapia ca.1917; three children. Inaugurated President of Mexico 01DC1920; his term marked end of violent revolution and beginning of educational, land and labor reforms. Retired to farming 1924; re-elected President 1928 but assassinated 17JY1928 before taking office.

Source: Hall, Linda B., Álvaro Obregón. College Station, Texas: Texas A&M University Press, 1981.

Overlock, Charles Alton born 26SP1859 Bangor, Maine to Jacob and Elvira (Nowell) Overlock. In 1882 Tombstone as carpenter; married there 1885 Anna Driscoll; three sons. Ranched in Sulphur Springs Valley (12AP1891E and 16MY1894P). With brother Lemuel had Tombstone and Bisbee butcher shops (03JA1896P). Ventured into mines, other projects (26FB1921I). With Alfred Paul Sr. and other friends claimed portion of Douglas town site 1900. Erected first building there -- office for his Douglas Lumber Co. Started real estate/insurance business 1907. Douglas' first elected mayor and first postmaster. While U.S. Marshall 1909-14, lived in Tucson. Returned to Douglas 1915; started feed store. Postmaster again when died 18FB1926. Anna died 16OC1949 in Calif. (19OC1949D); a descendant lives today in Bisbee.

Sources: "Charles A. Overlock, ... Dies Suddenly At Home Here," Dispatch, Feb. 19, 1926. Arizona Bureau of Vital Statistics birth and death certificates. Theobald, Arizona Territory Post Offices & Postmasters.

Paul, Alfred born 27JA1878 Dresden, Germany to Alexander and Albertine (Stildoff) Paul, who moved to U.S. 1880. As young man in western towns made living as miner, sometimes merchant. Joined C.A. Overlock and others in 1900 filing on Douglas town site. Provided smelter lime 1903-14 from Lee Station quarry, north of Douglas. Moved operation west of Douglas 1914; village of Paul Spur grew up around plant.

Married 05JU1902 Tombstone native Mabel Swain, daughter George W. and Martha E. Swain (04JY1902R). George, attorney and judge, owned Gladiator Mine with Vickers. George killed 02SP1911 by fall into mine (04SP1911I). Alfred and Mabel's children born in Douglas: Winifred Albertine, 11MR1903, and Alfred Raymond, 12OC1919. Alfred Jr. managed Paul Lime 1930s-50s. After his health faltered, Winifred's son, Howard Ames Jr., managed business. Alfred Sr. died 23SP1959. Family sold Paul Lime 1971 but family members remain in Cochise County.

   Sources: Arizona Bureau of Vital Statistics birth and death certificates. Hayostek, Cindy, "Our Mining Heritage," Pay Dirt Magazine, December 1997. Sloan, History of Arizona, Vol. 4.

Pollack, Thomas E. born 15JY1868 near Lake Geneva, Wis. Ran Iowa bank and mercantile before arriving 1895 in Flagstaff, Ariz. Raised sheep and cattle on Three V Ranch, north of Seligman; Grand Canyon and Willaha Cos., north of Williams; and Red River Land & Cattle Co., northern New Mexico. Established Apache Lumber Co. 1916 in McNary, Ariz.; developed associations with Santa Fe Railroad. Owner/president Flagstaff's Central Bank with Williams and Kingman branches. President Diamond Coal Co., Gallup, N.M. Married Mary Morton 22NV1909. Director Northern Arizona Normal School (03JY1902R), Arizona State Fair Commission. Died 27FB1938 in Flagstaff (03MR1938D).

   Sources: Connors, Who's Who In Arizona. Smith, Dean, Brothers Five. Tempe, Ariz.: Arizona Historical Society, 1989. Myrick, David, The Santa Fe Route. Wilson, Calif.: Signature Press, 1998.

Pyeatt, Ben born ca.1876 into large clan. Patriarch was James Benton Pyeatt, born 21FB1827 Mo., who had 13 children with wife Margaret Warren. Among offspring: James Henry, born 1861, Packard foreman 1898-19, died 1942; Ben, Packard foreman 1898-19 (05FB1917I); Hughella, born 1870, Avery Curry's wife, died 1954; Anna, born ca.1853, John Aston's wife. Pyeatts still ranch in western Cochise County.

Sources: Arizona Bureau of Vital Statistics birth and death certificates. Pyeatt oral history supplied by Gene Pyeatt. 1896 and 1902 Cochise County voting registration. Correspondence with Marie Pyeatt.

Randolph, Epes born 1856 in Virginia. Designed railroads and bridges before becoming Southern Pacific (SP) Tucson Division Superintendent 1895. President/general manager Cananea, Yaqui River & Pacific Railroad 1902. Manager SP affiliates known as "Randolph Lines" 1904. Involved in Tucson's Santa Rita Hotel and California Development Co.'s irrigation project. Married Eleanor Taylor JA1886 in Kentucky. Died 22AG1921 Tucson.

Sources: Connors, Who's Who in Arizona. Myrick, Railroads of Arizona Vol. I.

Rice, Harry Briggs born 31AG1863 Glenwood, Iowa. Worked briefly in Cheyenne, Wyo., where married Elizabeth Waring 1886; four sons. Worked in San Diego before assistant store manager Detroit Copper Co. Mercantile in Morenci 1899 (18JY1903R). Served on 1903, 1905 Territorial Council. To Douglas 1905 as assistant manager PD Mercantile; manager 1916. Active in Douglas Chamber of Commerce, Country Club; served on school board. Retired 1922 to California, where died 29SP1938. Two sons became prominent Douglas residents: Rex, owner real estate/brokerage firm; Caleb, Douglas Postmaster.

Sources: Goff, Territorial Officials, Vol. VII. "H.B. Rice, ... Dies At Santa Cruz, Calif., ...," Dispatch, Sept. 30, 1938.

Richardson, David A. born ca.1866 Crockett, Texas. Practiced law there until 1900 move to Nogales; then Douglas 1903. Defended Graham in El Tigre case (07OC1905R); published *Manual of Mexican Mining Law* (29OC1910I). Rosales Mining Co. secretary (27JY1907R); organized Cosac Mining Co. near El Tigre (30OC1911I). Partnered with Francisco

Elías in Agua Prieta tannery (12NV1919I); with Howell, Frank Hillman and others in Occidental Cattle Co. (11DC1917I). To El Paso (24OC1921I); died in Tucson 21NV1923 (22 and 23NV1923I).

Source: Connors, Who's Who in Arizona.

Rivera, Helidoro born ca.1875 Mexico; to Douglas ca.1906 with wife, Juana. Four children born in Douglas. Established Douglas grocery store (30JY1908I); with S.A. Gardanier rebuilt it into wholesale grocery/customs brokerage (09DC1916I). Founded Bancaria Mercantile y Agricola de Sonora with Gabilondo brothers, Elías and Soto (17DC1917I). Cattle and mining interests 1920-1. Killed in flash flood 12SP1926. Daughter Concepción married Antonio Gabilondo 03MY1928; her sister and brother joined American Consular Service.

Sources: 1920, 1920 U.S. Census. 1907-28 Douglas City Directories. "Popular Merchant Was 80 Yards Down Stream Under Auto," Sept. 14, 1926, Dispatch. "Gabilondo-Rivera Wedding ...," May 6, 1928, Dispatch. "Clark Rites Will Be Held This Morning," Oct. 31, 1944, Dispatch.

Ruiz, José Gutiérrez born ca.1867 in northern Spain. At age 14, stowed away on ship to Mexico. Owned two large Sonoran ranches, including Rancho Gallardo after Neel-Thompson. Superintended Agua Prieta-Bavispe road construction (07JA1934D). Married Eloisa Elías, sister of Sonoran Gov. Francisco Elías Suárez. She born 1877 Tecoripa, Son., to Manuel Elías Perez and Elosia Suárez Duarte. Ten surviving children, including Jose "Cowboy" Ruiz, elected Sonoran Sports Hall of Fame and Agua Prieta mayor. Other descendants still ranch in Sonora. Jose died 26JA1941 (28JA1941D); Eloisa 15JU1945 (17JU1945D).

Source: Elías, Armando C., The Elías Family. Tucson, Ariz.: U.S. Press & Graphics, 2008.

Serrano, Mother born Ana María Serrano Gámez 14NV1888 in Aguascalientes, A.C., Mexico. Entered novitiate 1910, vows 1916, arrived Douglas 1926. After moving into Packard's 10th Street house, she and three other nuns established Company Of Mary, an order devoted to education and charity. Novitiate in house; later classrooms/playground where Packard Herefords once grazed. Noted for artistic skills, especially embroidery, piano playing (her brother Francisco Serrano was well-known concert pianist). Also founded Elfrida's Catholic Church. Became U.S. citizen 1945. Died 17JU1972 in Douglas.

Sources: Naturalization papers held in Cochise County Clerk of Court Office. "Mother Serrano dies in convent," June 19, 1972, Dispatch.

Shattuck brothers **Enoch Austin**, **Jonas Henry** and **Lemuel Coover**, all born near Erie, Penn., sons of Henry Shattuck; Enoch and Jonas by first wife Emily Parker, Lemuel by second wife, Phoebe Ann Coover. In 1880s, brothers ranched as Cochise County's first cattle corporation, the Erie. Enoch served as Slaughter's undersheriff before he and Jonas moved the Erie to Kansas during 1890s drought. Lemuel stayed, becoming owner of mines, Bisbee Lumber Co., St. Louis Beer Hall and Miners & Merchants Bank. Married Isabella Grenfell 13AP1891; six children. Served on Bisbee City Council, Cochise County Board of Supervisors. Involved in Lucky Tiger-Combination Gold Mining Co., Shattuck-Denn Copper Co. and Winterhaven (Calif.) Commercial Co. After Isabella died 24OC1924, married Mary O. Wilson 25NV1926. Lemuel died 07SP1938 in Bisbee.

Sources: Connors, Who's Who in Arizona. Fathauer, Lemuel C. Shattuck. Bailey, Silk Hats.

Slaughter, John Horton born 02OC1841 Sabine Parish, La. to Benjamin and Minerva (Mabry) Slaughter. Reared in Texas, Confederate vet, Texas Ranger. Arrived 1880 San Pedro

Valley with cattle (07OC1880E); acquired San Bernardino land grant 1883. Used grant's artesian water to develop farm/ranch; built house there (19AP1891E). Cochise County Sheriff 1887-91; Arizona House 1907. Married Eliza Adeline Harris 04AG1871; two surviving children. Eliza died 1877; married Cora Viola Howell 16AP1878; several adopted children. John died 17FB1922 and Viola 01AP1941, both in Douglas. Ranch restored by Johnson Museum of Southwest in 1980s; open to public.

Sources: Connors, Who's Who in Arizona. Goff, Territorial Officials, Vol. VII. Erwin, Allen A., The Southwest of John Horton Slaughter. Spokane, Wash.: Arthur H. Clark Co. 1965.

Smith, Marcus Aurelius born 24JA1852 to Frederick C. and Agnes B. (Chinn) Smith in Cynthiana, Ky. Educated, admitted to bar there. Prosecuting attorney San Francisco 1879; married California native Elizabeth Rathbone; no children. Arrived in Tombstone 1881; held several mining interests. Cochise County Attorney 1883-85; eight terms Arizona's Congressional Representative 1887-1909; three terms U.S. Senate 1911-20; International Boundary Commissioner, 1921-24. Elizabeth died 16OC1899 in Tucson; he 07AP1924 in Washington, D.C.

Sources: Goff, Territorial Officials, Vol. III. Connors, Who's Who in Arizona.

Soto, C. Ignacio (aka Ygnacio) Martinez born 12MY1890 Bavipse, Son. to Jesús Ángel and Trinidad (Martinez) Soto. Educated in Moctezuma; working in Banco de Moctezuma when Packard transferred him to First National (28JU1910I). Married 31OC1912 Rosa Durazo in Moctezuma (09NV1912I); seven surviving children. Founded: International Commission Co. with S.A. Gardanier (16SP1915I); Bancaria Mercantile y Agricola de Sonora with Gabilondo brothers, Elias and Rivera (17DC1917I); Club Social de Agua Prieta (21FB1921I); Servicios Publicos de Agua Prieta (21 and 30SP1927D); Banco de Agua Prieta (19AG1928D); Cemento Pórtland Nacional S.A. (06JU1930D). Served Mexican Chamber of Deputies as Treasurer, 1924-28; Sonoran Governor, 1949-55. Died in 1962.

<small>Sources: Hayostek, Cindy, Borderland Chronicles No. 11, 2010. "El Gobernador Caballero," Sept. 28, 2008, La Jornada, Hermosillo, Son.</small>

Stebbins, Asa Harvey born ca.1840 in Massachusetts. Enlisted 44th Mass. Regiment 1862; discharged as lieutenant 1864. Married ca.1873 unknown woman who died ca.1877; two children. Arrived in Tombstone ca.1879; involved with Syndicate Mining Co., numerous other mines. Living in Jennie (Mrs. Casper) Taylor's boarding house when died 10JY1889.

<small>Sources: Cochise County Probate closed 226. "Obituary," July 11, 1889, Epitaph. 1881-86 Cochise County voting registration.</small>

Stephens, George Dixon born 04JU1884 Yolo County, Calif. Moved to Douglas 1904, homesteaded San Bernardino Valley 1908. Ranched with W.L. Hennessee until 1921 when bought him out. Married 03JU1908 Elizabeth Hassett, who'd lived 5-6 years at Slaughter's. After she died 27MR1911, married Rachel H.; two children. Son George married Adrienne Ames, Winifred (Paul) Ames' daughter. George Sr. died 30SP1973 in Douglas; Rachel 20AG1981.

<small>Sources: Cochise County Marriage Book 5, p. 448. Arizona Bureau of Vital Statistics death certificate. 1881, 1886 Cochise County voting registration. Cochise County Probate 12028 and 14082. "G.D. Stephens succumbs," Oct. 1, 1973, Dispatch.</small>

Sweet, Frederick Arnold born ca.1860 Rhode Island. Arrived Bisbee 1887; assistant CQ surgeon 1890; chief surgeon 1891. Married Julia Harkness in Brooklyn (20FB1897P); two sons. Active in Democratic politics, fund-raising to build Bisbee's Episcopal Church. Following his 15AP1903 death, church built as St. John's Sweet Memorial Church with prominent stained glass window dedicated to Sweet. In 1974, Sweet's son, who bore his name, gave lecture in Bisbee. Born two months after Sweet's death, second son became director of Chicago Art Institute. (17FB1974R).

<small>Sources: Hodge, Virginia F., St. John's 90th Anniversary Calendar. Privately printed, 1993. "Dr. Frederick Arnold Sweet," April 16, 1903, Arizona Republican.</small>

Taft, Kimball C. "Tim" born ca.1849 Michigan. Arrive Bisbee late 1890s. Drove stagecoach between Naco and Nacozari (28MY1899WO); then between Nacozari and Fronteras (07MR1902R). Worked Wisconsin (17NV1904D) and Esmeralda (01JY1905R) mines and managed mine for Bell & Pearson Co., all near Nacozari (01OC1905R). With wife Margaret moved to Phoenix (18JA1918I), but then to Douglas and watchman job at CQ smelter (24MR1922I). Died 27MR1923 in Douglas.

<small>Sources: Arizona Bureau of Vital Statistics death certificate. Cochise County voting registration.</small>

Teachout, Harlow (aka Harold) M. born 06DC1832 Vermont, probably nephew of Mary Ann Teachout, who married John W. Hohstadt Sr. Harlow married May Doud, born 08JU1865 Vermont to Albert and Lucinda (Sayer) Doud. The couple joined Hohstadts ranching in Sonora ca.1888. Teachout place near Cos, Son. Before his 22MC1921 death in Douglas (24MR1921D), Harlow briefly farmed near Yuma. May broke hip (30MR1927D) and became bedridden. Friends, including Jimmy Douglas and Packard, regularly called upon her. Daughter Verlie W. Ream cared for May until she died 20JA1935 in Douglas (27JA1935D).

<small>Sources: Baker-Reynolds, Some Came Sailing. Interview with Mary H. Robinson, 01FB2008 in Douglas. Arizona Bureau of Vital Statistics death certificates.</small>

Thompson, Rufus M. "Babe" born 1859 Bell County, Texas; one of three sons. Married in Texas; four daughters. Drove cattle into Cochise County 1886 and stayed. Got nickname by rescuing a baby (16AG1913I). Foreman Greene

Cattle Co. (26JY1903R); Turkey Track manager (02NV1907R). With Neel leased Gallardo Ranch (06 and 17SP1913I). After 29JY1914 death, Packard said Thompson was "one of the most conscientious men with whom I have an acquaintance. His idea of right and wrong was of the kind that precluded any idea of injustice to anyone."

Sources: Cochise County Probate No. 862. 1896-1900 Cochise County voting registration. "'Babe' Thompson Is Victim Of Pneumonia," July 30, 1914, International.

Tovrea, Edward Ambrose born 20MR1861 Sparta, Ill. to Arthur T. and Rosa (Hood) Tovrea. Freighting, 1883; overseeing irrigation construction, 1885-88; running butcher business, 1889; all in central Arizona. Partnered with Mossman to buy Lem Overlock's butcher shop (02MR1901R); soon added three more (07AG1903R). Organized Arizona Packing Co. (13DC1919I). Married 1885 Lillian (Richardson); four sons. Divorced 26DC1908; married 26DC1908 Della Gillespie. Moved 1914 to Phoenix; 1931 bought what's now known as Tovrea Castle. Died 07FB1932 in Phoenix. Son Phillip ran Arizona Packing, which made over $8 million in 1941; sold to Cudahy 1947. City of Phoenix restored castle in 1993; now open to public.

Sources: Sloan, History of Arizona. 1902-16 Cochise County voting registration. Carlson, Raymond, "Tovrea's, The Story Of An Adventure In Beef," March 1942 Arizona Highways. Cochise County Civil No. 5476. Cochise County Marriage Book 6, p. 48.

Tweed, Henry A. born ca. 1843 Florida to Charles Austin and Ruth G. Tweed. Charles arrived Prescott 1870 as Arizona Associate Supreme Court Justice. Henry arrived Tombstone ca.1880. Married Harriet Kimball Dodge, born ca.1844 Boston to William H. and Harriett W. (Etheridge) Dodge.; four children. Bought Vizina Mine 1883; involved with Bothin, Tweed & Co. (27MY1885T); Dragoon ranch (26JU1885T). After financial troubles, moved to Phoenix (23AP1889P) where developed real estate (15MR1892P). Died 18NV1895 Phoenix (22NV1895P); Harriett 19MY1911. Grandson Charles H. Tweed Jr., pioneer orthodontist, founded Charles H. Tweed International Foundation for Orthodontic Research and Education in Tucson.

<small>Sources: Goff, Arizona Territorial Officials Vol. 1. Arizona Bureau of Vital Statistics birth and death certificates. 1850, 1870, 1880, 1910 U.S. Census. www.tweedortho.com/</small>

Vail, Walter L. and **Edward L.** born 13MY1852 and 19SP1849 in Nova Scotia; grew up in New Jersey. Walter moved west 1875; with partner bought Empire Ranch 1876. In 1879, Edward joined venture, which prospered on Tombstone beef sales and Total Wreck Mine. Incorporated 1883. California marketing linked brothers to Carroll Gates and J.V. Vickers' CCC and other firms. Walter served 1879 Territorial House; Pima County Board of Supervisors. Married Margaret R. Nehall 1882; seven children. Edward served as Pima County Supervisor and county treasurer. Never married. Walter moved to California 1896. After he died there 02DC1906, family sold Empire to Gates (05JA1910I); retained Vail & Vickers Co., including Santa Rosa Island, off California coast. Edward died 15OC1936. Succeeding Vail generations managed island, which National Park Service acquired in controversial manner. Vail & Vickers dissolved 2011.

<small>Sources: Goff, Arizona Territorial Officials, Vol. VII. Bailey, Silk Hats. "Arizona Suffered Loss...," Dec. 8, 1906, Star; "Death Reaches...," Oct. 16, 1936, Star.</small>

Vickers, John Van born 02MR1850 to Paxson and Ann (Lewis) Vickers in Chester County, Penn. Educated there; took on family business upon father's death. Married Anna Mary Childs 1872; five daughters. Established Tombstone real estate office (03JY1880E and 05AG1880WN); added insurance agency (18FB1882N). Bought, sold Old Guard, other Arizona mines (02OC1890P). Agent/broker for Hohstadts (11SP1885R-E), other ranchers. Founded CCC with Theodore White, others; treasurer Erie Cattle Co. (11MR1895P). Tombstone School Trustee (26JU1885T); Cochise County Treasurer, 1888-89, 1895-96; Arizona Livestock Sanitary Board (10AP1889P); Territorial Council (20JA1891P). Anna ran business when husband held elective offices (04AP1895P). Moved to California 1898. Also owned Panhandle Cattle Co. in Texas, Santa Rosa Island, San Diego packing business, Huntington Beach oil and real estate; Kelso, Wash. coal interests. Alex Bayless managed latter (03JA1892E). Sold out CCC 1909. Died 28DC1912 in Los Angeles (02JA1913I).

Sources: 1860-80, 1900-10 U.S. Census. Goff, Arizona Territorial Officials Vol. VII. Bailey, Silk Hats.

White, Theodore Frelinghuyson born 13AG1844 to James and Lydia (Jarrett) White in Upper Dublin, Penn. Educated as engineer there; to Arizona 1871 as federal surveyor. Married 14AP1874 Annie Maxwell, born 10FB1854 in California; four children. Founded El Dorado Ranch ca.1880; incorporated CCC with Vickers 1885. President Tombstone Stockgrowers Association (02JA1886T); Cochise County Supervisor (16JY1885T). Sold out of CCC ca.1902. Prospered with California street paving business. Died 27JA1914 (30JA1914I).

Sources: Info provided by Nan Orshefsky (White's granddaughter), Wainscott, N.Y., to author 18AP1997. Bailey, Silk Hats.

Wood, Robert Clifton born 20FB1828 Virginia; reared Missouri. Moved to California 1854. Raised, led Wood's Battalion in Missouri during Civil War. Married Virginia Reynolds; five children. Following war Kansas City businessman; moved first to Prescott, then Tucson 1873. Bought lower San Pedro River ranch (04FB1880S); Turquoise-area mines (27JY1880E) but concentrated on Tucson business. Died 12OC1902 in Tucson; Virginia 16AP1920.

Sources: "Pioneer Dies," Oct. 13, 1902, Star. Arizona Bureau of Vital Statistics death certificates.

Bibliography

Books

A History of the Town of Portville, 1805-1920, Portville Historic and Preservation Society, 1986.

Arizona, The Youngest State, Vol. III&IV. Chicago: S.J. Clarke Publishing Co, 1916.

Adams, William, ed., Historical Gazetteer and Biographical Memorial of Cattaraugus County, N.Y. Syracuse, N.Y.: Lyman, Horton & Co., 1893.

Axford, Joseph "Mack," Around Western Campfires. Tucson, Ariz.: University of Arizona Press, 1969.

Bailey, Lynn R., The Dragoon Mountains. Tucson, Ariz.: Westernlore Press, 2008.

Bailey, Lynn R., Tombstone: Too Tough To Die. Tucson, Ariz.: Westernlore Press, 2004.

Bailey, Lynn R. and Chaput, Don, Cochise County Stalwarts, Vol. I-II. Tucson, Ariz.: Westernlore Press, 2000.

Bailey, Lynn R., We'll All Wear Silk Hats. Tucson, Ariz.: Westernlore Press, 1994.

Baker-Reynolds, Muriel, Some Came Sailing. Seattle, Wash.: privately printed, 2004.

Bisbee City Directories

Blake, William P., Tombstone and its Mines. New York: Cheltenham Press, 1902.

Brands and Marks of Cattle, Horses, Sheep, Goats and Hog, Livestock Sanitary Board of Arizona, 1908.

Brown, Clara Spaulding, Tombstone from a Woman's Point of View. Tucson, Ariz.: Westernlore Press, 1998.

Chafin, Carl, editor, The Private Journal of George Whitwell Parsons, Vol. II. Tombstone: Cochise Classics, 1997.

Clark, Ethel Maddock, Arizona State History of the Daughters of the American Revolution. Greenfield, Ohio: Greenfield Printing & Publishing Co., 1929.

Cleland, Robert Glass, A History of Phelps Dodge. New York: Alfred A. Knopf, 1952.

Clements, Eric L., After the Boom in Tombstone and Jerome, Arizona. Reno, Nev.: University of Nevada Press, 2003.

Connors, J., Who's Who In Arizona. Tucson, Ariz.: Arizona Daily Star job department, 1913.

Douglas City Directories

Elías, Armando C., Familia Elías. Tucson, Ariz., privately printed, 2008.

Eppinga, Jane, Arizona Sheriffs. Tucson, Ariz., Rio Nuevo Press, 2006.

Erwin, Allen A., The Southwest of John Horton Slaughter. Spokane, Wash.: Arthur H. Clark Co., 1965.

Faulk, Odie B., Tombstone Myth and Reality. New York: Oxford University Press, 1972.

Fathauer, Isabel Shattuck, Lemuel C. Shattuck, A Little Mining, A Little Banking, and A Little Beer. Tucson, Ariz.: Westernlore Press, 1991.

Foner, Eric, A Short History of the Reconstruction. New York, Harper & Row, 1990.

Goff, John S., Arizona Territorial Officials, Vol. I-VI. Cave Creek, Ariz.: Black Mountain Press, 1996.

Goff, John S., George W.P. Hunt and His Arizona. Pasadena, Calif.: Socio Technical Publications, 1973.

Hait, Pam, The Arizona Bank, Arizona's Story. Phoenix, Ariz.: Heritage Graphics, 1987.

Hall, Linda B., Álvaro Obregón. Power and Revolution in Mexico, 1911-1920. College Station, Texas: Texas A&M University Press, 1981.

Hatch, Vernelle A., Illustrated History of Bradford, McKean County, Penn. Bradford: Burk Bros., 1901.

Hopkins, Ernest J., Financing The Frontier, A Fifty Year History of the Valley National Bank. Phoenix, Ariz.: The Arizona Printers, 1950.

Hunt, Norman K., The Killing of Chester Bartell. Phoenix, Ariz.: Cowboy Miner Productions, 2006.

Jordan, Terry C., North American Cattle-Raising Frontiers. Albuquerque, N.M.: University of New Mexico Press, 1993.

Jorgensen, Avis A.K., Early Danish Pioneers. Tucson, Ariz.: Privately printed, 2012.

Kelly, George H., Legislative History 1864-1912. Phoenix, Ariz.: Manufacturing Stationers, 1926.

Klein, Maury, The Power Makers. New York, NY: Bloomsbury Press, 2008.

Limerick, Patricia Nelson, The Legacy of Conquest. New York: W.W. Norton & Co., 1987.

Lyon, William H., Those Old Yellow Dog Days. Tucson, Ariz.: Arizona Historical Society, 1994.

Machado, Manuel A. Jr., The North Mexican Cattle Industry, 1910-1975. College Station, Texas: Texas A&M University Press, 1981.

McClintock, James H., Arizona, Prehistoric, Aboriginal, Pioneer, Modern; The Nation's Youngest Commonwealth Within A Land Of Ancient Culture, Vol. II, III, IV. Chicago: S.J. Clarke Pub. Co., 1916.

Milner. Clyde A. II; O'Connor, Carol A; and Sandweiss, Martha A., editors, The Oxford History of the American West. New York: Oxford University Press, 1994.

Myrick, David F., Railroads of Arizona, Vol. I. Berkeley, Calif.: Howell-North Books, 1975.

Nichols, Charles A., Dear Old Cochise. Unpublished manuscript in author's possession.

Parson, George W., A Tenderfoot in Tombstone. Tucson, Ariz.: Westernlore Press, 1996.

Press Reference Library, Notables of the West, Vol. II, no publication data, 1915.

Raat, Dirk W., Revoltosos. College Station, Texas: Texas A&M University, 1981.

Rynning, Thomas H., Gun Notches, A Saga of a Frontier Lawman. San Diego, Calif.: Frontier Heritage Press, 1971.

Schwikart, Larry, A History of Banking In Arizona. Tucson, Ariz.: University of Arizona Press, 1982.

Sharp, Robert L., Bob Sharp's Cattle Country. Tucson, Ariz.: University of Arizona Press, 1985.

Shillingberg, Wm. B., Tombstone, A.T. A History of Early Mining, Milling and Mayhem. Spokane, Wash., Arthur H. Clark Co., 1999.

Sloan, Richard E., edit., History of Arizona. Phoenix, Ariz.: Record Publishing Co., 1930.

Sonnichsen, C.L., Colonel Green and the Copper Skyrocket. Tucson, Ariz:, University of Arizona Press, 1974.

Thames, John L., Blacksmiths of Tucson. Prepared for the 2000 Conference of the Artist-Blacksmith Association of North America held in Flagstaff, Ariz.

Theobald, John & Lillian, Arizona Territory Post Offices & Postmasters. Phoenix, Ariz.: Arizona Historical Foundation, 1961.

Tombstone General and Business Directory, 1883-84.

Wagoner Jay J., Arizona Territory 1863-1912, A Political History. Tucson, Ariz.: University of Arizona Press, 1970.

Wilson, John P., Islands in the Desert. Albuquerque, N.M.: University of New Mexico Press, 1995.

Zimmerman, Warren, First Great Triumph, How Five Americans Made Their Country A World Power. New York: Farrar, Straus & Giroux, 2002.

Family History

Roland "Buster" Pyeatt oral history
Ashley B. Packard research

Governmental Sources

Arizona Bureau of Vital Statistics
Arizona State Prison records
Arizona State Archives
Arizona State Census
California Death Index
California Voter Registers
Cochise County Board of Supervisors' Minutes
Cochise County Recorder's Office
Cochise County Archives (Treasurer's Office)
Cochise County Clerk of the Court
Maricopa County Recorder's Office
Pima County Recorder's Office
U.S. Bureau of Investigation
U.S. Federal Census

Newspapers

Arizona Daily Star
Arizona Quarterly Illustrated

Cynthia F. Hayostek

Bisbee Orb
Bisbee Review
Bisbee Weekly Ore
Cochise Quarterly
Douglas Dispatch
Douglas International
Tombstone Epitaph
Tombstone Nugget
Tombstone Prospector
Tombstone Record-Epitaph
The Tombstone
Tucson Citizen
Weekly Tombstone Nugget

Magazines

Arizona Journal of History
Borderland Chronicles
Journal of the West
Pay Dirt Magazine

Pamphlets, Papers

"An Historical Sketch," Young Men's Christian Association Railroad Branch, May 1917, no printer listed.

Bahre, Conrad J., "Wild Hay Harvesting in Southern Arizona," Journal of Arizona History, Spring 1987.

Christiansen, James E. and Jean M., The Felix and Ada Christiansen Home and Ranch, A Bit of Arizona-Mexico Border History. Privately printed, 2006.

Farrell, Mary M. and others, Tearing Up the Ground With Splendid Results: Historic Mining on the Coronado National Forest. Heritage Resources Management Report No. 15, USDA Forest Service Southwestern Region, 1995.

Fritz, Scott, "Impact of Economic Change on the Anglo, Jewish and Hispano Mercantile Communities in New Mexico and Arizona, 1865-1929." Paper given at 2003 Arizona Historical Society convention.

Hadley, Diana, "Cattle and Drought on the San Pedro River," paper given at 2003 Arizona Historical Society Convention.

"Historical Sketch, St. John's Church, Bisbee, Arizona," no date or author, from church office files.

"History of the Empire Ranch" brochure and other material provided by the Empire Ranch Foundation.

Hart, Mary Nicklanovich, "Merchant and Miner, Two Serbs in Early Bisbee." Arizona Journal of History, Autumn 1988.

Jeffrey, Robert S., The History of Douglas, Arizona. Master's thesis, University of Arizona, 1951.

King, Frank M., "Colonel Packard Will Be Missed," March 28, 1935, Western Livestock Journal.

Miller, Ernest C., Pennsylvania's Oil Industry. Gettysburg, Penn.: Pennsylvania Historical Association, 1974.

Mumme, Stephen P., "Battle of Naco: Factionalism and Conflict in 1914-15." Arizona and the West, Summer 1979.

Peplow, Edward H. Jr., "Memories of the Old Adams," Phoenix Magazine, May 1975.

Roberts, Virginia Culin, "The Mosons And The Martins, Pioneer Ranchers of Arizona and Sonora." Arizona Journal of History, Autumn 2004.

Santiago, Dawn Moore, "Charles H. Bayless." Arizona Journal of History, Autumn 1994.

Tellman, Barbara and Hadley, Diana, Crossing Boundaries: An Environmental History of the Upper Sam Pedro River Watershed, Arizona and Sonora. Tucson, Ariz.: Arizona State Museum et al., 2006.

Vail, Edward, Day Book in University of Arizona Library Special Collections.

Wagner, Jay J., Journal of Arizona History, Vol. II.

Wiggins, Genevieve, "A History of Douglas the Douglas Public Schools 1901-1965," unknown publishing information.

Wilson, Roscoe G., Pioneer and Well Known Cattlemen of Arizona. Phoenix, Ariz., McGrew Commercial Printery, 1956.

Wood, Charles L., Journal of the West, January 1977.

Worlds' Fair Edition of Bisbee Review "An Historical Sketch," Young Men's Christian Association Railroad Branch, May 1917, no printer listed.

Cash book of Mexican Methodist Episcopalian Church, ca. 1920. Photocopy in author's possession.

Websites

www.aphis.usda.gov
www.azstatefair.com
www. findagrave.com
www.genealogy.az.gov
http://herrick.alfred.edu/special/archives
http://papermoneyofsonora.com
www.tweedortho.com

Index

Adams Hotel, **120**, 138
Adams, John C., 120, 136-7, *236*
Adamson, John C., 219, *236*
Agua Prieta, Son., 175-6, 182, 193
Ah Lum Co., 124-5
Ajo Mountains, Son., 128, 181
Alfred, N.Y., 9-10, 150, 218
Angius, John B., 145-6, 168, *236-7*
Anshutz, Charles, 87, 106
Apache Indians, 11, 55, 65-6, 68, 83
Archibald, John R., 5
Arizona & Colorado Railroad, 156
Arizona Livestock Sanitary Commission, 119, 260, 272
Arizona Rangers, 132, 138, 151, 155, 170, 173
Arizona & South East Railroad (A&SE), 74, 78, 80, 129, 151
Arizona Territorial Council, 107, 111-2, 116, **118**, 119, 133
Arizona Territorial (State) Fair, 136, **137**, 138, 188
Arizona Trust & Banking Co., 157, 163, 188
arms embargo, smuggling, 195-6
Arthur, Chester A., 50-1
Ash Canyon, Ariz., 68, 75, 90
Aston, Henry J. and family, 79, 106, 147, *237-8*
automobiles, 1-2, 189-90, 207
Axford, Mack, 67, *237*
Babocomari, 82-4, 94, 254
banking operations, 1, 158, 163, 166-7, 179, 185, 188, 194, 216, 220-2
Bank of Bisbee, 146-7, 154
Bank of Douglas, 156-7, 178, 220
Barron, Augustus, 33, *238*
Barr, Robert W., 147, 169
Barrow, Sam M., 122, 140
Bayless, Alexander H., 72, *239*
Bayless, Charles H. and William H., 72, 89
Beauchamp, Henry C., 178, *240*
Behan, John H., 54, 59
Benson, Ariz., 19, 86
Bessemer Hotel, 110, 122

bimetallism, 111
Bisbee, Ariz., 38, 73-4, 106, 111, 127, 131, 137, 145, 149
Blinn, Lewis W., 26, 55
border trade, 86, 115, 151, 167, 179, 182-3, 205
Boston & Arizona Co., 19, 24, 32-4, 36, 82-3
bovine babesiosis (Texas fever), 115-6, 183
Bothin, Julian C., 51-2, 54, 61, 77
Bothin, Tweed & Co., 52, 61, 64
Bradford, Edward C., 185, 199, 234
Bradford, Penn., 8-9
Brodie, Alexander O., 131, 134
Brooks, John and Ross, 170
Brophy, William H., 146, 149, 156
Bryan, William Jennings, 67, 111, 130, 162, 184
Bullionville, Ariz., 19
Burnett, James C., 80, 122-5
Calles, Plutarco Elías, 177, 192-5, **196**, 216
Calumet & Arizona Mining Co., 151, 202, 218
Camou, Jose Pedro and family, 77, 87, 129-30
Camp Harry J. Jones (aka Camp Douglas), 178, 187, 194-5
Cananea Cattle Co., 179, 183
Cananea Consolidated Copper Co., 135, 147, 156, 179
Cananea, Son., 126, 128, 155, 157
Cananea, Yaqui River & Pacific Railroad (CY&P), 146, 155
Carranza, Venustiano, 182-3, 193, 19-6
Cattaraugus County, N.Y, 4, 60, 211
Charleston, Ariz., 15, 19
Chinese people, 53, 124
Chiricahua Cattle Co., 73, 94, 115, 147, 169
chloriders, 20, 25-6,
Christiansen, Hans L., 214, *240-1*
Christiansen, Hans M. family, 82, *240*
Civil War, 4
Civil War of Incorporation, 48
Claiborn, Bill, 49
Clanton, Ike and Bill, 48-50
Clapp, Milton B., 47, 72
Clark, Harry A., 218, *241*
Clarkson, Alec and family, 230
Clum, John, 24, 48, 62

Cobre Grande Copper Co., 126, 128
Cochise County Fair, 202-3
Cochise County Supervisors, 55, 107
Cochise County Treasurer, 54, 107
Coleville, Penn., 7
Company of Mary, 216
Conlon, Hugh, 106, 115, 148, 169, **204**, *241-2*
Constitutionalist faction, 182-3, 187, 192-5, 200
Contention, Ariz., 19
Contention Mine, 15, 25, 61
Contention Consolidated Mining Co., 19, 82
copper production, 74, 111, 116, 151, 158, 181, 202
Copper Queen Consolidated Mining Co., 74, 80, 135, 151
Corbin, Frank, Elbert and Phillip, 15, 29-30, 61
Corcoran, Katie, 121-2
corriente cattle, 74, **85**, 114,
Cottrell, Max B. and family, 150, 157, 161, 179, 205, **215**, 224, 231
court actions, 23, 27-8, 30-2, 34, 36, 52, 77, 81, 83, 87, 180
Courtland, Ariz., 156, 160
Cowen, James G., 153, 160
Crystal Springs, Ariz., 79-80, 87, 124
Cunningham, Michael, 146, 149, 156
Curry, Avery and Joe, *242*
dams, 87, 90 110, 122-23, 125
Davis, Jr., John H. "Jack," 1, 217, 223
Dawe, George, 178, 219, *242-3*
Democratic Party, 6-7, 48, 130, 133, 138, 148, 150
Des Moines and Tombstone Mining & Milling Co., 20
Dexter Stable, 54, 56, 59, 62
Diaz, Porfirio, 173-4
Doan, Fletcher and Frank, 160, 163, 166, 189, 195, 209, 217, *243-4*
Double Adobe, Ariz., 209
Douglas, Ariz., 131, 152, 202
Douglas City Bank, 156, **164**
Douglas International newspaper, 173-4
Douglas, James and James S., 146, 151, 156, 220
Douglas, Walter, 136, 155, 198
Douglas schools system, 187-8, 206, 209
Dragoon Mountains, 26-7, 46, 64, 68-9, 160, 192
drought, 93-4, 98, 133, 149

Dunbar, John, 54-6, 106, 113, *244*
Dunbar, Thomas, 54-6, 59, 89, 106, *244*
Dunn, Edward H., 13, 31, 119
Earp, Wyatt, Virgil, Morgan, 48-50
El Dorado Ranch, 72, 272,
Elías, Francisco, 188, 197, 203, 207, *244-5*
Ellis, Charles O., 156, 184
El Paso & Southwestern Railroad (EP&SW), 151, 160
El Tigre Mine, Son., 153, 177, 193, 250, 264
Emanuel, Alfred H., 22, 68, 88, 90, 124, *245*
Empire Ranch, 71, 147, 169
Epitaph newspaper, 14,
Erie Cattle Co., 71, 94, 115, 126, 192, 209
Etchells, Charles T. and family, 165, *245-6*
Exposition, Columbia (1893) and Louisiana (1904), 95-6, 105, 134
Farish, Thomas and William, 76, 90
farming operations, 67, 110, 124, **161**, 179, 188, 205, 210, 214
Fay, Artemis E., 14
fencing, 107, 126-7, 205
Filkins, Charles H., 9-10, 13, 20,
fire, 24-6, 46-7, 153, 162
First District Court, 23, 27, 30, 32, 125
First National Bank of Douglas, 156-9, 163, **164**, 166, 176, 178, 180, 185, 194, 205-6, 212-3, 216, 230-1
Fort Huachuca, Ariz., 54, 56, 114,
Four Bar Ranch, 192, 260-2
Fronteras, Son., 166, 176-7
Gabilondo family, 177, 197, *246*
Gadsden Hotel, 177, 189, 193, 231
Gallardo Rancho, 192-3
Gallen, Simon P., 87, 110, 123,
Gardanier, Henry A. and Sutter A., 187, *246-7*
Gates, Carrol and Egbert G., 127, 147, *247*
Gird, Richard, 14, 17, 29-30,
Gleeson, Ariz., 156, 160
Glenn, Will D. family, 167, 230
Gomez, Hilaria, 87, 124
Graham, Benjamin F., 153, *247-8*
Grand Central Mine, 15, 25, 61
Graves, Elbridge W. and family, **165**, 166, 175, **196**, 205, 212, 220-

1, 230, *248*
Gray, John P., 48
Great Depression, 217-22
Greene and Tanner Ditch, 75
Greene, Ella (first wife), 75, 123, 125
Greene, Ella and Eva (daughters), 75, 121-2
Greene, Mary (Proctor) (second wife), 147
Greene, William C., 75-6, 82, 87, 89-90, 98, 105-6, 110, **113**-14, 117, 121-23, 125-6, 135, 139-41, 147, 153-57, 170, 179-80, 198, *248*
Half Moon Ranch, 67-8, 90, 110, 153
Hall, B. Frank and James K.P., 18, 20
Hanks, Lewis C., 156, 163, 165, *249*
Harsell, Katherine S., 206, *249*
Hart, Harry, 183, *249*
hay, 55, 105, 154, 161, 205
Haynes, John, 32
Head Center Mining Co., 20, 33
Helms, Charles E., 64-5
Hempel, Eugene C., **186**, 234
Henness, Kelvin and Russell, 216, 218
Hereford, Ariz., 79, 87, 107, 124, 152
Hereford cattle, 2, **85**, 117, 127, **152**, 189, 203-5, 212, 218-**19**, 230
Hillman, Frank, 214, 230
Hohstadt, John W. family, 83, 86, 91, 115-6, 151, 183, *250*
Holbrook, Albert A., 132
Holland, Walter E. family, 230
Holliday, John, 48-50
Holly, Lavina C., 34-5, 41
Hood, James T. "Tom" and Joseph E., 115, 209-10, *250-1*
Hopkins, Alphonius A., 9-10, 16, 26, 28-32, 34-6,
horses, 2, 4-5, 59, 135, 137-8, 161, 181-2
horse racing, 42, 58, 63, 135, 137, 224
Howell, James A., 163, *251*
Huachuca Mountains, 47, 68
Huachuca Water Co., 47
Huerta, Victoriano, 177, 182-3
Hulings, Marcus and Willis, 15, 39
Hunt, Charles P. family, 191, *252*
Hunt, George W.P., **118**, 207

Hunter, John S., 27, 32
International Commission Co., 187, 195-6
Ives, Eugene S., 121, 133-5,
Johnson, Peter J. and family, 148, *253*
joint statehood (AZ and NM), 134, 136
Jones, Mary "Mother," 174
Joyce, Milton B., 55
Kansas, 86, 94-5, 104, 108, 153, 162, 179, 183, 192, 219
Kelton, Carlton B., 82, 98, 156, *253-4*
Kibbey, Joseph H., 133, 138, 155, 162
Kimball, Floyd C., 218, *254*
King, Frank M., 210, 217
Knoxville Mine, 28, 30-1, 33-4,
Kosterlitzky, Emil, 128
Kruger, Louis P., 157, 225, *254*
Kyrene, Ariz., 115, 126, 154, 179, 205
La Morita, Son., 115-6, 128, 139,
Land, Edward and William C., 82, 84, 117, 133, *254-5*
Lawhon, Wright W., 166, 185, 188, 207, 234, *255*
Leatherwood, Robert N., 10, 41, *255*
Lenormand, Emile, 81, *256*
Levy, Ben and family, 218, *256*
Lewis Springs, Ariz., 87
Lopez, Arturo "Red," 175
Lucas, John H., 23, 32, 35
Lucky Cuss Hill/Mine, 14
Lucky Tiger Co., 153
Lutley, William, 115, *257*
Mababi, Hacienda/Rancho, 166, 181, 198
Madero, Francisco, 175
Main Settlement, N.Y., 4, 5
Marley, David V., 230, *257*
Maynard, Benjamin F., 36, 58
Maytorena, José M., 177, 183, 192
McCord, Myron H., 121
McGowan, James B., 23
McCullagh, William J., 9,
McInernay, Bessie, 167, **186**
McKean County, Penn., 8
McLaury, Tom and Frank, 49

McNair, James C., 115, *257-8*
Meade, W.C., 89, 162
Meadows, John, 115, *258*
Metcalf, George A., 76, 155, *258*
Mexico & Colorado Railroad, 160
Mexican Revolution, 168, 174-5, 182, 192, 196
Miller, John M., 35-6
Miller, William G., 209-10, *259*
Mills, Charles E., 185, 212-3
milling operations, 19, 69
Miners & Merchants Bank, 153, 157
Mining Law of 1872, 23-4, 31
mining operations, 13-17, 18-19, 27-8, 31, 33, 43-5,
Mitchell, George, 127, 156, 158, *259*
Moctezuma Banking Co., 159, 167-8, 178, 180
Moctezuma, Son., 76, 159, 175-6, 179, 192
Moeur, Benjamin B., 220, 225
Mollison, W.S., 27, 68
Moore, Peter and family, 79-83, 209, *259-60*
Moson family, 76, **85**, 142,
Mossman, Burton C., 132-3, 152, 224-5, *260-1*
Mule Mountains, 74, 80
Naco, Ariz. and Son., 128, 146-7, 151, 157, 184, 193, 216
Nacozari Railroad, 160, 175-6
Nacozari, Son., 116, 151, 176-7, 183, 197, 202
Neel, William H., 115, 192, *261*
Nichols, Charles A., 160, 222, *261*
Obregón, Álvaro S., 177-8, 181, 193, **196**, 197, 216, *261-2*
Ochoaville, Ariz., 115,
oil industry, 8-9,
Old Guard Mine, 37
Olean, N.Y., 4,
Ojo de Agua, Son., 78, 105, 117, 130, 147, 181-2, 184, 207-8, 214
Orion Silver Mining Co., 30-1, 34
Ord Hotel, 157
Orneo Mine, 27
Osborn Station, Ariz., 74, 110, 115-6, 152
Overlock, Charles and Lemuel, 114, 150-2, 174, *262*
Owl's Nest Mine, 14, 29
Packard, Ashley Burdette Jr. (grandson), 1-2, 188, 214, **215**, 217,

223, 232
Packard, Ashley Burdette Sr. (son), 59, **96**, 98, 100, 104-5, 127, 132, 150, 160, 162, **186**, 205-6, 209, 212, **215**, 217-18
Packard, Ashley Giles (father), 5-6, 64, **96**, 118
Packard, Burdette Aden,
ancestry, 5-6, 12; arrival in Tombstone, 3, 12; banker, 159, 179; birth and childhood, 5-6; business owner, 5, 52, 56, 95, 137; cattle broker, 77, 84-6, 110, 115, 117, 126, 131, 142, 154; cattle inspector, 69-70, 74, 88; cattleman, 94, 105-6, 117; character, 1-2, 43, 57, 69, 184, 213; community service, 135, 148, 175, 159, 205, 207, 210-11, 222; death, 224; domestic life, 22, 57, 60, 69, 99, 101,146, **159**, 160, 179, 189; encounter with Ike Clanton, 49-50; Episcopalian, 148, 195; farmer, 66-7, 80; hawker, 5, 7; horse trader, 4; humor, 84, 112, 210, 213, 216; illness, 113, 149, 203, 214, 224; legislator, 111-12, 118-9, 121, 133-4; marries Ella Lewis, 9; marries Lottie Holbrook, 131; merchandiser, 5, 52; mine owner, 16, 26-32, 34-6; nicknames, 179; oil man, 7, 9-10, 208; photographs of, 5, 16, 112, 116, 118, 149, 203-4, 219, 221; physical appearance, 1; politician, 48, 107, 111, -12, 116, 117-18, 133-4; rancher, 79, 84, 86, 126, 178, 183; road developer, 208, 211, 218; traveler, 10-11, 22, 30, 33, 70, 95-6, 132, 135, **165**, 207, 211-12.
Packard, Carlota "Lottie" "Dixie" (Wood) Holbrook (second wife), 131-2, **159**, 162, 179-80, **196**, **215**, 230-1
Packard Cattle Co., 79, 87, 127, 130, 147, 157
Packard, Dorothea Lewis (daughter), 87, **96**, 98, 104-5, 132, **159**, 160, 162, 179, 194, **208**-09, 212, 221-2, 231
Packard, Ella (Lewis) (first wife), 9-10, 22, 57, 69, 77, 95, **96**, 97-104
Packard, Gertrude Louise (daughter), 59, **96**, 98-9, 104-5, 127, 132, 150, 157, 161, **189**, **215**, 231
Packard, Gertrude Louise (granddaughter), 150, 218, 222
Packard Investment Co., 161
Packard, Rachel (Williams) (daughter-in-law), 187-8, **215**
Packard, Rebecca (Rose) (grandmother), 59, 211
Packard Station, Ariz., 80, 124
Packard, Virtue V. (Crandall) (mother), 5-6, **96**
Panic of 1873, 6
Panic of 1893, 95
Panic of 1907, 157-8, 163
Parker, John A., 195, **208**, 221
Parsons, George W., 47, 90

Paul, Alfred and family, 151, 191, **196, 230**, *262-3*
Paul Spur, Ariz., 191, 230
Pearce, Ariz., 111, 114, 123-4, 156
Pennsylvania oil, 5, **8**, 13
Pesqueria, Elena, 78, 117
Phelps Dodge Corp., 74, 148, 151, 202
Phoenix, Ariz., 54, 111, 149
Pilares, Son., 70, 76, 89, 116
poker, 10, 44, 178, 205
Pollack, Thomas E., 136-8, 158-9, 178, 180, 184, 205, 225, 230-1, *263*
Portville, N.Y., 4, 96, 113, 118, 211
Price, Lyttleton, 23
Progressive movement, 134, 173, 222
Pullman, William A., 14
pumping operations, 25, 59
Pyeatt, Ben and family, 184, *263*
Quakers, 4, 75
railroad operations, 73-4, 114, 139
ranching operations, **71**, 73-5, **78**, 79, 93-4, 105-6, 108-9, 127, **152**
Randolph, Epes, 136, 155, 157-9, 178, 181, *264*
Recession of 1920s
Republican Party, 6, 48, 51, 138, 162
Rice, Harry B., 133-4, 162, *264*
Richardson, David A., 153, 157, 166, 174, 189, 192, *264-5*
Richardson, Richard R., 27, 68
Ricketts, L.C., 185, 213
Rivera, Heliodoro, 187, *265*
Rixford, Penn., 7, 9
Roberts, Edward J., 76, 89, 122
Roper, Fordyce A., 9, 13, 37
Ross, Daniel D., 148
Roy Mining Co, 179, 205
Ruiz, Jose G., 218, *265*
Rynning, Thomas H., 155, 170
Safford, Anson P.K., 15, 23, 45, 47, 61
San Domingo, Son., 113-4, 117,
San Pedro River, 15, 54, **78**, 80-1, 91, 98, 121, 125, **152**
San Pedro Valley, 80, 94, 98. 106, 114, 123, 125
San Rafael del Valle, 87, 130, 147, 153

Sarabia, Manuel, 173-4, 197
Say, Asa W., 17-19, 28, 30-1, 35-6
Scranton, Levi, 82, 87, 126
Second District Court, 36, 77
Schieffelin, Ed and Albert, 14
Serrano, Mother, 216, *266*
Shattuck, Enoch, Jonas and Lemuel C., 71-2, 146, 153, *266*
Shattuck School, 127, 217, 223
Sherman, William Tecumseh, 50, 61
Stonewall Mine, 26-7
shotgun policy, 29-30
Silver Cloud Mine, 27, 40, 56, 160
Simonson, Ernest W., 195, 217, 222, 224
Simmons, W.A., 32-3, 46
Slaughter, John H., 73, 93-4, 108, 150, 163, **204**, 205, *266-7*
Slaughter, George M. and Robert L., 192-3
Sleeper, J. Henry, 13, 31
Smith, Marcus A., 62, 98, 136, *267*
Smithman, Jonathan B., 14, 18,
Soto, C. Ygnacio (aka Ignacio), 167, 175-6, 179, 185, **186**-7, 194-6, 233, *267-8*
Southern Pacific Railroad, 10, 68, 73, 86, 124, 155, 183
stagecoach, 5, 11, 61, 128, 176
Stebbins, Asa H., 54, 69-70, *268*
Steinburn, James W., 21, 29, 39
Stephens, George D., 197, *268*
Stephenson, Bruce, 209
Stonewall Mine, 27-37, 43
Stonewall No. 2, 31-4, 37
Sulphur Springs Valley, 55, 70, 94, 115, 126, 188, 191
Sunset Mill and Mine, 17-20
Sunset Silver Mining Co. 17-18, 20
Sweet, Frederick A., 112, **130**, 148-9, *268-9*
Swisshelm Cattle Co., 115
Sycamore Springs Water Co., 46
Taft, Kimball C. "Tim," **128**, *269*
Taylor, Casper, 9, 18, 24-5, 56
Taylor, George, 115, 154, 161
Taylor, Jennie, 24, 56
Tammany Hall, 7, 121

Teachout, Harlow M., 115-16, 151, *269*
Tevis, Perrin, Land & Co., 82
Thirteen Club, 160
Thompson, Rufus M. "Babe," 147, 163, 192, *269-70*
Tombstone, Ariz., **21**-2, 26, 37-8, 42, 44, 51, 53, 56-60, 212
Tombstone Mill and Mining Co., 15, 30, 61
Tombstone Epitaph, 24, 48, 62
Tombstone Record, 62
Tombstone Record-Epitaph, 56, 62
Tombstone Republican newspaper, 56, 62
Toughnut Mine, 14
townsite controversy, 23-4
Total Wreck Mine, 71
Tovrea, Edward A., 151, *270*
T-P Ranch, 65, 68-9
Transvaal Copper Mining Co. 178-9
Tranquility Mining Co., 33, 37
Tres Alamos, Ariz., 54
Trost, Henry C., 146, 157
Turkey Track Ranch, 79, 126, 147, 161, 181, 183
Turquoise Mining District, 26-7
Turkey Track Ranch, 79, 90, 142, 162, 192
Tweed, Henry A., 25-6, 51-2, 58, 62, 64-5, 113, *270-1*
Tweed, Harriet K., 53-4
Tweed-Packard (T-P) Ranch, 65-6
Vail, Edward L. and Walter L., 70-1, 89, 127, 147, 169, *271*
Valencia onions, 209, 214
Valley National Bank, 184-5, 194, 212, 230-1
Villa, Francisco "Pancho," 175, 192-3
Vickers, John V., 45-**46**, 72-3, 75, 87, 89-90, 93-4, 105, 107, 127, 169, *271-2*
Vizina Building, 22, 35, 45, 47
Vizina Mining Co. **21**, 22-5
Vizina, James, 27, 42, 45
Vizina Mine, 15-16, 20-4, 26, 37, 56, 68
Walker, Thomas E., 15, 17
water, 25, 46-7, 59, 67, 125, 161
water rights, 81-3
Whitbeck, Henry, 77, 90
White, Theodore F., 72, 89, 169, *272*

White, William W., 13, 18, 31
Willcox, Ariz., 54, 95, 111, 119, 124, 156
Williams, Ben and Lewis, 74, 119, 146, 148
Wings of Angels Foundation, 232
Wood, Robert C., 132, *272*
YMCA in Douglas, 202, 207
Zulick, C. Meyer, 70, 76, 88-9

Connections: The Life and Times of B. A. Packard

Cynthia F. Hayostek

ABOUT THE AUTHOR

Cindy Hayostek grew up hearing stories about B.A. Packard because his grandson was her father's best friend. Then she began encountering the Cochise County pioneer in history books as "B.A. Packard, the cattleman and banker ... ." Knowing there had to be more to his story, Hayostek began looking for it.

She started in 1993 by searching Cochise County public records, and then by reading local newspapers. Finding much new information, she became fascinated by the way so many historical figures connect to Packard.

Hayostek also came to admire Packard's unquestionable integrity, and how it was passed on to his descendants. They include his great grandchildren, who are now the author's friends.

While researching and writing Connections, Hayostek graduated Phi Beta Kappa from the University of Arizona with a bachelor's degree in history. She also worked at a small daily newspaper and at a trade journal, and published four books. The most recent is Douglas, issued by Arcadia Publishing.

She also publishes Borderland Chronicles, a quarterly history journal about the borderlands in southeastern Arizona. For more info: borderlandchronicles.com.

Connections: The Life and Times of B. A. Packard

CPSIA information can be obtained
at www.ICGtesting.com
Printed in the USA
FSOW03n0921091015
12028FS